CONTINUITY ANI

This is a fascinating must-read and highly readable book; even if you disagree with the author's arguments, you will reconsider much of the rhetoric that we take for granted regarding Maoism. **Roxanne Dunbar-Ortiz**, author of *An Indigenous Peoples' History of the United States*

Continuity and Rupture is Moufawad-Paul's theorization of a political and revolutionary thought of today. This book offers an active framework for understanding the Maoist turn in Marxism, which the author grounds in a challenging vision of history and a necessity for social change. **Julian Jason Haladyn**, author of *Boredom and Art*

Capitalism is headed for disaster. Any serious attempt to alter the course of history requires revolutionary theory. Whether you agree with J. Moufawad-Paul's conclusions or not, this book raises the questions we all need to ask. **Gabriel Kuhn**, author of *Life Under the Jolly Roger* and *Turning Money Into Rebellion*

Calling all organizers, anti-capitalists, and people who care about anticolonial struggle—this book is for you. Beautifully clear, Moufawad-Paul lays out the concepts that we almost never get to learn in our schools or in our social movements—the concepts that many have struggled to grasp and apply—the concepts that are necessary for revolution. Placing the tools of western philosophy in the service of explicating the significance and necessity of actually-existing Maoism, this book is an accessible and compelling primer in science, theory, philosophy, and revolution. This book is just in time. At its heart, it is an historical materialist account of the unfolding of revolutionary praxis through the rupture and continuity of Marxist-Leninism and Marxism-Leninism-Maoism. Moufawad-Paul begins his periodization and clarification of Maoism from the revolutionary theory of the Community Party of Peru and the Communist (Maoist) Party of Afghanistan situated in the global struggle against capitalism-imperialism. And for you, eurocentric academic Marxists: you have been put on notice—you can't say you haven't been told.

Rachel Gorman, Associate Professor in Critical Disability Studies, York University

Moufawad-Paul's *Continuity and Rupture* is a much welcomed attempt to bring philosophical clarity to political debates which all too often are wrapped around vague terms at the expense of conceptual clarity. Its central thesis claims that Maoism is a coherent theoretical development that both continues the revolutionary content of Leninist theory and breaks with its historical limitations, thus opening up a new set of theoretical possibilities ultimately rooted in the scientific propositions of historical materialism. It is a provocative thesis, but one that is lucidly explored by Moufawad-Paul. This is a book that should renew interest in historically concrete forms of Marxist theory and produce spirited, but invaluable, debate on the nature of Maoism. Highly recommended for both practical and philosophical reasons!

Esteve Morera, author of *Gramsci's Historicism* and *Gramsci, Materialism and Philosophy*

Continuity and Rupture

Philosophy in the Maoist Terrain

Continuity
and Rupture

Philosophy in the Maoist Terrain

J. Moufawad-Paul

Winchester, UK
Washington, USA

First published by Zero Books, 2016
Zero Books is an imprint of John Hunt Publishing Ltd., Laurel House, Station Approach,
Alresford, Hants, SO24 9JH, UK
office1@jhpbooks.net
www.johnhuntpublishing.com
www.zero-books.net

For distributor details and how to order please visit the 'Ordering' section on our website.

ISBN: 978 1 78535 476 2
978 1 78535 477 9 (ebook)
Library of Congress Control Number: 2016936941

A CIP catalogue record for this book is available from the British Library.

Design: Lee Nash

Printed and bound by CPI Group (UK) Ltd, Croydon, CR0 4YY, UK

We operate a distinctive and ethical publishing philosophy in all
areas of our business, from our global network of authors to
production and worldwide distribution.

CONTENTS

For comrades Gabrielle, Christophe, and Hamayon

Clearly, both continuity and rupture are part of the process of the evolution of every science, because this process of evolution—of every phenomenon in the natural realm, society and human thought—is informed by the unity of opposites.
—Communist (Maoist) Party of Afghanistan

Whence a revolution in Marxism, the Maoist revolution.
—Alain Badiou

Abbreviations

CmPA = Communist (Maoist) Party of Afghanistan

CPI (Maoist) = Communist Party of India (Maoist)

CPI (ML) = Communist Party of India (Marxist-Leninist)

CPI (ML) Naxalbari = Communist Party of India (Marxist-Leninist) Naxalbari

CPI (ML) PWG = Communist Party of India (Marxist-Leninist) People's War Group

CPN (Maoist) = Communist Party of Nepal (Maoist)

CPP = Communist Party of the Philippines

CWG (Marxist-Leninist) = Communist Worker's Group (Marxist-Leninist)

GPCR = Great Proletarian Cultural Revolution

MCC = Maoist Communist Centre

MIM = Maoist Internationalist Movement

MKP = Maoist Communist Party of Turkey

nPCI = The New Communist Party of Italy

PCI (Maoist) = Communist Party of Italy (Maoist)

PCMF = Maoist Communist Party of France

PCP = Communist Party of Peru

PCR-RCP = Revolutionary Communist Party of Canada

PPW = protracted people's war

RCP-USA = Revolutionary Communist Party, USA

RIM = Revolutionary Internationalist Movement

RU = Revolutionary Union

TKP/ML = Communist Party of Turkey Marxist-Leninist

WCP = Workers Communist Party of Canada

Prologue
Maoism and Philosophy

Before 1988 Maoism did not exist. I begin with this counter-intuitive statement in order to clarify the particular theoretical position that is the concern of this book. In *The Communist Necessity*, the polemical "prolegomena" to this book, I argued that there needed to be a "new return" to the concept of the revolutionary party—a reclaiming of the theoretical tradition marked by world-historical revolutions—and that this new return was to be found in the "three-headed beast" of Marxism-Leninism-Maoism. Unfortunately some of my critics, unaware that *The Communist Necessity* was primarily a polemical intro-duction to a philosophical intervention that still needed to be written, made the mistake of conflating my demand for a "new return" with the very "old return" that I warned about: they assumed that, by arguing for a Maoist party of the new type, I was arguing for an unqualified and uncritical return to the party-building experiments, and actually-existing socialisms, that had reached their limits in the mid-20th-century. In point of fact, and this is one of my main claims, Maoism is not an old-fashioned Marxism but, unlike all of those demands to "return to Marx" (again fashionable following the crisis of 2008 and the onslaught of austerity), a modern theoretical terrain.

The moment one speaks of returning to the concept of a revolutionary communist party, and motivates this return with a reclamation of past categories of struggle (i.e. the vanguard, proletariat-bourgeoisie, revisionism and anti-revisionism, revolutionary science), every defense mechanism conditioned by the collapse of the Eastern Bloc and the supposed triumph of world capitalism is mobilized to inoculate the reader from ideological contamination. There is a common assumption that such a demand is "orthodox" despite the fact that a rejection of the party might also be orthodox: it is the orthodoxy of a movementist understanding of reality, the contemporary first-world left's dogma, or even the orthodoxy of a return to a pre-Lenin Marx untainted by revolution. Then there is the rejection of applying the category of science to Marxism which is seen by some as old-fashioned but might be a misidentification with the general category of science with its "natural" and "hard" iterations. There is often scant investigation of what is meant by the employment of the categories of "party" and "science" or what theoretical constellation could be mobilized under the rubric of a "new return".

Thus, at the outset of this project, it is necessary to declare two qualifications that will hopefully undermine these imprecise criticisms. First of all, I am interested in declaring fidelity to a heterodox revolutionary tradition that occupies a political sequence between the twin orthodoxies of party monolithism and movementist utopianism. If the demand for some sort of return to a revolutionary party is "orthodox" then so too is the demand for a return to disorganized non-party utopianism which was the kind of organizing that existed before, during, and after Marx. Just as modern movementists return to the latter approach without necessarily being orthodox, I believe we can embrace a new return to the former for the same reason. Secondly, I think it is worthwhile to speak about theory with some sort of scientific rubric in order to determine why historical materialism is preferable to another theoretical approach. Those Marxists who reject the category of "scientific" have no legitimate reason to privilege historical materialism because they cannot say why it is superior outside of theoretical taste. Although it might be the case we need to define science according to an older sense of the term, or maybe just content ourselves with the qualifier of "scientific approach", we can only dispense with this distinction and retain the significance of historical materialism by playing with semantics.

The very fact that I need to make these qualifications, though, demonstrates that in the imperialist metropoles, there has been very little understanding amongst the contemporary mainstream left about the history of the name *Maoism*. Since this mainstream left's discourse is often determined by anarchist, autonomist, and Trotskyist/post-Trotskyist understandings of history, Maoism is a term attached to a vague understanding of the Chinese Revolution—that is, it is the Marxism practiced by the Chinese Revolution led by the figure of Mao Zedong—and is thus immediately relegated to the past. To speak of "Maoism" is to render oneself more than half-a-century out of date, or worse to enunciate a "Stalinism" with Chinese characteristics. Leaving aside, for the moment, the fact that some of these analyses of Maoism are themselves over-determined by an out-of-date Marxism, there is also the fact that they pass over the anti-revisionist Marxist-Leninist period in silence.

Therefore, there has been a lacuna in the comprehension of the New Communist Movement of the late 1960s–1980s that gripped the majority of the world. I attempted to speak to this lacuna in *The Communist Necessity* when I indicated the significance of the anti-revisionist Marxist-Leninist movement. As Aaron Leonard and Conor Gallagher, among others, have demonstrated in *Heavy Radicals*, the New Communist Movement, where the name "Maoism" was first raised as a standard (for it was not used prior to the 1960s, not even during the Chinese Revolution in 1948) in the context of the Sino-Soviet Split, was extremely significant. Indeed, according to Leonard and Gallagher, the New Communist Movement in the US greatly eclipsed the New Left; the anti-revisionist Marxist-Leninist movement, that usually called itself "Maoist", was so pervasive that it was designated as *the* security threat by the FBI.[1]

Outside of the US the situation was much the same: we can discover (despite the fact that many of these movements erupted only to spectacularly disintegrate or slowly degenerate) a massive world-wide communist movement that mobilized under the name of Maoism. In Canada, the Workers Communist Party and En Lutte became mass parties, seeding their members into the ranks of organized labor, in a manner that had not been accomplished since the 1930s, only to be absorbed and collapse. In the UK, the Revolutionary Communist League of Britain was temporarily able to pull the masses into its orbit so as to launch one of the first significant critiques of Eurocentrism.[2] In the European continent, particularly in France, the anti-revisionist Marxist-Leninist movement was at the heart of May 1968, producing intellectuals such as Jacques Rancière and Alain Badiou who, though now departing from their "Maoist" past, still cannot help demonstrating some fidelity, in their own particularly ways, to this experience. Most important, however, in places such as the Philippines and India, the New Communist Movement would persist and develop, continuing to this day, transforming into the contemporary Maoist movement. These are just some examples of this period, a time when the name "Maoism" was temporarily en vogue, and it is disheartening that contemporary Marxist intellectuals are either unaware or disinterested in making sense of this past.

But even this poorly apprehended New Communist Movement preceded Maoism proper. Regardless of its mobilization of the name *Maoism*, it was only a precursor of contemporary Maoism—its skeleton, its DNA—and was ultimately conditioned by the fossil remains of a Leninism that had reached its limit, despite those moments where it yearned for more than Leninist orthodoxy. So if those who did not understand the context in which I demanded a new return to the communist necessity were incapable of even grasping the significance of the anti-revisionist period of struggle, they were largely incapable of understanding what was intended by the concept of Marxism-Leninism-Maoism. I was indicating a theoretical terrain that had only emerged at the moment capitalism declared itself the end of history, years after even the New Communist Movement had collapsed.

Maoism Did Not Exist?

Let us return to my initial claim: prior to the end of the 1980s, Maoism did not exist. The controversial, if not erroneous, nature of this assertion seems obvious since there were indeed organizations and individuals that referred to themselves as "Maoist" before the 1980s. Thus, to claim that there was really no such thing as Maoism before 1988 is indeed counter-intuitive, possibly a willful denial of history. But it is precisely this claim that is my point of departure, a line of demarcation that is only absurd insofar as the entire practice of philosophy is absurd.

Indeed, if the practice of philosophy is to demand conceptual clarification, then philosophical statements often manifest as absurd in the context of the real world where conceptual clarity is generally abjured in favor of nomological confusion. Take, for example, Aristotle's old claim that there is no such thing as *human being* outside of the social. One might counter, without being wrong, that Aristotle's definition is absurd since human beings can and do exist outside of social contexts—hermits who live on mountains, lonely desert wanderers, rugged individuals who live "off the grid"—and content oneself with the obvious absurdity of philosophy. Aristotle would reply, however, that his point was misunderstood since the human species cannot *be human*, and be recognized as human, without recourse to the social: the human can only be human in a space wherein other humans exist; the human can only be human after it is socialized, growing to adulthood, in this same space. Whether or not we agree with Aristotle's definition of human being is not the point here; I simply wish to indicate that his argument, regardless of its internal merits, is no longer absurd once it is understood as an argument that is meant to draw conceptual boundaries.[3]

Therefore, what we find with the example of Aristotle's definition of human being is an attempt to provide clarity to a concept
that exists beyond the name: it is absurd insofar as it denies
conceptual meaning to the name itself when it is used to
contradict the concept, it is possibly rational insofar as it
attempts to excavate the conceptual meaning behind the name
and fix this meaning in a specific context that is both spatial and
temporal. And this is precisely what is meant by arguing that
Maoism did not exist before 1988: a coherent conceptual content
was not fixed prior to the end of the 1980s, the term "Maoism"
was as conceptually incoherent as Aristotle's bare human prior to
the event of socialization that ascribed meaning to the name.

Upon leaving the absurd realm of philosophy and entering
the realm of the social wherein theory emerges, let us examine
the end of the 1980s when Maoism, I argue, begins to emerge as
Maoism proper. The communist-led People's War in Peru, a
revolutionary eruption right at the moment when capitalism was
declaring itself "the end of history", produces this statement:

> While Marxism-Leninism has obtained an acknowledgement
> of its universal validity, Maoism is not completely acknowl-
> edged as the third stage [of revolutionary science]. Some
> simply deny its condition as such, while others only accept it
> as 'Mao Tse-Tung Thought.' [...] The denial of the 'ism'
> character of Maoism denies its universal validity and, conse-
> quently, its condition as the third, new, and superior stage of
> the ideology of the international proletariat: Marxism-
> Leninism-Maoism.[4]

Here, then, we have a theoretical statement that is drawing a
boundary between the previous usage of "Maoism" and a
concept of Maoism that is supposedly new: a theoretical
tendency apparently guiding a revolution that manifested
following the supposed defeat of communism. Before the above

statement was made, even those responsible for making it spoke of a *Mao Zedong Thought*, short-handed as Maoism. And though, in 1981, these same Peruvian revolutionaries began to think of the possibility of *Maoism* (in a document entitled *Towards Maoism*), it was not until they had reached the apex of their revolutionary movement that they declared the "universal validity" of Maoism as a "third stage" of revolutionary science. Hence the supposedly controversial claim that Maoism did not exist before 1988: it did not exist as a properly coherent theoretical terrain.

Even still, 1988 was not the crucial moment where the concept of *Maoism* crystallized; it was still too vague, still burdened by conceptual confusion, to be anything more than a provocative suggestion made by an organization that was, at the time, reigniting revolutionary praxis. The moment of rupture, wherein the theoretical continuity of Marxism-Leninism was forcefully disrupted, would be 1993… But before I explain this in further detail, I want to provide an introductory background to this book's existence and subject matter.

The Exclusion of Maoism

In 2012 I wrote a pamphlet-sized polemic entitled *Maoism or Trotskyism*[5] in an attempt to not only respond to what I felt were bad faith engagements with Maoism, most of which presupposed the Trotskyist narrative and definition of Maoism, but to also clarify the grounds of the debate between two divergent theoretical trajectories that were claiming to be either the proper representative or further development of Marxism-Leninism. My intention was to define the basic conceptual terms of the debate, to clear up misunderstandings, and at the very least, if the reader was faithful to a Trotskyist-influenced tendency and had no intention of gravitating towards Maoism, provide grounds for appreciating the actual meaning of Maoism rather than promoting and debating straw-person versions.

Furthermore, *Maoism or Trotskyism* was written in the context of my frustration with the silence and ignorance surrounding Marxism-Leninism-Maoism amongst popular first-world academic Marxists. For example, *The Critical Companion to Contemporary Marxism*,[6] which purports to provide a map to every significant Marxist tendency, possessed no chapter on Maoism (although it did, ironically, possess chapters on Marxist tendencies that were inspired by Mao Zedong and the Chinese Revolution), a rather strange omission even if one was to identify Maoism only with the Chinese Revolution. The fact that Marxists could be silent about a Marxist trajectory that has been responsible, since 1988, for multiple people's wars, and thus exclude a significant contemporary phenomenon, was a glaring oversight.

This quietus regarding Maoism, however, was not entirely surprising. My own introduction to Marxism was one that was decidedly silent on the theoretical trajectory inspired by the Chinese Revolution. Indeed, my understanding of Leninism was heavily influenced by a discourse that, echoing Cold-War propaganda, assumed that Stalin was a mass murderer and that Mao was a tragic echo of Stalin. It was not until I was confronted with revolutionary traditions and movements in the global peripheries that this discourse was challenged and I came to understand it as partially the result of Trotskyist ideology, and partially a result, I suspect, of an orientalism that is more interested in European expressions of Marxism than the tendencies that developed in the so-called third world.[7]

By placing Maoism in confrontation with Trotskyism, my polemic was also meant to address two related issues: the ignorance regarding Maoism that is promoted by a Trotskyist-influenced discourse; the fact that Marxism-Leninism-Maoism was indeed quite significant because, unlike other tendencies, it was the ideology that influenced every existing communist people's war—it was actively attempting to make revolution.

The need to expand on aspects of this polemic that were more important than the polemic's thesis became clear after Montreal's

Maison Norman Bethune began to produce and sell *Maoism or Trotskyism* as a pamphlet only months after I had cast it into the internet ether. What was most evident was the fact that the philosophical investigation of the terms *Maoism* and *Trotskyism* masked the need to explain many of the assumptions behind the term to which I was declaring fidelity (Maoism) that I had treated as a priori. Simply demanding that people accept Maoism over Trotskyism was not enough; I also needed to further explain, beyond my quick summations, why Maoism was a "new stage" of revolutionary science after Leninism, as I claimed, beyond the axiom of "universal applicability" gleaned from world-historical revolution. It was not enough to just provide an inventory of what was universally applicable in Maoism but, based on the ensuing and invigorating discussion, it was also clear that the meaning behind these claims required further elaboration.

For example, my claim that Maoism did not exist as *Maoism proper* until the late 1980s and early 1990s was received with some confusion. As I have already indicated, though, clearly the term "Maoism" existed prior to this time period. I was arguing, though, that these "Maoisms" were generally unscientific hypotheses that, despite sometimes having the germ of what we can call *Maoism-qua-Maoism* (that is, Marxism-Leninism-Maoism), were still examples of a vague rather than coherent concept. Even though I tried to explain the difference between the name and concept of Maoism, and why the events of 1988 and 1993 were something of an epistemic break that necessarily established the beginning of Maoism as a stage of revolutionary science, I had started to realize that both in the pamphlet and elsewhere (on my blog *MLM Mayhem* and in a manuscript I was working on at the time) this claim demanded further elaboration.

As I have argued above, philosophical practice is generally about drawing distinctions and establishing definitions; philosophy is, to put it simply, a discipline that is concerned with discussing the meaning of concepts and theoretical terrains and, in this discussion, hopes to provide a measure of clarity. Hence, the difference between name and concept, and the need to explain a concept coherently in a way that does not simply assume that the emergence of a *name* means the emergence of a *concept* is important to grasp. For example, the name and concept of "atom", though connected, demonstrate an important philosophical disparity: the pre-Socratic "atomists" did not have the same coherent understanding of atomic structure as modern particle theory, though it is clear that physicists borrowed the term from the ancients. In both instances the name is identical; the concept diverges.

Of course, a philosophical polemic (such as *Maoism or Trotskyism* or even *The Communist Necessity*) necessarily has to be narrow because to be focused, by definition, means a *narrowing* of the philosophical gaze. When we examine an object in order to understand this object, we temporarily and primarily focus upon it at the expense of everything else. Eventually, however, we must connect this object to other similar objects as well as contrary objects, for nothing exists in a void, but still a certain measure of focus is required or we cannot arrive at definitions. And it is this *eventually* that began to concern me after multiple discussions and arguments surrounding the initial pamphlet.

Several philosophical interventions in the terrain of Marxism-Leninism-Maoism were required: this concept not only needed to be explained, defined against the simple name *Maoism*, but its significance also required clarity. For there were other people who read my pamphlet and argued that one could not speak of *Marxism-Leninism-Maoism* because there could only be Marxism-Leninism—either dogmatically in some sort of "Stalinist" sense, or critically in the sense that the problems of Marxism-Leninism had still not been superseded and thus could not be superseded through something called Maoism.

Philosophical Clarity

The result of the discussions around *Maoism or Trotskyism* led me to realize that Marxism-Leninism-Maoism in some ways lacked a coherent philosophical constellation. This is not to say that it was lacking as a science, that it lacked a theory and various exciting theoretical sub-categories (which all sciences possess), but that, since it was still only a few decades old and necessarily outside of the realm of academic privilege, it had not yet produced a series of philosophical interventions aimed at clarifying its theoretical terrain.

This lack should not be surprising. Marxism lacked a coherent philosophy for many decades after it was proposed as a science, and philosophers such as Louis Althusser spent their entire lives trying to figure out how philosophy could be practiced within the Marxist terrain. When scientific paradigms emerge, and necessarily produce a theoretical process in which new concepts continuously erupt, it takes some time for us philosophers, who are generally a boring and out-of-touch group of misanthropes, to recognize the importance of these theoretical terrains. All of the pieces for a philosophical elaboration are usually contained within a scientific paradigm but, since philosophy is ultimately nothing more than an attempt to narrow down concepts for the sake of clarity and thus force meaning, philosophers may be slow to recognize the importance of a given theory or concept.

Moreover, if Marxism is a living science that is always open to the future, that is engaged in a developing truth process where new understandings of concrete reality are established through militant practice and most importantly world-historical revolution (for Marx and Engels argued that the motion of history was class struggle, and this was their scientific hypothesis of history and society), then philosophy must necessarily lag behind. Since a revolutionary theoretical terrain develops within the crucible of revolution on the part of the wretched of the earth, philosophers are generally divorced from these moments of theoretical development. Just as the majority of philosophers do not spend most of their time in scientific laboratories where new concepts of the so-called *hard sciences* are developed, they spend even less time in the laboratory of militant class struggle.

Philosophy cannot establish new theoretical concepts for a given scientific terrain, even if its practitioners would like to pretend otherwise, and is ultimately limited to the narrow realm of introspection: we take what is given, we try to elaborate on the given, we attempt to explain what this given means. Even the supposed "queen of philosophy", ontology, is limited by the established truth processes of the scientific paradigms that have produced its possibility. One cannot imagine Plato's theory of forms without the prior establishment of mathematics; one cannot imagine Spinoza's metaphysics without Euclidian geometry; one cannot imagine Alain Badiou's most recent ontological attempts without an entire host of scientific truth processes that make his investigations possible let alone correct.

The truth is that Maoism doesn't need philosophy in order to develop its concepts any more than physics or mathematics need philosophy to persist as physics and math. Just as the physicist and mathematician are often best left alone by interloping philosophers, so too are revolutionary Maoist movements usually best left unhindered by philosophical interventions. To my mind, the only job of philosophy in these contexts is to provide clarity for people who are confused by conceptual impasses and to speak some sort of meaning to these concepts that would be developed even without this speaking.

Therefore, if Marxism-Leninism-Maoism currently lacks a parallel development of philosophical intervention, this has nothing to do with the theoretical strength of this supposed revolutionary science; all it does is demonstrate that philosophers of politics, specifically philosophers of Marxism, are lagging behind—and we always lag behind.

But in this lagging behind maybe we can provide some clarity, some light shed from the rear-guard of a theoretical movement, so as to draw the attention of critically minded people who are looking for clarity in these supposed theoretical impasses. Within this context, however, philosophers are only capable of examining the concepts and phenomena at hand; we cannot produce theory, and if we imagined we could we would be undermining the basis of the science we claim to be clarifying. In this context, a philosophical intervention is little more than an act of interlocution, rarified interpretation, and if it imagines it is something more it misses its mark.

All of this is to say that my attempt to provide some basic interventions in the terrain of Marxism-Leninism-Maoism will be an extremely limited exercise. A philosophy of any Marxism cannot produce theoretical concepts, even if it sometimes imagines it can, but can only engage with concepts presented by class struggle. In this narrow engagement, though, philosophy will demand a clarity of terms, work to reveal the structure of the theoretical terrain, attempt to force a choice, and argue why one option is more valid than another—why an entire theoretical terrain is either rational or irrational according to its own terms.

Beyond this, philosophy has nothing more to say.

Maoism as Continuity and Rupture

In the following pages, then, I am interested in examining the general boundaries of Marxism-Leninism-Maoism that have already been established by the most recent conceptual rupture of revolutionary science that labels itself *Maoist*. My aim is not only to provide clarity for these boundaries, but to map out some of the debates within these boundaries, how they are different from the boundaries drawn by Marxism-Leninism, and what still needs to be addressed within the conceptual terrain. Most importantly, I am concerned with the notion that Maoism is a stage that is continuous with Marxism-Leninism (just as Leninism was continuous with Marxism) while being, at the same time, a rupture from Marxism-Leninism (again, just as Leninism was a rupture from Marxism): the dialectical tension of *continuity-rupture* is something I take seriously as a philosopher, because it can explain so much of the meaning of Maoism, and will be addressed, from various angles, in the following chapters. As the Communist (Maoist) Party of Afghanistan has maintained, "the principal aspect of the continuation of Marxism-Leninism is summed up, and short-handed, in the phrase *Marxism-Leninism-Maoism*," with *Maoism* simultaneously being a moment of rupture.[8]

Hence, one of the axiomatic claims behind this book is that Maoism is a theoretical development that is continuous with the revolutionary communism that has evolved from Marxism and through Leninism because it possesses fidelity to the principal claims of historical materialism. At the same time, while it is continuous with Marxism-Leninism, it is also a theoretical rupture because, like Leninism, it was a moment of theoretical orthodoxy that, emerging from the limits of Leninism, was a heterodox rearticulation of the theory. Here, a rupture with the limits of one scientific paradigm was necessary in order to proclaim fidelity with the science as a whole. The theoretical rupture does not emerge from a vacuum but in direct and continuous relation to the tradition of which it is a part, a tradition that it upholds (with which it possesses continuity) *by the very fact of its rupture*:

There is no doubt that Leninism was a rupture from Marxism, a rupture from its secondary or subordinate mistakes and inadequacies (including, in specific cases, ruptures from elements that, until Leninism, were understood as basic and fundamental), but at the same time Leninism is also the continuation of Marxism. Therefore, in the stage of Leninism, the ideology and science of proletarian revolution was not entirely recast; it was only recast to the extent required by the ideological content of this development. In this partial recasting, Marxism was not entirely erased and replaced by Leninism; rather, the principal feature of Marxism was summed up in the term *Marxism-Leninism*. Furthermore, there is no doubt that Maoism, while expressing partial ruptures (a rupture from its secondary and subordinate mistakes, inadequacies, and unscientific aspects, as well as a rupture from some of its accepted fundamental elements) mainly upholds the continuation of Marxism-Leninism.[9]

Maoism, then, is not simply an addition to Marxism-Leninism (as it was generally understood prior to 1988 under the rubric of *Mao Zedong Thought*), but a theoretical development of the science that sums up its continuity in the formula *Marxism-Leninism-Maoism*. Additional thoughts and theoretical insights are not the same as a theoretical break; the latter is similar to what Gaston Bachelard and Thomas Kuhn, speaking of science in general, categorized as an *epistemic rupture* or *paradigm shift*, respectively—a break that, while continuous with the field of science, simultaneously alters that field by producing new theoretical boundaries.

If we understand Maoism as being a moment of theoretical rupture, rather than simply the addition of key insights within the terrain of Marxism-Leninism, then our engagement with its terms is conditioned by a respect for the actual boundaries it claims to draw. Even if we choose to reject Maoism after being aware of precisely what it claims to be, at the very least our rejection will be based on a proper understanding of its definition rather than the meaning some have erroneously ascribed to its name. Indeed, the polemic that inspired this book was itself inspired by several false attributions—hence the reason for its inclusion in this book as an appendix.

Obviously this book is incapable of being the definitive intervention in the theoretical terrain of Marxism-Leninism-Maoism. If every scientific paradigm necessitates its own philosophy, then much more than what I have offered herein will be required. Therefore, I have intentionally limited myself to the problematic of *continuity and rupture* which might be able to serve as the basis for a sustained and fruitful philosophical investigation into the realm of Maoism. That is, in the following pages I am interested primarily in how and why Maoism, as a theoretical terrain, is in continuity with the radical kernel of Marxism by the very fact of its theoretical rupture.

My hope, then, is that the following chapters will become part of a larger movement within radical philosophy to bring clarity to what I take to be the most exciting development of real-world communism to date. Thus: several small steps in the direction of a philosophy of Maoism—far less significant than the exciting strides made, through class struggle itself, in the theoretical terrain that I am attempting to clarify.

Notes

1. Aaron Leonard and Conor Gallagher, *Heavy Radicals: the FBI's Secret War on American Maoists* (Winchester: Zero Books, 2014).

2. This critique, *Eurocentrism and the Communist Movement* (Montreal: Kersplebedeb, 2015) has recently been revised by its primary author, Robert Biel, and republished.

3. Obviously I am simplifying, for the sake of argument, Aristotle's definition of the human animal. Although Marx drew on Aristotle's concept of *zo'on politikon* (the human as the animal of the polis) in a progressive manner, it is worth noting that Aristotle intended this concept to exclude women, slaves, and foreigners. In some ways the concept itself explains Aristotle's attempt to confine it to chauvinist categories—being a social animal himself, he was influenced by the dominant ideology of his time—but this is a philosophical can of worms that only tangentially concerns this book's subject matter.

4. Communist Party of Peru, *On Marxism-Leninism-Maoism*.
5. An edited version of this polemic is included in this book as an appendix.
6. Boston: Brill, 2008.
7. Although, in my opinion, this problem might be connected to the influence of Trotskyism on first-world Marxist academia, since Trotskyism is one of the most Eurocentric expressions of Marxism.
8. Communist (Maoist) Party of Afghanistan, *A Response to the RCP-USA's May 1st 2012 Letter*.
9. Ibid.

Chapter 1

The Terrain of Maoism-qua-Maoism

Marxism-Leninism-Maoism is a universally applicable, living and scientific ideology, constantly developing and being further enriched through its application in making revolution as well as through the advance of human knowledge generally.
—Revolutionary Internationalist Movement, *Long Live Marxism-Leninism-Maoism!*

General Axioms

I will begin this chapter by providing a basic definition of Marxism-Leninism-Maoism. My aim, here, is to provide the reader with the framework of the book by summarizing some key axioms that might otherwise lurk implicitly in the background. If philosophy is to intervene in a given theoretical terrain in order to clarify conceptual problems and attempt to force meaning, then it is necessary to provide the reader with a rough sketch of the terrain that is being explored. The exploration of this terrain, the focus of the entire book, will mainly concern the axioms summarized below and the philosophical problematics they produce.

Axiom 1: Since the name "Maoism" existed before the concept of "Marxism-Leninism-Maoism", while it is important to recognize that the latter shares some of the DNA of the former, I label contemporary Maoism *Maoism-qua-Maoism*. Similarly, before Leninism was codified conceptually as a theoretical terrain (that is, where its key theoretical developments were universally applicable in all instances of class struggle), it had already existed as a name: for some it simply meant fidelity to the revolution led by Lenin, and thus fidelity to V.I. Lenin the

1

person and his politics; for others, as Roland Boer has pointed out, "far from being an invention by comrades after the October revolution, 'Leninist' was initially a term of abuse from opponents, an accusation of splitting".[1]

Axiom 2: I historically locate the emergence of Maoism-qua-Maoism, the period of time in which Maoism became a coherent concept, as a process that began in 1988. My argument is that Maoism was properly established as a concept first in 1988 during the people's war led by the Communist Party of Peru [PCP], "the first organization to refer to Maoism as a new stage of Marxism-Leninism".[2] Then, following a process of international debate, Maoism was coherently summarized (that is, conceptually crystallized) by the Revolutionary Internationalist Movement [RIM] in 1993. Obviously there are other interpretations of Maoism that do not declare fidelity to this historical narrative; my contention is that the coherent notion of Maoism as the third stage of revolutionary science produced by this process is the conceptualization of Marxism-Leninism-Maoism shared by the majority of significant contemporary Maoist organizations.[3]

Axiom 3: I presuppose that historical materialism is a *science*, a notion that has fallen out of favor with some but a claim that is necessary in order to properly understand the meaning of the theory initiated by Marx and Engels. Although I do not adhere to a crude conceptualization of this science (i.e. that materialist dialectics is the "queen of the sciences" that can explain everything and thus speak with authority about the substantial concerns of physics, biology, astronomy, chemistry, etc.), I believe that it must be understood as a science according to its own terms in order for it to have any significant meaning. Hence, what makes historical materialism important as a theory is its adherence to the basic notion of *science* that defined enlightenment thought: its ability to provide an explanation according to its own boundaries, historical/social causes for historical/social phenomena, rather than appealing to supernatural and mystified explanations; its ability to theoretically develop according to its fundamental laws of motion (i.e. that class revolution is the motive force of history) and thus be open to the future rather than a closed circuit in which no new truths/insights can be developed; its ability to produce theoretical moments that are universally applicable in particular instances. Historical materialism might not be the "queen of the sciences" but I presume, as an axiom, that it is the science of history and, based on its fundamental premise, the science of revolution. In the second chapter I will elaborate on this conception of revolutionary science.

Axiom 4: I understand Maoism as a third stage of revolutionary science, scientific because its key theoretical insights are universally applicable in every particular instance. In this way it represents both *continuity* and *rupture* with Marxism-Leninism, just as Leninism represented continuity and rupture with Marxism: a paradigm shift in revolutionary science, produced by coherently summarizing the experience of the second world-historical communist revolution (the Chinese Revolution led by Mao Zedong), that could only implement this shift, and thus the emergence of a new theoretical terrain, by also being a continuation of the universal aspects of the previous stage of revolutionary science. By claiming that Maoism is a third stage of revolutionary science, as the PCP first declared in 1988, I am also claiming, in line with the RIM's statement of 1993, that "without Maoism there can be no Marxism-Leninism. Indeed, to negate Maoism is to negate Marxism-Leninism itself."[4]

Axiom 5: In order to understand the necessity of Maoism as the current stage of revolutionary science, we need to understand the theoretical limits of Marxism-Leninism. The theoretical rupture, which is at the same time a continuity, only makes sense after we examine the limits of the previous scientific paradigm. Even an anti-revisionist Marxism-Leninism of the kind that used to be short-handed as "Maoism" is now inadequate for building a revolutionary movement.

The point of a philosophical intervention in the terrain generally defined by the above axioms, however, is not to focus on theorizing Maoism but to clarify and explore the already-existing theoretical terrain of Maoism. As will become clear in this chapter, the basic meaning of Marxism-Leninism-Maoism was clarified between 1988 and 1993. I am more interested, as a philosopher, in intervening upon a terrain that already exists (in this case, the terrain indicated by the above axioms), describing the boundaries of this terrain, and attempting to provide conceptual clarity for further exploration. Contemporary Maoists, unlike the majority of past Maoists, claim that Maoism is a new stage in revolutionary science; the job of a philosophy that places itself in the service of this theory (and philosophies and their philosophers always, even if unconsciously, dedicate themselves to an ideological position) is to explain *why* this is the case and explore its implications.

Thus, my main reason for outlining these axioms is simply to mark out some fundamental characteristics of the terrain under investigation. In this book I am not primarily interested in justifying the existence and necessity of this terrain, although this is a secondary concern, but am simply indicating the key landmarks of the conceptual geography I hope to illuminate. A navigator who finds himself adrift in a vast river that others have already discovered does not waste too much time wondering whether they should be travelling this river in the first place; rather, they attempt to navigate the currents of this body of water by referring to the pre-given boundaries provided by those who have charted its geography. So while it might be the case (though I do not think so) that I have found myself upon a river that will only lead to a dead-end, my focus is on explaining the pre-given boundaries I plan to navigate. In charting my route, clearing up misconceptions and dealing with various dogmas, my hope is that the resulting cartography will provide clarity for both Maoists and non-Maoists alike.

"Maoism-qua-Maoism"

To reiterate, I am making a distinction between the name and the concept of Maoism; hence my use of the laborious philosophical term "Maoism-qua-Maoism"—meaning, *Maoism as being Maoism.* More accurately, I mean *Maoism as being properly understood as the Maoism of today.* That is, the Maoism that is espoused by the most significant organizations, as well as what we can call "the worldwide Maoist movement", that define themselves according to this name—the Maoism understood by almost all of us who identify according to this term—possesses a specific conceptual meaning that differs from the meaning of organizations prior to 1988 that shared the name.

Even within the revolutionary tradition shifts in the meaning of a term are not uncommon: as aforementioned, before the theoretical codification of *Leninism* that transformed it into what we understand it to mean now, Leninism was used by those who rejected the Bolshevik political line to mean "sectarian": here a name is shared, but there are clearly two different concepts. The conceptual distinction is far more important than the shared name; those of us who declare fidelity to Leninism do not mean the same thing as those who might still maintain the earlier definition of the name.

Similarly, the majority of those of us who now identify as *Maoist* believe that there is a significant conceptual difference between our Maoism and the Maoism(s) of the past, even if we share the same name. Since this distinction might seem rather vague, it is necessary to examine it in more detail. Hopefully this examination will allow for a philosophical investigation of *Maoism-qua-Maoism*; in order for there to be such an investigation we must be able to explain the meaning of the concept under examination.

Before 1988 and 1993 there was indeed something called Maoism, but this iteration of Maoism is what today's ascendant world-wide Maoist movement often calls *Mao Zedong Thought.* In this period, those who called themselves or were called "Maoist" generally took the name to mean anti-revisionist Marxism-Leninism. A paradigm example of this definition can be found in the programme of the Canadian Communist League (Marxist-Leninist)—the organization that would eventually become one of Canada's most important anti-revisionist communist parties in the 1970s and 1980s, changing its name to the Workers Communist Party [WCP]. In 1975, this nascent party formation began its manifesto by defining its ideology as *Marxism-Leninism-Mao Zedong Thought* and clarified its Maoism, in the manner of most anti-revisionist communist organizations, as meaning nothing more than a reclamation of the Marxism-Leninism abandoned by those parties following the Soviet Union under Khrushchev. Maoism for the WCP primarily meant "struggle against modern revisionism"—fidelity to the revolutionary essence of Marxism-Leninism abandoned by the Marxist-Leninist parties in "most countries" that "degenerated and became revisionist".[6]

Therefore, before the late 1980s Maoism was understood as anti-revisionist Marxism-Leninism, and the Maoists of this period were generally anti-revisionists who privileged China over the Soviet Union. With few exceptions, Maoism was not grasped as a new stage in revolutionary science but merely a correct way of thinking—a return to a proper and revolutionary Marxism-Leninism that had been undermined by the Soviet Union under Khrushchev. Following the political line of the Chinese communists under Mao, and the polemics exchanged between the Chinese and Soviet parties, Maoism in this context was a name that stood primarily for the adherence to the revolutionary principles of Leninism.

At that time, the emergence of an exciting anti-revisionist revolutionary current made sense. On the one hand there was the bankrupt communism of Khrushchev's Soviet Union that was speaking of a "peaceful co-existence" with capitalism; on the other hand there was the "New Left" that not only denounced the mainstream communist parties following Khrushchev's line but also the history of Leninism. The New Communist Movement, unhappy with either of these choices, declared fidelity to the Chinese Revolution, which had not yet capitulated to the capitalist road, as well as the world-wide anti-imperialist movement. This fidelity was quite often called "Maoist" even if it lacked a clear theoretical line beyond a commitment to anti-revisionist Marxism-Leninism and the Chinese Revolution led by Mao.

There were, of course, debates in this period regarding the meaning of this Maoism, and sometimes significant differences emerged between Maoist groups. There were even a few attempts to think through the meaning of a coherent theoretical terrain of Maoism that, in some sense, prefigured today's theoretical terrain of Maoism. None of these conceptualizations, however, were coherent and systematic enough to push past the terrain of an anti-revisionist Marxism-Leninism. Most importantly, outside of the North American context, there were theorists such as Jose Maria Sison (Philippines) and Charu Mazumdar (India) who were leading parties engaged in people's wars and developing a more thorough understanding of Maoism's possibilities. Even still, there was no significant attempt to defend the privileging of *Maoism* over *Mao Zedong Thought*—those who tried to do so prior to 1988 were unable to produce a concrete and coherent theorization regardless of what they claimed. Indeed, most Marxist-Leninist-Maoist organizations today recognize that "[i]t was the PCP who said that Maoism was a step above Marxism[-Leninism] and that the ideology that should now guide the communist international movement was Marxism-Leninism-Maoism".[7]

Until the late 1970s, when China was still arguably revolutionary, it was difficult to provide a thorough assessment of the experience of the Chinese revolution, and thus understand the meaning of its successes and failures, as had been done by China with respect to the Soviet Union. Hence, this previous Maoism was under-theorized and even if it contained the seeds of what we now call Marxism-Leninism-Maoism it could only be under-developed due to the very nature of a science that develops according to the condition of revolutionary praxis. Regardless of how its anti-revisionism was short-handed, this tendency was still Marxism-Leninism, but a tendency that was reaching the limits of the Leninist terrain and that, upon reaching these limits, would be forced to deal with contradictions that were not solved until the New Communist Movement collapsed.

Indeed, the fact that the old "Maoism" could not think beyond its Marxist-Leninist limits was demonstrated in the clichéd formula that Leninism was "the Marxism of the imperialist era". Such a formula, though doubtlessly useful for operationalizing Lenin and demonstrating how it possessed a particular universal importance (i.e. it was a development of Marxism that not only understood the imperialist era of capitalism but possessed the tools to wage class struggle in this epoch), was ultimately unscientific because it could only produce a dogmatic conceptualization of Marxism-Leninism where *Leninism* became the absolute limit of the theory and Maoism, in this sense, could only ever be the anti-revisionist "thought" dedicated to its appreciation. Since this understanding of both Leninism and Maoism (that is, "Mao Zedong Thought") might still be a roadblock for understanding how and why Leninism can be overstepped, it is worth discussing in some detail.

The first problem with this formulation is that it is an impoverishment of Leninism. By reducing it to a summation of Marxism within a particular era, rather than recognizing one aspect of its universality in its grasp of this era, this formulation cannot explain why Leninism is noteworthy. Leninism thus becomes a phenomenon that is important because of a time—a time, no doubt, that will exist as long as capitalism exists—and not because of the theorizations it has produced regarding this time. The formulation is too large and thus unwieldy; it explains nothing of itself by a reduction to the unscientific notion of a *zeitgeist*. Here we find an unconscious Hegelianism, the philosophy that Marx and Engels broke from, in that it becomes something of a speculative system: Leninism as the accomplishment of the world spirit of revolution.

The second problem with this conception of Leninism, following the first, is that it fails to recognize that imperialism existed prior to Lenin and that the Marxism of Marx and Engels was also a "Marxism of the imperialist era" but, clearly, a different era of imperialism. It is not as if Marx and Engels did not discuss this imperialism; indeed Marx's discussion of "so-called primitive accumulation" in the first volume of *Capital* is very aware of the imperialist dimension of capitalism during his time. Of course, Lenin's discussion of imperialism is an examination of an imperialism transformed by capitalism, and is thus a significant and universal development of theory, but the point here is that the "era of imperialism" pre-exists Lenin.

Moreover, since imperialism is, as Lenin put it, the "final stage" of capitalism (more precisely, the consummation of capitalism where the imperialism that pre-dated and developed capitalism is transformed by capitalism and thus part of its moribund period), then to name Leninism the "Marxism of the imperialist era" is to also make the claim that there can be no further development in revolutionary science. Why? Because if Lenin was correct (and those who refuse to recognize a development beyond Leninism presume that this is the case), then the era of imperialism will only end with the termination of capitalism. Thus, according to this definition of Leninism, the science of revolution is completed in Leninism, and every theorist post-Lenin can only be an addition or qualification to these final revelations. There can never be a Marxism that is post-imperialist era without a calamity that sets history back several centuries or a revolution that brings about the communist horizon. Lenin, then, becomes the final word on the class struggle of the present since imperialism is the threshold. In this sense, there can be no scientific development: those who argue that Maoism can never be a true -*ism* according to this qualification, then, have rigged the game by making Leninism similar to the Absolute in Hegel's *Logic*—a final systemization of the science that cannot admit future development, is beyond historicization, and, in a word, is pseudo-science.

To be closed to the future is to no longer be scientific. A science is that which develops and does not claim to encompass the entire future in its paradigm. Once we define a stage in science in overly broad terms it no longer makes sense: if Leninism is the Marxism of the imperialist era, and this is all Leninism means, then we are dealing only with a dogmatic formula. *What* made this formula possible in the first place? Lenin's analysis of imperialism, his conceptualization of the state and revolution, his theorization of the party. Very well! These developments, among some other things, are the content of Leninism; not the *periodization* of Lenin, that he also happened to analyze, which has nothing to do with Leninism-qua-Leninism aside from an attempt to lock it into a dogmatic form—a permanent Leninism, a science closed to the future and thus *not* a science because, in order to be a science, the closure of the future horizon cannot happen. Science is that which is open to the future, its truth a process rather than an absolute accomplishment determined by a closed circuit. Hence, those who rely on this definition of Leninism (and thus the possibility of Maoism) would do well to remember Engels' words in *Feuerbach and the End of Classical German Philosophy*: "by declaring that his knowledge of the absolute idea is attained... the whole dogmatic content of the... system is thus declared to be absolute truth, in contradiction with [the] dialectical method, which dissolves all dogmatism. Thus the revolutionary side is smothered beneath the overgrowth of the conservative side."[7]

To define Leninism as the "Marxism of the imperialist era"—and thus to refuse scientific development—is indeed conservative due to the broadness of the definition. Failing to recognize the particular meaning of Leninism, and how it is actually distinct from the science initiated by Marx and Engels, leads to a closure of the science itself. One might as well declare that the Newtonian paradigm is "physics in the era of causality" and thus damn the science to closure: Einstein's intervention, then, becomes just an addition to Newton and not a transformation of the entire terrain of theory—Albert Einstein Thought!—not to mention all of those developments post-Einstein.

How, then, do we "dissolve" the "dogmatism" according to the "dialectical method" and thus avoid being "smothered" by the "conservative side" of thought evinced by the above definition of Leninism? By abandoning this hackneyed definition of Leninism and Mao Zedong Thought that was the hallmark of the New Communist Movement and grasping the dialectic of continuity-rupture that defines the unfolding of every scientific terrain. If we are to agree that there is something about the imperialist era that signifies the emergence of Leninism, then we must also recognize that the advent of actually existing socialism changes the meaning of the imperialist epoch examined by Lenin. In this sense, Maoism could be called the communism of the socialist era—the Marxist ideology that can explain class struggle in the context of socialism—since socialist revolutions, despite the defeat of the two world-historical socialist revolutions, alter the meaning of global imperialism. Even this definition, though, is not entirely correct: i) it fails to satisfy the conditions of science in general, as discussed above, by closing science in abstract historical epochs that might not admit the very thing that defines science—the fact that truth is a process that cannot be closed; ii) it fails to satisfy the conditions of revolutionary science in particular, based on the axiom that class struggle is the motor of history, where the possibility of successive stages is initiated by world-historical revolutions.

Some Broad Brushstrokes

The people's war led by the Communist Party of Peru, as noted above, was significant because it was the first time an organization engaged in a revolutionary insurgency was more than simply the proper name of anti-revisionist communism. Rather than speaking of a Marxism-Leninism understood properly through "Mao Zedong Thought", in 1988 the PCP, at the height of its people's war, claimed that Maoism was indeed a proper scientific "-ism" and was thus the third stage for revolutionary science: Marxism-Leninism-Maoism. Then, following the PCP's initiative, revolutionary organizations from all over the globe met under the auspices of the Revolutionary Internationalist Movement to assess the successes and failures of the Chinese Revolution so as to succinctly define Marxism-Leninism-Maoism, crystallizing a basic theoretical terrain for Maoism in 1993.

This conceptualization of Maoism was so important that eventually other revolutionary organizations would accept and adopt the theorization manifesting in RIM's 1993 statement. For example, around a year after the RIM statement of 1993, the Communist Party of India (Marxist-Leninist) People's War (formerly known as the People's War Group) would discard *Marxism-Leninism-Mao Zedong Thought* for *Marxism-Leninism-Maoism*. Eventually, this organization would merge with other parties to form the Communist Party of India (Maoist) [CPI (Maoist)] which is now spear-heading a people's war.[8]

Claiming that Maoism became Maoism through this process—from 1988 to 1993—is important because definitions are important. Regardless of the eventual fate of the PCP and the RIM (or even how some Marxist-Leninist-Maoist organizations today may be critical, for good reason, of the PCP and the result of the RIM experience), the basic theory that they helped make manifest is the Maoism that has been expressed by the most revolutionary and popular communist movements since the fall of the Eastern Bloc. While it is true that other attempts to conceptualize the name of Maoism have not vanished—just as fidelity to Marxism-Leninism-Mao Zedong Thought has not vanished—it is a fact that the Maoism that is now theoretically hegemonic amongst Maoists throughout the world is related to the Marxism-Leninism-Maoism originally conceptualized by the PCP and the RIM. Similarly, after Stalin wrote *Foundations of Leninism* and the term Marxism-Leninism became hegemonic amongst the international communist movement, at that time it did not really matter that Trotskyists claimed an alternate version of Marxism-Leninism: the origin of the term became irrevocably wed, rightly or wrongly, to Stalin's theorization.

Once again, I need to reinforce the fact that I am only explaining the pre-existent boundaries. Whether or not these are proper boundaries is a second-order question—one that both myself and others have attempted to answer and justify elsewhere—and not the focus of this book. In this chapter, again, I am simply attempting to explain the vicissitudes of a course that has already been charted. The point is to indicate the distance between the name and concept of Maoism, bridging this gap by quickly explaining the most thorough and historically significant (if we accept, as communists, that historical significance is established by concrete revolutionary struggle) conceptualization of the word.

In any case, this specific conceptualization of Maoism claimed that *Maoism* was a third stage of revolutionary science because it produced new theoretical insights beyond Leninism that were equal to Leninism because they were also *universally applicable*—theoretical concepts which are necessary for revolution because they can be applied in every social context. I will describe the broad brushstrokes of the development of revolutionary science that moves in a Maoist trajectory without, keeping my above point about pre-existent boundaries in mind, providing too much elaboration. Such elaboration has been provided elsewhere and is the concern of theory. Hence, since philosophy follows theory it must begin by assuming that which has already been theorized limiting itself to an intervention on a pre-existing terrain. In the following paragraphs I will define the general contours of this terrain without providing significant elaboration; this is because the theory already exists, and so I feel no need to over-reproduce its description.

First, we understand that Marxism is universally applicable because it produced the first scientific analysis of capitalism, grasped that history's movement is defined by class struggle, and that we are now in the period where the proletariat is the agent of history, capable of ending capitalism. This general aspect of its universality is buttressed by various interior scientific concepts: the theory of the mode of production where a social formation's meaning is understood, in the last instance, according to the interplay of productive forces (the combination of tools, machinery, and labor power) and productive relations (the social, class-based relationships in which humans engage with forces of production); the understanding that the economic base of productive forces/relations informs a political, legal, and social superstructure—an analogy that means that the latter cannot exist without the former, since it is impossible to imagine particular political/legal/social modes of being without the prior existence of a particular mode of production[9]; a thorough analysis of the capitalist mode of production and its origins; the first codification of a materialist approach to history and society.

Next, we claim that Leninism is universally applicable because we believe that it is only possible to establish socialism through a revolutionary party, that a state commanded by the proletariat must be instituted to suppress the bourgeoisie so as to possibly establish communism (i.e. the dictatorship of the proletariat), and that we are now in the imperialist stage of capitalism. To these insights we can add: the theory of socialism, where the dictatorship of the proletariat *is* socialism, a transitionary social formation that is to communism as mercantilism is to capitalism, and thus the theorization of class struggle to socialism; a theorization of "opportunism" based on the revisionism of Bernstein and Kautsky[10]; and the germinal conceptualization of "the national question" that explains how communists ought to understand the anti-colonial struggles of oppressed nations.

Finally, after 1993 and the assessment of the successes and failures of the second world-historical communist revolution, we should recognize that Maoism is universally applicable because: class struggle continues under the dictatorship of the proletariat (socialism is a class society), the revolutionary party must also become a mass party and renew itself by being held to account by those it claims to represent (the mass-line), the struggle between the revolutionary and revisionist political lines will happen within the revolutionary party itself, and that the strategy of people's war rather than unqualified insurrection is the strategy for making revolution.[11] To these insights we can add: a further elaboration of the theory of base-superstructure where it is understood that, while the economic base might be determinate in the *last instance*, it is also true that *this last instance might never arrive* (a point made by Althusser, following Marx and Engels) and thus we can conceive of instances where the superstructure may determine and/or obstruct the base;[12] the theory of New Democratic Revolution, which applies *universally* to the *particular* instances of global peripheries (universal in the sense that it applies to every so-called "third-world" context) and explains, for the first time in history, how regions that are not capitalist by themselves and yet are still locked within a system of capitalist exploitation (that is, regions that are the victims of imperialism) can make socialism; and a further anti-colonial development of "the national question", refracted through Mariategui and Fanon but established in practice by those Maoist people's wars (i.e. Peru, Nepal, India) that encountered the necessity of mobilizing multiple oppressed nations.[13]

The overall point, here, is that revolutionary theory develops through class revolution, specifically through world-historical revolution, and that there have only been three world-historical communist revolutions: the Paris Commune which, in its successes and failures, taught Marx and Engels the basis of a proletarian revolutionary science; the Russian Revolution which consolidated this basis by establishing a socialist state; the Chinese Revolution which, in launching the Russian Revolution, consolidated Leninism as a moment of rupture-continuity in the chain of revolutionary science. Since revolutionary struggle is open-ended, and is thus capable of establishing its theory in the manner of a living science, we should recognize that another revolution that goes further than the Chinese Revolution and yet still fails to produce communism—i.e. fails in an even more spectacular manner than China—would have to be assessed in order to understand the next theoretical moment beyond Maoism.

World-Historical Revolutions

The broad brushstrokes discussed in the previous section can also be understood as significant by examining the history of revolutions, particularly the ones I have called (borrowing from Samir Amin) *world-historical*, according to the problematic of failure. After all, it is one thing for me to list a series of significant characteristics of revolutionary science and assert that they are significant because they are the characteristics the Maoist tradition deems as characteristic; it is quite another to prove that this is a fact when there are competing interpretations within the larger Marxist terrain. A facile but rather compelling counter-argument to my claim(s) might assert that the very fact that all of the previous revolutions eventually failed is enough to treat each of them as singular instances, without any universal qualities, proven to be singular by the very fact of their failure.

But since it is not enough to dismiss an argument we do not like by labeling it *facile*, let us give this counter-argument its due. The failure of these revolutions is indeed significant. After the failure of the Paris Commune, and the execution of the communards, an entire generation of radicals in Europe was thrown into confusion. Because the success of the Chinese Revolution overlapped with the waning Russian Revolution there was no gap of disillusionment between these two instances of revolutionary rupture, as there was between the Commune and the October Revolution, but there was the confusion caused by the Sino-Soviet split and, later, the massive disillusionment produced by the combination of the fall of the Eastern Bloc and China's decision to choose the capitalist road.

Although I have argued elsewhere that it is important not to dismiss revolutionary successes because of their eventual failures, this is not enough to diffuse the counter-argument. Why not? Because the Maoist tradition, even before the advent of Maoism-qua-Maoism, has dismissed other revolutionary possibilities that did not accord to the scientific trajectory it accepted as fact, arguing that certain strategies and approaches will be doomed to failure because they do not grasp what was established by the world-historical revolutions. We make these judgments all the time. For instance, I have claimed that the Arab Spring, though a significant rebellion, would fail to become a revolution because of its movementist dimensions—the lack of a revolutionary party meant that other, non-revolutionary forces that were organized (i.e. either Political Islam, the liberals, or the military institution) would end up directing the disorganized energy of rebellion—because of the conditions established by the three world-historical revolutions and this rebellion's failure to meet these conditions. As it turned out, those of us who made these arguments were correct. At the same time, however, a very similar argument can be made about those revolutions that accord to the characteristics I used to dismiss the Arab Spring: for instance, the failure of the people's war in Nepal was used by various critics to argue that the approach of the CPN(Maoist) was deluded: some argued that this was because they were following a "Stalinist" political line ("socialism in one country") that Trotskyism had proved was doomed, as both the failures of the Russian and Chinese Revolutions supposedly proved; others argued that the revolution in Nepal was doomed because it followed a "Leninist" model of a vanguard party that, again as history has supposedly proven, can only lead to failure. All of these arguments concerned the *meaning* of failure, and what it should constitute, and it is important to understand which arguments about this meaning are correct.

Let us look at another example. The event of the victory of Allende's Socialist Party of Chile was seen, and for good reason, as a new development in anti-capitalist struggle in the early 1970s. But some aspects of the anti-revisionist Marxist-Leninist current argued that its failure was prefigured in the very way in which it had assumed power: by winning in an election, and not through a revolution, it had failed to smash the bourgeois institutions that, under an elected socialist party, would immediately become the sites of counter-revolution. Here, the argument was that without the establishment of the dictatorship of the proletariat, the dictatorship of the bourgeoisie will remain (since this dictatorship is a social totality and not something that can be voted away as it is the police, the military, the economic structure, etc.), and that Allende's victory was the most radical variant of the revisionist thesis of "peaceful co-existence with capitalism". The revisionist thesis presumes that socialism can be established peacefully, possibly through elections, without a revolution aimed at demolishing those institutions upon which a capitalist society is premised, or those institutions (like the military and the police) that exist to defend bourgeois class power. As it turned out the assessment of the tragic limitations of Allende's Chile was correct because the counter-revolution came from those institutions that were previously devoted to defending the dictatorship of the bourgeoisie and, because Allende's party took power through an election, were not smashed and replaced by institutions built through revolutionary mass power. We need to ask, though, why should this assessment even matter when those who made it relied on the examples of the Russian and Chinese Revolutions, both of which were already in the revisionist camp when this critique was made. (Russia, before Allende's election, had put forward the thesis of "peaceful co-existence". By the time of the coup in Chile, the capitalist roaders had already won and, to the horror of Chilean anti-revisionists, recognized Pinochet's coup.) On what basis does this assessment stand when the counter-position that it argued *also* produced failure?

These are questions that should not be dismissed dogmatically; the only way to make sense of them is to establish a distinction between the failures of world-historical revolutions and those that lurk in these revolutions' penumbra. But in order to establish this distinction, to avoid dogmatism we first need to provide an argument as to why we recognize a particular revolutionary set as the *core* concept of revolutionary theory and all that fall outside of this set as *penumbral*.

Establishing the Paris Commune, Russian Revolution, and Chinese Revolution as world-historical standards for revolutions pursuing communism is not entirely difficult. The Paris Commune was the first attempted break from capitalism in history and, since its event, has been recognized as such: its memory is constantly recalled by progressives, its failure is still treated as trauma, and there was no anti-capitalist in Europe at the time who was not invested in its existence: both the Marxist and anarchist traditions recognize that this is a fact, including traditions outside of Europe that continue to conjure its memory.

The Russian Revolution is similarly easy to establish as world-historical: for the first time in history we have the emergence of a state that declares itself socialist and that, because of this first-time status, becomes *the* world enemy of the imperialist camp: we do not have to cite the Cold War as an example of its world-historical status, which pushed it into the primary counter-capitalist pole, for we can also examine how it was recognized by progressives everywhere, at the moment of its emergence, as *the* break with the state of affairs: every left-wing journalist directly following the October Revolution recognized this was the fact, even its left-wing critics (from Rosa Luxemburg to a quickly disenchanted Emma Goldman to Leon Trotsky's attempted Fourth International). Similarly, the Chinese Revolution manifested upon the historical stage like a hurricane: for the first time in history we witnessed a non-European nation breaking with European imperialism and establishing economic independence that was socialist; the entire decolonization movement in Africa and Asia was inspired, in various ways, by the Chinese revolution. Thus, we have three first instances of revolution (though not entirely *first* because they followed each other, learning from each other's mistakes) that have not yet been rivaled on the historical stage. Other socialist revolutions were either attempted replications, or fell short of these moments.

These are the truth-producing events of revolutionary science.

Inversely, we can also understand which revolutions were not world-historical simply by asking whether they revealed any new universal insights for humanity as a whole. If we define a world-historical revolution as that which is revolutionary for people everywhere while simultaneously revealing new theoretical universals, then there are many revolutions that are barred from this category. For instance, going back before these three proletarian revolutions, and examining the two main contenders for bourgeois revolution (the American and the French examples), we can say that whereas the French Revolution

20

was a world-historical *bourgeois* revolution (and thus, to be clear, not one of the three examples we're looking at in terms of proletarian revolutionary science, but still important for Marxism), the American revolution, though initiated first, was not world-historical—nor was it necessarily a bourgeois revolution.[14] Indeed, whereas the ideology and theory mobilized by the French Revolution possessed a global dimension—at the very edge of Jacobin ideology we find the Santo Domingo Slave Revolution that formed the most radical sequence of the French Revolution[15]—the American Revolution was simply a revolt of slave-owners, a movement of secession. There was nothing in the American Revolution that could be adopted, universally, by all of humanity; every slave-in-rebellion and abolitionist sided with the British Empire.[16]

Falsification

Let us return to the examples of the three world-historical communist-oriented revolutions. Establishing their significance is not enough to explain the distinction between their failures and those of other revolutionary sequences. At this point we are simply establishing that the lessons gleaned from these revolutions possess a *universal status* because of these revolutions' *world-historical aspect*: the former is dependent on the latter because how else can universality be established? Only on what is world-historical, meaning *global*: that which can be applied in every case, though mediated by various particularities (i.e. the universality of the establishment of the dictatorship of the proletariat may not look the same in China as it did in Russia). But establishing a particular sequence of revolutions, and thus the lessons learned from these revolutions, as world-historical should lead us to understand the distinction between *four categories of failure*: a) those possible failures that are encountered because they result from new questions the previous revolutions did not encounter; b) those possible failures that the most recent world-historical revolution encountered but did not solve; c) those possible failures that the most recent world-historical revolution encountered and *did* solve; d) those failures that were solved *prior* to the most recent world-historical revolution, by earlier revolutions in the sequence.

Let us streamline these categories: the first two deal with failures that lurk either *at* or *beyond* the horizon of revolutionary history; the second two deal with failures that are contained *within* or *before* revolutionary history. We will call the first two categories *live failures* and the second two categories *dead failures*. The former have yet to be solved; the latter have already been solved. Those potential revolutions that fall into the category of *dead failures* (i.e. they go about their revolutionary business as if certain questions were not solved and instead try to reinvent the proverbial wheel) are those that generally lack revolutionary potential due to their inability to recognize the successes and failures already established by the revolutionary sequence... just as an artist unfamiliar with Marcel Duchamp who produces "ready-mades" is someone we would not recognize as a very good artist.

Hence, these four categories and the way they are grouped are significant because they can inform our understanding of revolutionary failure, and how to make a distinction between a gradation of failures that are not identical. Chile's failure in the 1973, which was already proved at the time to be a *dead failure*, is not identical to Russia's failure in the years that spanned between Stalin and Yeltsin: this was a *live failure* that had already established the basis upon which Chile's failure could be understood. The Arab Spring's or Syriza's failure is even less significant because these do not even approach the failure of Allende's Chile! For if Allende's Chile cannot meet the bare minimum of what constituted failure for the world-historical revolutions (that is, the most important and truth-producing events of revolutionary science), and yet was still more politically advanced and consolidated (again judged by the same truth-producing events) than the Arab Spring and Syriza, when we make political judgments about the Arab Spring and Syriza we are dealing with events that are far below the standard of revolutionary failure: these are definitively *dead failures* or potential *dead failures*.

To be clear, I am not arguing that rebellions and revolts that fall into the categories of *dead failure* should be mocked or dismissed out-of-hand. We should always support the masses when they rebel against the structures of global capitalism.[17] All such rebellions challenge capitalism's state of affairs and function as openings, as I will argue in a later chapter, in which a possible revolutionary sequence can thrive. Rather, the point I am making about failure is this: there are failures that have already been encountered by history that should inform us about every rebellion in the present. When we encounter a revolutionary approach that is not aware of the ways in which past failures were recognized and/or overcome, then we encounter approaches that, by themselves, will necessarily make the same mistakes—that proverbial attempt to reinvent the wheel. Hence, we need to understand how the recognition of failure develops according to the three world-historical revolutions.

1. *The Paris Commune.* This world-historical revolution proved, decades in advance, that the revisionist thesis of "peaceful co-existence with capital" was unacceptable because its revolutionary event only manifested through an insurrection—the ruling class could not be reasoned with or elected out of its hegemony. Any rebellion that does not meet this standard (which recognizes that one needs to take up arms to make a revolution and that the state's military and police will mobilize to put down a revolution, *as they did with the communards*) that is outside of the revolutionary sequence is definitively a dead failure. If we understand the Paris Commune according

to its failure, then, we should grasp precisely what Marx and Engels grasped: the failure of the communards to establish a dictatorship of the proletariat, to take over the state, smashing its bourgeois institutions in the process, and consolidating class power.

2. *The Russian Revolution.* The successes that were universally applicable were discussed in an earlier section. So what failures of this part of the sequence are universally significant, i.e. *live failures*? The failure to recognize how and why class struggle continues during socialism within the dictatorship of the proletariat and, in this context, how to consolidate a mass-line.

3. *The Chinese Revolution.* Again, the universally applicable successes of this moment of the overall sequence was explained earlier. The universality of its failures, though, is what we are required to solve today: how to consolidate the cultural revolution so as to win the class struggle that continues socialism, how to properly grasp the strategy of making revolution *in toto*.

Every rebellion since the Chinese Revolution has fallen extremely short of reaching the points at which this revolution failed. Most often we're asking questions that were foreclosed by the Paris Commune or the Russian Revolution, wasting our time trying to solve problems that were already solved and thus encountering the failures the above sequence overcame. This is why an understanding of the categories of failure allows us to make certain judgments: if an event falls short of solving what a failed world-historical revolution *already solved*, and thus is not even approaching the threshold of failure that this world-historical revolution encountered, then it is exhibiting a dead failure.

The overall point, then, is that if we understand this sequence we can also understand how to make sense of failure and the conditions in which failure is possible. This sequence, of course, is largely inductive because, based on causal reasoning that is not formally deductive (we are not establishing mathematical syllogisms but instead functioning according to an inference to the best explanation), we are only establishing probability. That is, a potential revolution that does not fit the above qualifications because it is something we would otherwise classify as a *dead failure* is only highly unlikely to fail—historical flukes are possible, just as there can be empirical experiments in chemistry which violate the rules established by previous experiments, though to date I cannot think of one example of an exception. More significantly, though, the above sequence establishes a very high level of explanatory power: it can explain the reasons for a revolutionary failure better than an account that is not premised on these three world-historical instances. For example, the failure of the revolution in Nepal is better explained by its inability to satisfy the conditions grasped by the second and third world-historical revolutions (particularly in the way in which the second revolution was grasped by the third)—that is the line struggle within the party, the failure of the left political line to defeat the right political line—then according to a vague, and thus very unscientific, explanation regarding the failures of Leninism or Nepal's Stalinist "socialism in one country" approach, both of which were explanations that demonstrated very little attention to the phemonena they were attempting to explain.

As an aside, this way of making sense of revolutionary theory through failure demonstrates the very thing that Karl Popper assumed was lacking from historical materialism, thus allowing him to dismiss it as a pseudo-science: the principle of falsification.[18] Apparently Popper understood very little about the interior controversies of historical materialism and took the popular Cold-War codification at its word: a theory that does not permit testing, that establishes the future and the present as total. The claims made by historical materialism were not, as he assumed, about the testability/falsification of communism itself which, he was correct in pointing out, was the utopian hypothesis that, like God, could never be scientifically tested and thus lurked only as a potential threshold break from history. The historical boundary of communism exists only as a hypothesis that might never arrive, a way to judge the sequence of making socialism, which is indeed testable. Thus, as historical materialists, we do have a way to test for falsification, the possibility that our theories might be proven false: the very thing that determines the motion of history, class struggle.

Ruptural Process

With the problematic of world-historical revolution and falsification established, let us return to the theoretical terrain of Maoism-qua-Maoism and how to make sense of its operations according to the boundaries and description we have described. Marxism-Leninism-Maoism is not simply the algebra of all of Mao's writings and the manifold event of the Chinese Revolution. Maoism-qua-Maoism exists above and beyond Mao Zedong the individual, whose name is only ascribed to this theoretical terrain because it serves as a convenient historical cipher. Although I have argued that Maoism did not properly emerge until the closing decades of the 20th-century, the substance by which this theoretical terrain was established is the theory produced by Mao Zedong, treated as significant due to the world-historical nature of the Chinese Revolution led by the same individual. But only the substance.

Similarly, and as aforementioned, Leninism was not established as a theoretical terrain simply through the sum-total of everything Lenin wrote and did. After all, Lenin's theory of the party was derived from Kautsky; Lenin's theory of the state was derived from both Kautsky and Marx/Engels; Lenin's theory of imperialism, in opposition to Kautsky's, was a historical materialization of several bourgeois theories. What, then, is the moment where theoretical labor that is simply in continuity with a contemporary theoretical terrain becomes also a moment of rupture so as to become a new terrain? Obviously this moment of continuity-rupture does not happen simply by writing theory, engaging in revolutionary practice, and imagining it as more significant than it actually is; under this interpretation everything thus becomes "rupture" and hence the concept, as well as the concept of theory itself, is rendered meaningless. But if we chart the process in which Leninism emerged as a theoretical terrain, we can also understand the development of Maoism.

First, there is the October Revolution, the principle theorist of which was Lenin, which was a world-historical revolution: the significance of the revolution retroactively forced significance upon the theoretical work most clearly connected to this event. If there was no October Revolution, then the writings of Lenin would remain theory within a general Marxist terrain, an interesting and perhaps discursively useful province that did not pushed the terrain further: it may provide theoretical clarity and debate regarding certain native problems, but without any practical proof that its declarations about reality are universally applicable this is all it can do. Here, the only universal applicability would be whether or not this theory is in line with the general conception of the historical laws of motion, a universality inherited from Marx and Engels, and the particular expression of this universality. A world-historical revolution premised on the work of this theorist, however, alerts us to the fact that we are dealing with the germ of an emergent terrain. Something is different here: Lenin's theoretical practice is thus not simply in continuity with every other contemporary Marxist; it also promised rupture.

The October Revolution was not, however, enough to found Leninism even if Lenin's theoretical practice was part of its point of origin. The origin of a given theory is not equivalent to this theory or its significance; to assume otherwise is an epistemic fallacy. If such an equivalency relation held, then Darwin's theory of natural selection would be equivalent to Malthus' theory of populations, and we would be hard-pressed to find any biologist who seriously agrees that natural selection is reducible to Malthusian ideology.[19] Therefore, we do not encounter the Leninist terrain simply through the event of the October Revolution which, by itself, was simply the first communist revolution where the Bolsheviks operationalized Marxism, as best evinced by the theoretical practice of Lenin. What was thus required for the emergence of Leninism as a salient theoretical terrain was a declaration on the meaning of the event that forced its significance; through this declaration of meaning, a successive organizing of the theoretical data was necessary: a *theoretical operationalization*. The point, here, is to discover what is universally applicable, what ruptural understanding this emergent terrain may or may not possess.

Stalin's *Foundations of Leninism* is perhaps the first significant and molar process of theoretically operationalized Leninism. The problem with this early attempt, however, is that there are counter-operationalizations of Leninism, based on counter-assessments of the October Revolution, written by Trotsky and others. Here we discover a theoretical struggle over the meaning of a terrain during its germinal stage. And yet we can still learn something about the meaning of this eventual terrain simply by examining the points of intersection that speak in the language of universality. This tortured process of theoretical struggle, where Leninism was becoming Leninism-qua-Leninism, would finally be accomplished in the Communist Party of China's polemical document *Long Live Leninism!* where the universal aspects of Leninism would be adequately summed up in the face of revisionism. Here the process had crystallized within a terrain that could be named and described, summarized in a salient form, so as to argue that the rejection of Leninism *by the very party that Lenin had established* implied a rejection of Marxism as a whole.

Indeed, just as the Russian Revolution was the first Marxist world-historical revolution, insofar as the Bolshevik Party under Lenin operationalized Marxism, the Chinese Revolution was the first Marxist-Leninist revolution because the Communist Party of China under Mao was operationalizing (and theorizing) Leninism. Hence, the New Communist Movement that was influenced by China was, as aforementioned, an anti-revisionist Marxist-Leninist movement (the explosion of multiple anti-revisionist communist organizations throughout the world has been referred to by some as a period of *ML* groups), the first widespread manifestation of Leninism-qua-Leninism that, the Hoxhaite trend notwithstanding, was often called "Maoist".[20]

The above assessment of Leninism's emergence as Leninism should provide key insights regarding the justification of Maoism as a theoretical terrain and the process of its emergence. We can summarize these insights according to the following criteria:

1. *A world historical revolution provides the origin point of any significant and ruptural theoretical development.* The Chinese Revolution was the second communist world historical revolution insofar as it was able to systematize the lessons of the first world historical revolution, operationalize these lessons to learn from its failures, and, by going further, encounter new failures. The theory produced in this crucible would contain the seeds of new universal insights that still required time and struggle to comprehend.

2. *The assessment of the theoretical practice behind a world revolution begins the process of developing a theoretical*

terrain, based on what theoretical insights, in light of the revolution, are universally applicable. Following the success of the Chinese Revolution we encounter a vast body of theoretical work produced by Mao Zedong and other revolutionaries produced before, during, and after the revolution, and we are faced with the difficulty of deciding which aspects of this theory are unique and universalizable. In this process, where the terrain's germinal form is developing towards its first clear articulation, we encounter various trends that may or may not develop into something more significant; it is often difficult to declare on the meaning of the event of the revolution and its theory due to our proximity. Hence, the various anti-revisionist groups that would endorse the theory of Cultural Revolution, but only and purely as a safeguard against revisionism (where Leninism is allowed to accomplish its aims), would often and also endorse the "three-worlds theory"—a cosmetic division of the world that, when treated as universally applicable, led to some strange positions. Also, during the Great Proletarian Cultural Revolution in China we can observe a multiplicity of divergent theoretical trends, all declaring fidelity to Mao Zedong Thought.

3. *The new theoretical terrain emerges when this struggle passes beyond the limits of the previous terrain and begins to produce a new stage of struggles according to its assessment, synthesis, and decision of universality.* Leninism's boundaries were fully understood when the revolution formerly led by Lenin became openly revisionist and the Chinese Revolution, already beyond the limits of the terrain understood by Lenin and his fellow revolutionaries, could grasp the full meaning of the theory that was produced by the struggle in that terrain so as to deliver a

judgment upon those who labored under its name but failed to grasp its concept. In doing so, however, they were also part of a process that would establish something *beyond* these boundaries once this theoretical struggle crossed the Leninist limits. These limits were necessarily passed when China itself became revisionist and the New Communist Movement that had hoped to inoculate itself with an anti-revisionist Marxism-Leninism disintegrated. Here is where something we can properly call *Maoism* emerges: the shores of a new theoretical terrain that were waiting beyond the limits of the previous terrain's exhaustion.

Glimmers

None of this is to say, of course, that there were not glimmers of today's Maoism in the past Maoisms, that the eventual emergence of the concept was not prefigured by daring and significant attempts on the part of those who adopted its name. A conceptual break in the field of a science does not emerge from an abyss, even if it might occasionally appear as if it does, and after the moment of break it is always possible to look back and grasp the process of continuity that permitted rupture.

Prior to this rupture, therefore, one can see the glimmers of its emergence in the theory and practice of various revolutionary organizations: the Communist Party of India (Marxist-Leninist) under Charu Mazumdar, the Communist Party of the Philippines under Joma Sison, the Communist Party of Turkey Marxist-Leninist under Ibrahim Kaypakkaya—all of which commanded People's Wars under the auspice of Mao Zedong Thought, all of whose principal theorists developed germinal concepts that would feed into what would become Marxism-Leninism-Maoism.

Outside of these revolutionary theorists, there were notable political economists who spoke of Maoism and provided some foundational theoretical concepts. Samir Amin's early work, for example, is significant in this regard; his defense of the Chinese Revolution under Mao Zedong as world-historical would lead him, in *Class and Nation*, to claim that Marxism should be understood through the "heterodoxies" of Leninism and Maoism.[21] Even still, Amin did not possess an understanding of Maoism beyond what was articulated by the Chinese Revolution and the anti-revisionist movement it helped spark.

We can even see glimmers of a philosophical intervention into the terrain of Maoism, conceived by those Maoist philosophers who glimpsed the future possibility of Maoism and were thus attempting, though still caught in the terrain of Marxism-Leninism, to explain what could, and what might need to, emerge. Hence the insights of Louis Althusser, primarily a philosopher of Marxism-Leninism, who saw something significant in the Chinese Revolution and Mao Zedong. Similarly the early work of Althusser's student Alain Badiou, himself once a Maoist in name, was an attempt to philosophically excavate what had not yet come into being.

Indeed, Badiou's *Theory of the Subject* is worth examining in some detail because it both anticipates the universality of Maoism and prefigures, in an arguably eclectic manner, a philosophy of Maoism; it only misses the mark because it is written in the hope of Maoism-qua-Maoism without having access to the theoretical terrain that would only appear at the end of the 1980s. But even as he was writing this book, his last gasp as an anti-revisionist Marxist-Leninist, the rupture of Maoism was approaching. If anything, *Theory of the Subject* is a work of Marxist philosophy that contains all of the contradictions reached by Marxism-Leninism while being, at the same time, aware that these contradictions are contradictions insofar as they point to the necessity of a new rupture in revolutionary science.[22] For in *Theory of the Subject* Badiou talks about "the dialectical matrix whose operator is *scission*, and whose theme is that there is no unity that is not split"[23]—a recognition of continuity that is at the same time rupture, a demand for a "scission" that follows from Marxism-Leninism.

In *Theory of the Subject* Badiou is partially aware of some of what would eventually come to be understood as the universal aspects of Maoism and thus demands that these aspects be recognized as universal: class struggle within the dictatorship of the proletariat, the mass-line. But these glimmers, caught as they are in a philosophical project disconnected from a revolutionary movement capable of producing theory, could be nothing more than germinal insights waiting for a future that had not yet arrived. It is thus telling that Badiou would abandon this attempt to claim the name of "Maoism" as an ideological position by the time he wrote *Being and Event*.

Moreover, despite Badiou's demand for the Maoist contribution to Marxism-Leninism to be recognized as possessing a universal dimension, he still claimed that "Marxism is a phenomenon and, as such, it is periodized. It thus begins two times: with Marx and then with Lenin. 'Marxism-Leninism' is a name for this double seal—for the double name. The doctrinal One of the historical Two."[24] The argument here is that there are only two historical "periodizations" that produce the doctrine of Marxism, and this is precisely the claim of every Maoism that preceded contemporary Maoism; otherwise, Badiou would argue for three periodizations, a "doctrinal One of the historical Three", and it is significant that, despite his claims regarding the universal insights produced by Maoism, he is still arguing for a Maoist rectification of Marxism-Leninism (a philosophically concise rearticulation of Marxism-Leninism) rather than a Maoist rupture as significant as the Marxist and Leninist ruptures.

Therefore, Badiou's *Theory of the Subject* is significant insofar as it is looking forward to a third periodization but is incapable, and rightly so, of arguing that this periodization already exists. Being a philosopher, Badiou is only capable of investigating the problems inherent in the then-existent terrain of revolutionary communism, a terrain called Marxism-Leninism. He is perhaps demanding the necessity for a third periodization of the revolutionary doctrine but he cannot intervene in a terrain that had not yet emerged; historical ruptures are not produced by philosophers, as insightful as they might be, but by revolutionary praxis on the part of the masses. After all, a philosopher can declare anything they please to be a moment of historical rupture, and provide clever and well-reasoned arguments as to why this declaration is fact, but philosophy and clever arguments do not make history. Rather, any such arguments will only become fact, and a *contested* fact, if and when the historical rupture, the moment of periodization, arrives.

We can understand the extent of Badiou's pre-Maoist Maoism when he writes in *Logics of Worlds*, decades after *Theory of the Subject*, that "the Cultural Revolution effectively explored the limits of Leninism. It taught us that the politics of emancipation can no longer work under the paradigm of revolution, nor remain prisoner to the party-form."[25] Hence what we are presented with is a Maoism that was always understood as subterranean to Leninism and that, at the very most, points us away from continuity with Marxism-Leninism: a complete rupture.

None of this is to say that Badiou's work on the possible universality of Maoism, or other similar and germinal insights, are useless. Now that we can understand them as prefigurations we can mine them for insights. Most often we will discover that they are filled with innumerable speculative corridors where the imagination of the revolutionary thinker, like so many individuals embedded in academic production, has run amok; it is hard to confine oneself to the limits of a terrain that has not yet come into being.

Perhaps it is worthwhile to use some of Badiou's philosophical language, though in a way he might disown today, in order to understand these prefiguring-Maoist glimmers in light of the ruptural emergence of Maoism. Badiou often speaks of *evental sites* where "something that cannot be reduced to its ordinary inscription in 'what there is'" produces a subject.[26] Furthermore, Badiou claims that "[t]he event is attached, in its very definition, to the place, to the point in which the historicity of the situation is concentrated. Every event has a site in which it can be singularized in a historical situation."[27] For our purposes, which are not identical to Badiou's, it is worthwhile thinking of an event as a moment of historical rupture, as noted in the previous section, that forces conceptual meaning.[28]

The Maoist subject, therefore, is produced by the specific event in which Maoism is proposed as a rupture from Marxism-Leninism. Furthermore, since "a site is only 'evental' insofar as it is retroactively qualified as such by the occurrence of an event"[29] then this event requires a forcing of meaning that results from the "truth procedure" it is understood as initiating, grasped retroactively. The first evental site of Maoism is the world-historical revolution in China, particularly the Great Proletarian Cultural Revolution, but this is not enough to produce the theory of Maoism. The second evental site of Maoism is the People's War in Peru; the forcing of its meaning is the adoption of Marxism-Leninism-Maoism by the Revolutionary Internationalist Movement, that declared fidelity to the event of this People's War and its theory, in 1993.

Leaving the sometimes arcane and obtuse realm of Badiou's philosophy, we can put this in the "common" language of historical materialism, the more exoteric categories inherited by revolutionaries since Marx and Engels, and thus break from Badiou. Historical phenomena are the result of a process but are only understood as a result in retrospect. That is, although upon looking back we can understand a specific moment or thing as a historical necessity, it is not until this moment or thing emerges that we claim it as such; otherwise, all we have are contingent chains of circumstance. Historical necessity is not the same as historical destiny: while in the moment, history might take a different path, and it is not until a specific path is taken that we can explain *why* and *how* it took the path by glancing back at all the contingent moments that brought only the moment we now know as existent into being. Thus, we cannot speak of any historical moment or thing as existing prior to its emergence even if we now grasp glimmers of its emergence, and an historical argument for its emergence, when we examine the past. More to the point: we understand a given historical phenomenon's prefiguration, these glimmers, only because of its existence.

Hence, there could be no real understanding of the processes that produced capitalism until the historical emergence of capitalism: the militants of a bourgeois order that existed prior to the French Revolution, no matter how much their thought resounds with capitalist destiny, were speaking of something they could not possibly understand because it did not yet exist. To return momentarily to Badiou's language we can say *before capitalism the capitalist subject did not exist* although we now know, retroactively, that its precursor was existent and might even have used the same name. Similarly, we can say that *before Maoism the Maoist subject did not exist* although there was indeed a subject that went by the same name.

Universality and Particularity

To claim that Maoism is a third stage in rupture and continuity with revolutionary science is not to claim that its specific applications in the revolutionary movements that have erupted since the late 1980s need to be replicated identically in every social context. The universal aspects must always be separated from a particular instantiation (as is the case of every science), as Mao once argued when he tried to explain how the application of the general axioms of Marxism in the context of China, though still affirming the universality of revolutionary science, would possess a different form than their application in Russia or anywhere else.

Class struggle in China would not identically resemble class struggle in Russia or Western Europe; it would be dogmatic to assume otherwise, and more than one Marxist organization has entered a moribund existence by trying to identically replicate, for example, the particularities of the October Revolution (or, preceding this, even the Paris Commune) rather than produce a creative articulation of the general aspects of revolutionary theory based on a concrete analysis of a concrete situation.

It is important to note the relationship of universality-particularity—which intersects and parallels continuity-rupture—so as to defuse some of the more asinine criticisms of Maoism that are so prevalent as to have become common sense amongst the mainstream left at the imperialist centers. For instance, when we argue that we should learn from the revolutionary experience of the people's wars that began at the "storm centers" of revolution following the collapse of actually-existing socialism, a common response is that these experiences are useful only for the global peripheries and have nothing to teach revolutionaries in the metropoles. That is, Maoism is rejected as universal because it is treated as being a very particular application of communism local only to the global peripheries. The universality of a theory, after all, is that it can be applied in every situation.

This is an old charge and one that preceded contemporary Maoism. Indeed, one reason why Maoism was once rejected as an *-ism* was because it was seen as the description of an experience particular to China, or at most to contexts that were "semi-feudal and semi-colonial" (i.e. the global peripheries). Marxism-Leninism-Mao Zedong Thought, then, as one formalization of anti-revisionist Marxism-Leninism, expressed the assumption that this kind of "Maoism", when expressed in the global metropoles, was mainly about a fidelity to the Marxism-Leninism that had been rejected by the Soviet Union under Khrushchev. Hence, according to this interpretation, there could be Maoist people's wars in the peripheries since, if there was a

"Maoism", then it only had to do with a third-world experience; in the metropoles there was still the strategy of insurrection directed by an anti-revisionist Marxism-Leninism.

We can go further and note that various anti-Leninist doctrines of Marxism are premised on the same logic: the revolution in Russia, of which Lenin was the principal theorist, is alienated from the experience of the proletariat as a global whole because Russia in 1917 represented a unique state of affairs, alienated from the advanced capitalist centers of imperialism. From this analysis follows the desire to discover a Marxism before Lenin, a pure doctrine that is not tainted with any of these localizations that, due to their particularity, are incapable of providing universal lessons.

The most obvious and deeply logical problem with this critique, which undermines its right to make the critique to begin with, is that the situation of Western Europe described by Marx and Engels at the end of the 19th-century is itself a particularity that, if treated only as a particularity, has nothing to do with any contemporary social context. Post-structuralists and post-colonialists have already made much ado about this fact, and those who make similar critiques under the aegis of Marxism would do well to learn from this analysis since it is the logical result of their criticisms of Maoism or even Leninism: if you are going to argue that contemporary people's wars, the Chinese Revolution, or even the Russian Revolution cannot provide universal lessons about how to make revolution, let alone possess scientific status, then you might as well dispense with Marx and Engels for the same reason; they were also describing, at the most formal level, a particular concrete situation. Indeed, by the same token, the revolutionaries in Russia, China, or elsewhere should also refuse to adapt Marxism to their particular contexts since, according to this logic, its 19th-century and Western European particularities should forbid its application: this is, as noted, the argument made by post-structuralists and post-colonialists.

38

What, then, do Marxists claim when faced with the charge of the European particularity of Marxist theory? Some go so far as to argue that Marx and Engels weren't hampered by eurocentrism—the limits of a social consciousness produced by the social being of existing at the centers of 19th-century imperialism—but that their work has been *misunderstood*.[30] Perhaps it is this desire to defend a pure Marxism that is beyond reproach, and to argue against all evidence that Marx and Engels were angels who produced holy doctrine, that also produces a myth of a universal Marxism, prior to Lenin or Mao or any other social movement, that is always applicable, as if Marx and Engels could understand the entire world and the future of humanity. The more sophisticated response, however, is to argue that Marxism's universal aspects, to a greater or lesser degree, must be separated from the regional lacunae of its progenitors. Moreover, this argument is utilized to demonstrate the strength of historical materialism: if social being determines social consciousness then it makes sense that even the first historical materialists (who were not gods but real humans embedded in real societies) would possess a consciousness that was also determined by their social being. If we accept the second interpretation of historical materialism as correct, eschewing some dogmatic understanding where Marx and Engels are treated as individuals who could completely transcend their times, then we must also reject the claim that we cannot learn from revolutionary movements at the global peripheries or that these movements are incapable of producing universality. Such movements are not, for any real logical reason, more particular than the movements in which Marx and Engels were involved.[31]

The above analysis brings us to the second problem of this criticism of Maoism's universality (as well as, it should be noted again, of criticisms of Leninism's universality) which is as much ethical as it is logical: by what right do the revolutionary movements in Europe and its colonies, specifically Western

Europe, possess a claim to universality over and above the movements in the global peripheries? Only the right of eurocentrism, which is not a logical argument but an appeal to chauvinism. We are told we cannot look to the experiences of contemporary people's wars so as to understand the current conjuncture if and when we live at the centers of capitalism; at the same time, these communist movements at the peripheries are not told by other Marxists that they have no business applying the universality of Marx and Engels (and sometimes Lenin) to their contexts, contexts which are far different from the experience of Western Europe in the 19th-century, or even Russia in the early 20th-century. Moreover, the same people apply Marx and Engels to their social context with only a cursory nod at the differential of time and space; they were European after all and possess more authority than the non-European other that is told to look to Europe and its heirs while being denied historical authority.

And yet one of the universal aspects of revolutionary theory, once articulated by Lenin, is the fact that revolution happens first at the "weakest links" of imperialism, the global peripheries, rather than in those spaces that have become more antagonistic to revolution due to the benefits experienced from imperialist super-exploitation. Although those Marxists who reject Lenin for the reasons mentioned above can ignore this assessment in good conscience, those who do believe that the Russian Revolution possesses a universal dimension cannot reject the same assessment without being guilty of bad faith: there is no reason to apply the lessons of Russia without applying the successive lessons of China and the people's wars that mobilized the experience of the Chinese Revolution aside from chauvinism. And Trotsky's theory of permanent revolution, with its designation of the colonized and neo-colonized as "smaller peoples" bound to follow the more important revolutions at the centers of imperialism, is paradigmatic of this chauvinism.[32]

To claim that there is something universal in Maoism, and that we can learn from the Maoist people's wars at the peripheries, is not to claim that these experiences can be applied identically to every single context. We do not apply the particular experience of Marx and Engels to every social context, or even the experience of Lenin, but this is not what makes them important. Rather, the claim is that there are possible universal aspects to these experiences that can be wrenched from their particular articulation and, once grasped as universal, reapplied to other particular contexts in a creative manner. This is precisely what we have done with Marxism since its origination; any Marxist who thinks this is a mystery is either dishonest or misunderstands the theoretical terrain as a whole.

Thus, the process of continuity and rupture is internally defined by the process of universality and particularity. That is: begin with social investigation and an examination of the particular ways in which the universality of the proletariat-bourgeois contradiction is operationalized in a given social formation, how it is fractured and composited through other social contradictions, and thus what elements of the masses consciously experience exploitation and understand the necessity of revolution. Indeed, one reason why Maoism possesses universality is because it is aware, through the theory and practice of the mass-line, of the need for a "regionalization" (or, as Mao short-handed it in the context of China, a *sinification*) of Marxism, but one that is still in continuity with the universal aspects of the science developed through revolution.

Ideological Hegemony

The historical process that provided us with the theorization of *Maoism* as a new stage of revolutionary science, however, is one that is necessarily troubled by the retreat of communism leading up to this process. Here, it is important to note that Maoism appeared following decades in which innumerable Marxist tendencies competed for ideological hegemony, a competition that eventually became over-determined by the temporary *defeat* of actually-existing socialism. Declaring a new stage of revolutionary science, then, is a declaration that is automatically hampered by this legacy that must be taken into account.

There was a time when Marxism-Leninism possessed a significant level of ideological hegemony amongst the international communist movement, even if the name of *Leninism* was sometimes defined by embattled conceptualizations: there were those who followed the definition first tendered by Stalin, and those who followed the rebel definition represented by Trotsky and the so-called Fourth International. From this divergence followed successive divergences, along with a courageous anti-revisionist attempt to reassert a revolutionary concept of Leninism in the midst of worldwide revisionism, until the retreat and collapse of Marxism at the end of the 1980s.

Despite these divergences (and especially the Trotskyist divergence over the meaning of Leninism), Marxism-Leninism possessed an undeniable level of international hegemony amongst communist movements. Even if a Marxist group or individual rejected the hegemonic definition of Marxism-Leninism, even if they differed over minor meanings of the concept, it was still the primary form, for better or for worse, in which Marxism was ossified. After all, Trotskyism was always (and in many ways still is) a minoritarian Marxist trend, mainly popular at the imperialist centers, and the other competing Marxism-Leninisms that emerged prior to and during the anti-revisionist period of Marxism-Leninism *still* accepted a general theoretical terrain as a priori.

Marxism-Leninism-Maoism does not have the same ideological hegemony that Marxism-Leninism possessed by the time of the Chinese Revolution, nor does it have the same level of ideological hegemony that Marxism possessed by the time of the Russian Revolution in the European working-class movements.

And I want to suggest that ideological hegemony is important because, following the insights of Antonio Gramsci, it is necessary to make a revolutionary ideology "common sense" if people are ever to consent to its aims: a) first the people with an "advanced consciousness" (i.e. those drawn to pursuing the revolution, primarily those with a "proletarian consciousness") need to consent to the necessity of a revolutionary theory so as to agitate and organize on its behalf; b) secondly, through the process of building a revolutionary organization, this sphere of communist hegemony needs to grow in order to counter capitalist hegemony; c) and, thirdly, this process of *counter-hegemony* (where revolutionary hegemony is developing as a counter-current to the hegemony of the current ruling class) is only possible if a specific revolutionary theory is first consented to by those with an "advanced" consciousness.

While it is true that contemporary Maoist organizations possess a level of ideological hegemony within the contexts where people's wars have erupted (and that this fact should tell us that Maoism is theoretically significant), when it comes to the international communist—let alone the generally *anti-capitalist*—population, Marxism-Leninism-Maoism does not yet possess, globally, a coherent counter-hegemony. Other tendencies still abound: anarchist tendencies, anti-Leninist Marxist tendencies, Trotskyist and "Stalinist" tendencies, and even alternate Maoist tendencies. Such tendencies existed throughout the previous periods of communist struggle, true, but only as alternatives to the hegemonic Marxism-Leninism that even they understood, at the time, was the primary understanding of revolutionary communism: indeed, much of the work of these other anti-capitalist trajectories during the past epoch was to struggle against the hegemony of Marxism-Leninism, poke holes in its edifice, and exist primarily as alterities in rebellion against a Marxism-Leninism that, regardless of its own interior hetero-geneity, was simultaneously an ideological totality.

In fact, the reason why both Marxism and Marxism-Leninism were able to achieve this general totality was because of the ideological line struggles, and the concrete practices these struggles produced, that were waged by their militants. In order to achieve a clarity in political line, Marx and Engels engaged in innumerable line struggles with alternate currents in their radical milieu so that, by the time of Lenin, Marxism was a concept that stood above its name. Similarly, Lenin waged a series of theoretical line struggles with contemporary Marxists (i.e. Kautsky, the Mensheviks, etc.) in order to produce a concrete analysis of a concrete situation that would, as noted earlier, eventually result in universal applicability once Marxism-Leninism emerged as a theoretical terrain. This process was concretized by the Chinese Revolution and those militants who would declare, in the face of Soviet revisionism, *Long Live Leninism!*:

In the historical conditions of the epoch of imperialism and proletarian revolution, Lenin carried Marxism forward to a new stage and showed all the oppressed classes and people the path along which they could really shake off capitalist enslavement and poverty. [...] These forty years have been forty years of victory for Leninism in the world, forty years in which Leninism has found its way ever deeper into the hearts of the world's people. Leninism not only has won and will continue to win great victories in countries where the socialist system has been established, but is also constantly achieving new victories in the struggles of all oppressed peoples.[33]

But the ideological fragmentation that Marxism and then Leninism respectively experienced is not the same as the ideological fragmentation that persists today, amongst anti-capitalists in general and Marxists in particular, following the collapse of actually-existing socialism. Thus, Maoism emerged as a theoretical terrain, proclaiming itself the inheritor of the mantle of revolutionary science, at a moment of widespread fragmentation where radical tendencies proliferate in a confused and often arcane manner. Reclaiming scientific totality in this context, then, is a significant philosophical problem that cannot be dismissed simply by repeating, as if it is a magical formula, that Maoism *is* the new stage of revolutionary science.

The point, here, is that Maoism as a revolutionary theory is attempting to establish ideological hegemony in the midst of *the totalization of ideological fragmentation* and needs to recognize that it is fighting an uphill battle. The supposed defeat of Marxism and the proclamation of capitalist triumph has produced a theoretical malaise that undermines, in various ways, any claim to theoretical totality: the first question that must be asked of anyone who proclaims the correctness of a revolutionary trajectory is *why* this trajectory is more correct than other trajectories that might at first appear similar, and why the hegemonic totality of one trajectory should be embraced at the expense of others. Maoists will answer, of course, that the correctness of their ideology is proved in class struggle itself: following the collapse of Marxism-Leninism, and based on an assessment of the insights produced by the most recent world-historical revolution, it is the only revolutionary ideology that is actually making revolution. In some ways this claim is enough because, as I have argued, theory is produced by struggle and does not need philosophical intervention to develop as theory. And yet, on the very level of philosophical intervention, this problem of totality in the face of fragmentation needs to be examined because it might tell us something important about an embattled Marxism-Leninism-Maoism.

First of all, this problem should explain why Maoism is taking longer to establish its hegemony internationally than Marxism-Leninism, regardless of whatever (significant) regional hegemonies it has currently achieved. Marxism-Leninism was established in the historical process between the Russian and Chinese Revolutions, receiving its most anti-revisionist form during the height of the latter event. In this process there emerged innumerable philosophical interventions that drew lines of demarcation around the theory and, armed with this theory's articulation in the concrete fact of two world-historical revolutions, were able to further develop its hegemony in thought. When this process reached its historical limitations, however, the counter-revolution was so thorough and devastating that the ideologues of global capitalism were able to claim that capitalism was *the end of history*. The ensuing period of reaction, though resisted by the sudden emergence of Maoism, was the very totality that led to the fragmentation of revolutionary thought. One step forward, then, after many steps back.

Secondly, the need to struggle against the totality of ideological fragmentation should make us cautious of any and all attempts on the part of those militants who were formerly dedicated to Maoism to speak of a theoretical terrain beyond Maoism.[34] After all, if Maoism is still embattled and has not yet established ideological hegemony then how can one speak of transgressing its boundaries? This question should seem odd for anyone even marginally interested in Maoism, especially if they have not considered it seriously, for aside from the significant people's wars that have given a conceptual meaning to the name of *Maoism*, there has not yet been a world-historical revolution that has transgressed the limits of the prior world-historical revolution and, in this transgression, been assessed according to its successes and failures. Unfortunately, there are former Maoists who, regardless of once recognizing the formulation produced by the PCP and the RIM, now speak of a *post-Maoist* communism. But in order to transgress Maoism, it must first be established that Maoism has reached its limits; in order for Maoism to have reached its limits, it must have first achieved ideological hegemony so as to even cognize its limits. One would be better off claiming that Maoism is an erroneous theoretical line, a dead-end tributary of revolutionary thought, than to pretend that it is capable of being transgressed—a claim that would necessarily have to reject Maoism as a *concept* and think of it only as a transitory *name* that can be dropped as easily as any other failed name.

These two problems will be examined, from various angles, in later chapters. Hopefully they will be given clarity by the end of third chapter where the limits of Marxism-Leninism and the problem these limits present are thoroughly examined. If Maoism is the current stage of revolutionary science, though, then it cannot be understood as easily transgressed when it is still, in the midst of a period that clearly disparages revolutionary science, developing as a concept. Thus it is necessary to return to the distinction between the *name* and *concept* of Maoism and grasp what it means scientifically in order to steel ourselves against either spurious abandonment or dogmatic adherence.

Notes

1. Roland Boer, *Sectarianism Versus Ecumenism: The Case of V.I. Lenin*.

2. Revolutionary Communist Party of Canada, *Maoism Today*.

3. The type of Maoism that is inherited from the tradition of the Maoist Internationalist Movement [MIM], what would be called "Maoist Third-Worldism", rejects the RIM experience for a variety of reasons, one of which was the influence of the RCP-USA. Although I think part of the MIM's critique of the RCP-USA's involvement in the RIM is correct (particularly their claim that Bob Avakian's "Conquer the World" document was "crypto-Trotskyism"), I also think it is important to uphold the RIM experience because the parties involved at the time were significant revolutionary parties in the global peripheries and not primarily, as the MIM and Maoist Third-Worldist groups

were/are, organizations based at the centers of capitalism, specifically the US. Moreover, the RIM statement in 1993, *Long Live Marxism-Leninism-Maoism!*, was a statement made when the PCP was still the primary influence in the RIM and so its general framework for Maoism as a new stage, despite a few qualifications, would not be entirely different from what Maoist Third-Worldists believe is universal about Maoism. Indeed, despite the MIM's rejection of the RIM, it still declared fidelity to the PCP's people's war and its initial theorization of Maoism as a third stage of revolutionary science. Hence we are still forced to accept 1988 as a crucial point of conceptual clarity, regardless of the parting of ways of these two versions of Maoism.

4.   RIM, *Long Live Marxism-Leninism-Maoism!*
     (http://www.bannedthought.net/International/RIM/AWTW/
     1995-20/ll_mlm_20_eng.htm).

5.   Canadian Communist League (Marxist-Leninist), 11–12.

6.   Maoist Communist Party France, 27.

7.   Engels, *Feuerbach and the End of Classical German Philosophy*, 9.

8.   I am not arguing, here, that the CPI (Maoist) was a member of the RIM or even interested in joining. The Communist Party of India (Marxist-Leninist) People's War does not appear to have been interested in joining the RIM, and by the time the CPI (Maoist) formed the RIM was already in dissolution. At the same time, however, the Maoist Communist Centre [MCC], which was part of the foundation of the CPI (Maoist), was a RIM member, as was the Communist Party (Marxist-Leninist) Naxalbari that, years later, would merge with the CPI (Maoist). Moreover, the CPI (Maoist) was once very close to the Communist Party of Nepal (Maoist), before this organization abandoned its people's war, and in ideological agreement with its version of Maoism which was the RIM conceptualization of Maoism. Furthermore, the CPI (Maoist) saw the PCP's people's war and conceptualization of

Maoism as being extremely important and influential. Finally, the conceptualization of Marxism-Leninism-Maoism in the CPI (Maoist)'s theoretical documents is identical to the Maoism articulated and summarized in the aforementioned RIM document.

9. For example, if we take religion to be a particular social phenomenon, can we truly imagine the "Protestant Work Ethic" without capitalist social relations where the bourgeois way of relating to each other (individuals locked in competition who possess the liberty to better themselves through hard work) is mobilized according to the productive forces of factories, increased commodity production, market forces, etc.

10. Although we must admit that this either originated with or was better clarified by Rosa Luxemburg.

11. This last point, to be fair, is still controversial, which is why I plan to discuss it in significant detail in a later chapter.

12. For a thorough elaboration on this, see Mao's *On Contradiction*. In the interest of clarity, however, this concep-tualization of base-superstructure can be understood according to the persistence of patriarchal ideology well past the time where it would make sense for patriarchy to exist. Under capitalism, in an abstract sense, the economic base should not allow for a superstructure that excludes or oppresses women—it would actually make sense to exploit men and women equally without any reason for choosing which gender is designated for the sphere of reproduction (i.e. house work, raising the next generation of workers, etc.). Patriarchy is the superstructural product of previous modes of production that lingers well after it was deter-mined by a particular social base... and yet, *because it lingers,* has historically affected the way in which the economic structure of capitalism is articulated. Ideas produced by the logic of one mode production are not necessarily given up in

a successive mode of production, even if the core logic of this epoch could function abstractly without them. Rather, they are accumulated so as to become part of the way in which these successive mode of productions actually develop.

13. For further discussion on the topic of New Democracy, see the sections in the Appendix that compare the Maoist approach to this problematic with the Trotskyist approach. For further discussion on the topic of Maoist approaches to settler-colonialism see my doctoral dissertation, *A Living Colonialism*.

14. See, for example, Charles Post's *The American Road to Capitalism* that argues that it was the American Civil War, and not the American Revolution, that was the US's bourgeois revolution. Furthermore, even if Post is correct, the American Civil War was far from world-historical because: a) capitalist revolutions had already happened elsewhere; b) slavery was abolished elsewhere; and c) there was a significant slave revolution connected to the French Revolution.

15. See C.L.R. James' *The Black Jacobins*. James argues that the Santo Domingo Slave Revolution gained strength by theorizing itself within the contours of the French Revolution. Like the radical Jacobins, then, it also had to contend with the onslaught of Thermidorian reaction and the rise of Napoleon.

16. See, for a good historiography of the reactionary nature of the American Revolution, Gerald Horne's *The Counter-Revolution of 1776* and Dominic Losurdo's *Liberalism: A Counter-history*. Moreover, Roxanne Dunbar-Ortiz has argued that the American Revolution was largely resisted by Indigenous nations (forced to choose between imperialists from afar and the settler-colonialists at home) and experienced as an exterminatory event: "Throughout the war between separatist settlers and the forces of the monarchy,

armed settlers waged total war against Indigenous people, largely realizing their [genocidal] objectives" (Dunbar-Ortiz, 76).

17. We need to clarify this statement, though, by arguing for a critical analysis of rebellion so as to guard against supporting pro-imperialist and fascist revolts. The bizarre endorsements of the Free Syrian Army and the Libyan pro-NATO revolts amongst some sectors of the left—not to mention the initial leftist support of the fascists in Ukraine—are not what we should mean when we claim that "it is right to rebel".

18. See Karl Popper's *The Logic of Scientific Discovery*. Here it is also worth noting that Popper's claim that falsification should be the basis of the sciences is a claim made by a philosopher, and not a scientist, and also politically motivated: Popper was attempting, as a liberal democrat, to bar historical materialism from science. Although it is possibly correct to recognize the significance of *falsifiability* in scientific endeavor, to accept Popper's theory of *falsification* as the basis of scientific development is a philosophical rather than scientific position. Science does not explain the basis of its logic; philosophy is that which attempts to force meaning, and Popper's attempt at forcing meaning is not necessarily more or less valid than other philosophers of science who might have disagreed.

19. I am referring, here, to Darwin's claim, examined in detail by radical biologist Robert M. Young in *Darwin's Metaphor*, that he had difficulty figuring out the motor of evolution until he read Malthus and hit upon the concept of natural selection.

20. That is, although China originally led the defense of Leninism in the international communist movement of the time, the Albanian communists under Enver Hoxha would eventually distance themselves from the Chinese-influenced anti-revisionism and cling to the pure Marxism-Leninism of

Stalin's *Foundations of Leninism*. Despite some salient critiques made of Mao Zedong and Chinese foreign policy, the Hoxhaite variant of Marxism-Leninism was marked by a dogmatism that would lead to it being called, by the Mao Zedong Thought groups, "dogmato-revisionist".

21. Amin, 206.
22. In the third chapter I will examine the contradictions of Marxism-Leninism in more detail.
23. Badiou, *Theory of the Subject*, 4.
24. Ibid., 125.
25. Badiou, *Logics of Worlds*, 518.
26. Badiou, *Ethics*, 41.
27. Badiou, *Being and Event*, 178–179.
28. Since I am only interested in adopting this language to shed light on my examination of Maoism, I am also not planning to provide a proper exposition of Badiou's ontology or the terminology, such as "situation", that are indexed by these quotations.
29. Badiou, *Being and Event*, 179.
30. Kevin Anderson's *Marx at the Margins* is an example of a sophisticated version of this argument.
31. For more on Marxism and how it has been hampered by, while simultaneously challenging, eurocentrism, see Robert Biel's masterful *Eurocentrism and the Communist Movement*.
32. See the Appendix, *Maoism or Trotskyism*, where the intrinsic eurocentric chauvinism of Trotskyism is examined.
33. Revolutionary Internationalist Movement, *Long Live Leninism!*
34. That is, the various types of "post-Maoism" that are now being proclaimed by intellectuals such as Alain Badiou or organizations such as the RCP-USA and the Kasama Project.

Chapter 2

Science's Dogmatic Shadow

It has been forgotten that [Marx] only laid the basis for historical materialism and discovered the essential laws of capitalism. It has been forgotten that he had no other ambition, especially not that of depriving his successors of advancing the struggle under new conditions which he scarcely tried to predict. The best of his successors, Lenin and Mao, did not so deprive themselves: for a rigid dogmatist, what could be more heterodox than the contributions of Leninism and Maoism to Marxism?

—Samir Amin, *Class and Nation*

The Problematic of Science

By arguing that there is an important distinction to be made between the *name* and *concept* of "Maoism" I am attempting to demonstrate that Maoism-qua-Maoism is a theoretical tendency that is still rather new and, because of this newness, poorly understood. Many of its detractors conflate the concept with the name and, ignoring the process that generated Maoism as a concept, waste their time critiquing (and rather poorly) the Chinese Revolution and the period of anti-revisionist communism.[1] By clarifying the meaning of contemporary Maoism, specifically the Maoist variants adopted by the majority of today's worldwide revolutionary forces, I am also demanding that all would-be critics of Maoism focus on the actual rather than imaginary theoretical terrain.

More important than this demand, however, is the fact that the distinction between *name* and *concept* should teach us something about a theoretical terrain. We need to recognize that Maoism as a *concept* stands over and above the name of Mao Zedong, just as

Marxism and Leninism must stand over the name of Karl Marx and Vladimir Lenin, respectively. These are moments of theoretical development that are named after significant revolutionary theorists but that, in the final instance, merely take these names as ciphers for a set of concepts that go beyond the individuals for which they are named. Just as a critical Marxist should not accept that everything Marx claimed is sacrosanct, so too a critical Leninist or Maoist should not reduce Leninism and Maoism to the moment of naming. Again, Maoism is not reducible to the "thought" of Mao Zedong but is something that is derived from this thought through an assessment of the world-historical revolution in which this person was its principle theorist.

Obviously it would be easier to dispense with names altogether, especially since the naming of a theoretical tendency often pulls us back into an obsession with the individual person from whom this name originated. Past and present Maoisms share the name of Mao, after all, and in the moment of this sharing are easily confused—the concept is obscured by the name and its origin. It would be better, then, to speak simply of *revolutionary communism*, perhaps, rather than chain together the names of those theorists that represent the development of revolutionary communism as a science. After all, physics does not theorize itself according to similar chains: the contemporary physicist does not attach *Einsteinian* to *Newtonian* because they simply accept that the transformation from the Newtonian to the Einsteinian paradigm is a fact and that this fact is uncontroversial—there is no reason to create these hyphenated chains.[2]

But here is where the so-called "hard sciences" differ from the science of history and revolution. After the long march of scientific militancy, years after the moment of rupture has been accepted, the average physicist does not feel the need to conceptualize their terrain and worry about ideological line struggle. While it is true that there are always moments of reaction, where scientists will attempt to lose themselves in spiritualism and mystification, most scientists are able to prove, over and over, the necessity of a paradigmatic shift with equations, technologies, laboratory praxis.

I recognize that it is currently controversial to demand a return to the conception of historical materialism as a science. There is a hesitance amongst Marxist intellectuals to resort to what many of us feel is an "old-fashioned" term, particularly since it has been associated with Soviet orthodoxy and a very unscientific way of understanding Marxist theory. This approach to Marxist science, where everything could be explained according to an ontology of "dialectical materialism", was more of a mechanistic translation of a Hegelian notion of science—flip Hegel on his head, naturalize his dialectics (i.e. Engels' *Dialectics of Nature*), and call it science. Therefore, by urging a return to this conceptualization of Marxist theory I am not at arguing for an old return but, instead, demanding a new return to a better grasp of what it means to speak of historical materialism—and the way it has unfolded through Marx, Lenin, and Mao—as a scientific truth procedure. Such a return must necessarily recognize that every claim to science will indeed cast a dogmatic shadow, its parascientific double, and we not only have a history determined by this shadow but a present of similarly parascientific approaches: Marxisms that do not recognize themselves as science but are still, once we grasp what it means to theorize historical materialism as science, instances of parascience; more orthodox Marxisms, still using the older understanding of Marxist science, that refuse to recognize themselves as mechanical theologies by dogmatically repeating phrases like "materialist dialectics" and "mechanical metaphysics".

One of the reasons I believe it is important to recognize that historical materialism is a scientific-theoretical terrain is because it allows us to step outside of the ways in which philosophy and theory are often conflated by Marxism and thus provide clarity to both Marxist theory and the practice of philosophy within the realm of theory. Indeed, the conflation of Marxist theory with philosophy has resulted in an impoverishment of historical materialism and has undermined Marxist praxis. Thus, in order for Marxism to not be mistaken as little more than another ideology, another philosophy, or even another "social ontology" (even though it does generate ideological, philosophical, and ontological positions), the distinction between theory and philosophy needs to be maintained. Moreover, the recognition that historical materialism is a scientific-theoretical terrain, and the philosophy is an autonomous procedure affected, in various ways, upon this terrain, is of primary importance.

Marxism is thus not, essentially, a philosophy or ideology; it is a science. More precisely, historical materialism is a science that prefigures and determines philosophies and ideologies. If we begin by accepting this axiom, as old-fashioned as it might seem, then we can easily side-step the innumerable debates about whether or not historical materialism matters in the same way that any scientifically minded person would reject debates about whether physics, biology, or chemistry matter. The theoretical terrain first grasped by Marx and Engels matters because, as aforementioned, it is the scientific apprehension of social-historical phenomena... And it is the correct way of apprehending this phenomena, and not a speculative theoretical system made up just because it looks and sounds interesting, because it began as a concrete examination of concrete circumstances and, since it began, has demystified its object of study and provided an explanatory depth that no other social theory (all of which are truly "social ontologies") has been able to do without making recourse to the terrain of Marxism.

To maintain that historical materialism is a science results in an immediate clarification of conceptual territory. Although Marx and Engels used "philosophical" language to codify the foundations of this science (i.e. "being", "consciousness", etc.), such usage was more metaphorical than philosophical because they were not speaking about speculative matters. Similarly, other sciences mined the history of philosophy for their language (i.e. "atoms", "genetic", "elements"), and it would be entirely arrogant to assume that physics, biology, and chemistry can be determined under the philosophical category of *ontology* when such a category, being a speculative and quasi-religious conceit, is utterly alien to scientific practice.

Historical materialism is a science because it satisfies the basic definition of science of most textbook definitions of scientific reason: i) it provides a natural explanation for its given natural phenomena (i.e. it does not explain social-historical phenomena according to supernatural categories); ii) it provides the possibility for explanatory depth and inferences to the best explanation; iii) it hypothesizes a general law of motion (class struggle) that accounts for theoretical development; iv) its general law of motion is testable/falsifiable, despite Popper's claim to the contrary, according to moments of revolution and practice; v) it generates a truth procedure that determines how its theoretical terrain is open to the future.

Although some cynics might argue that such a definition of science is a type of "philosophical decision" in that it is wagered to decide, a priori, the boundaries of science, we should respond that it is only "philosophical" in retrospect. That is, if this definition is "philosophical" it is only philosophical in the kind of non-philosophical sense described by Feuerbach: a description, in philosophical terms, of what already *is*. Physics, biology, and chemistry also fit the above qualifications—but so what? Their truth procedures are not undermined by the philosophical decision of this description, and only a bargain-basement philosopher would declare them ontologically unsound because of this definition: these sciences, regardless of any philosophical complaint to the contrary, result in concrete affects. One might as well pretend that a car's engine cannot function because the definition of the sciences that have generated this technology (which, in fact, demonstrate the above definition of science) lack a proper philosophical basis.

Indeed, François Laruelle argues that Marxism is inhibited by a prior philosophical decision based on its conceptualization of the category of *matter*. That is, the concept of "matter" is a philosophical decision that "cannot form its own theory and that... needs an exterior theory, a theory with a philosophical origin; it needs an idealist complement in the form of a materialist *position*".[3] Now if it is indeed the case that the Marxist project remained "philosophical" then it would be correct to assume that its understanding of "matter" was entirely philosophical, and thus Laruelle's critique will retain its strength against every expression of Marxism that rejects the qualification of science: a non-scientific materialism will indeed find itself in the realm of philosophy and, if this is the case, such Marxism needs to philosophically define, and thus fall back into idealist categories, what "matter" means and why it *matters*. But if historical materialism is a science then Marx and Engels were not asserting the category of *matter* in an idealist sense, nor were they bothering with a philosophical decision: they were simply describing the world without resorting to speculative categories just as other scientists describe the world. And if Laruelle wants to dismiss these other scientists for their materialism he must, again, also dismiss the results of these sciences that philosophy by itself cannot produce.[4] A vaccine is not hampered by the fact that its creators declared fidelity to the philosophical decision of materialism.

Similarly, Marx's materialism is not a philosophical category: it takes the world as it is without presupposing questions of ontology and speculative philosophy. When Marx claims that "social being determines social consciousness", then, he is not asserting philosophical categories about an ontological being and an epistemological consciousness. The names are identical but their meaning has shifted. *Being* is not intended to imply a speculative philosophical category but simply what is, what exists, and people caught up within existence. Consciousness is just the apprehension of this baseline of socially embedded living.

While it is correct to note that historical materialism resorts to terminology that is philosophically loaded, to assume that this terminology still belongs to philosophy, or that Marx was founding a "social ontology" instead of a speculative ontology, is itself a philosophical decision, an attempt to pull a scientific terrain back into the realm of philosophical authority. As noted above, other sciences have also resorted to terminology inherited from philosophy, but all this demonstrates is that scientific terrains have been forced, at the moment of origin, to resort to a language that already exists and that is unfortunately philosophically loaded because the sciences emerged from, but eventually parted ways with, philosophy. As these sciences' truth procedures develop, though, a unique terminology also develops and demonstrates a widening gap between theory and philosophy. By the time of the Higgs-Boson discovery, for example, the terminology of particle physics evolved far beyond the language borrowed from the Atomists. Similarly, even when Marx was writing *Capital* we can witness a growing gap between terms borrowed from philosophy (being, consciousness, alienation, etc.) and a theoretical nomenclature that was devoted to demystifying social-historical phenomena (modes of production, productive forces/relations, tendency of the rate of profit to fall, etc.).

Here, it is worth noting that the origin of scientific theory might be a point of pride for philosophers: the sciences, upon separating from philosophy, were able to do what philosophy (and also religion) promised but could never fulfill. Namely, provide concrete answers about reality that could be proven, measured, tested, repeated, and thus produce real, material truth procedures. The Copernican hypothesis, for example, is a truth that no philosophical speculative endeavor could ever match; nor does philosophy produce technologies and vaccines. Before the theoretical terrains of science were recognized for what they were, ontology was the standard of truth. Being a speculative discipline that lacked the historical qualifications of truth that would be established with the "enlightenment break" from metaphysics, ontology did nothing but muse over the meaning of existence, the structure of being, and outside of the rules of logic and argumentation (which could be equally made by various competing ontologies) was incapable of establishing the kind of truth procedure that scientific theory *did* establish. What we find in philosophy are attempts to establish truth according to a speculative, non-testable systems of thought. Each ontology is no more or less logical than others; all are incapable of providing material results. Hence, we should understand Hegel's claim that his philosophy was a true "science" as a kind of rejection of the emergence of science in favor of ontology, a re-privileging of philosophy in the face of enlightenment demystification. Feuerbach, who was intimately familiar with Hegel's system, recognized it as the accomplishment of philosophy to date but still classified it as speculative theology.

This jealousy of scientific theory notwithstanding, we should also recognize that recourse to terms that, at first glance, appear to be philosophical permit attempts to pull historical materialism, and other sciences, back into the fold of philosophy. The fact remains: science does things; philosophy speculates and attempts to make sense of these things, as it does with every theoretical terrain.[5] The science of historical materialism not only demystifies the world in a way that other theories cannot but, because of this demystification, generates revolution. The proof of Marxism's efficacy as a science is that its practices, based on its fundamental law of motion, can and have been implemented: class struggle.

From the Scientific to the Dogmatic

Since the science of history bases its proof on class struggle, and since its laboratory is the entire social world, it cannot easily produce the same level of general acceptance that the other sciences often enjoy. There will always be those who, unable to properly grasp moments of failure, will be drawn back to the innumerable dead-ends of the theoretical past: those conceptual terrains that went nowhere and were incapable of further developing the science. The "hard sciences" also possess their parascientists, backwards practitioners who embrace past errors, but these people are generally understood as pseudo-scientists: someone may indeed appeal to outdated scientific categories to "prove" that the world is flat, that the Big Bang theory is erroneous, that ectoplasm is a material reality, or that the earth was created in six days, but they will never be taken seriously by the general scientific community.

Our parascientists, however, are not always recognized as such due to the general unwillingness, even amongst Marxists, to accept and/or understand Marx's and Engels' claims about the science of history. For example there are those who misunderstand the meaning of *revolutionary science* and imagine that something called "materialist dialectics" is the grand unifying science behind every science: Ted Grant and Alan Woods, for example, reject Einsteinian categories in favor of some nebulous Newtonianism because they believe that Marxism permits their intervention as meta-scientists in the categories of modern physics.[6] Outside of these obvious clichés, however, we can define Marxist parascientists as those who continue to conflate philosophy with science and are indeed engaged in pursuing social ontology.

While I think it is erroneous to claim that nothing can be learned from those historical-materialist tendencies that devolve into critical theory that remains at the level of social ontology—so many concepts can be pulled into a scientific milieu, and other sciences have done this—we do need to recognize that when these tendencies are alienated from an understanding of Marxism as a scientific terrain, and are thus philosophical normalizations of Marxism, they tend to be parascientific: they do not do what historical materialism is meant to do; they do not contribute to class struggle. In the worst instances they speak with the language of scientific authority while, at the same time, confirming Popper's complaint that Marxism is not testable (i.e. Trotskyist doctrines, such as "permanent revolution", which have never been tested and can never be tested, are put forward with authority despite the fact that this Marxist tendency has never led a revolution), thus functioning as clear examples of parascience. In other instances they openly abandon the claim to science but still believe, despite submerging themselves in the realm of philosophy, that they can legislate reality with something akin to scientific authority (i.e. the Frankfurt School, despite its theoretical importance, is paradigmatic of this problem), which should make us ask why they matter in the first place.

Perhaps in reaction to this crude understanding of science promoted by those who would have us believe that some form of Marxism is either the meta-science of *everything*, or the most complete social ontology, there are those who refuse to recognize that historical materialism can be a scientific methodology of even the phenomena it claims to represent, history and society.

Historical materialism is a science that attempts to explain the phenomena of history and society and can only grasp these phenomena scientifically if it recognizes class struggle as the motive force. The problem with this axiom, however, is that class struggle often prevents us from grasping the methodology of the science: if we are embedded in class societies then we are influenced by the ideology of the ruling classes. Such an ideology often prevents us from seeing clearly, convinces us that there is only a chain of ruptures, rather than also continuities, and that there is nothing universal to be gleaned from those great revolutions that have ultimately failed. Thus, it is tempting to reject the only scientific basis of understanding the development of science, class struggle universalized in the crucible of world-historical revolution, and either rejecting the concept of revolutionary science altogether or embracing some ineffectual meta-scientific approach, where historical materialism simply becomes the judge of all sciences *except* history and society, that is ultimately little more than parascience.

In this context, the militant of revolutionary science often finds themself struggling against innumerable rejectionist tendencies that are all demanding, in various ways, scientific abdication. Such a struggle, unfortunately, often produces its own form of dogmatism. Hence, Marxism-Leninism-Maoism is not yet immune to the very same dogmatic tendencies it has often rigorously critiqued.

The Basic Problem of Dogmatism

At this point it is worth noting that Maoism should reject any conception of a "pure" communism. There is no such thing as a pure communism; the very notion is idealist in that it mobilizes quasi-Platonic categories to explain a perfect concept of the political. Those Marxist trajectories that attempt to defend their purity by seeking justification primarily in what the prime "saints" of communism have written, rather than the method-ology and universal insights they have provided, are dogmatists. Ruptures in the science emerge due to a creative heterodoxy that declares fidelity to the past moments of universality, reinter-preting these moments in particular circumstances. It is not enough to claim that something is properly "communist" by citing Marx: we must be prepared to admit that the science initiated by Marx is universal because of its methodology but that not everything Marx wrote, simply because it bore his name, was also scientific.

Indeed, within the germinal anti-revisionist tradition that preceded Maoism-qua-Maoism there was a conceptual term used to disparage this "pure" communism: *dogmato-revisionism*.

Initially applied to Hoxhaites (that is, followers of the Albanian communist leader Enver Hoxha), dogmato-revisionism was understood as the revisionism resulting from ultra-orthodoxy.[7] That is, those who claim that their communism is "pure" because they can locate its precedents only in the writings of previous communist theorists that are taken, as individuals, to be beyond reproach, are themselves revisionists in that they reduce revolutionary science to the writings and claims of great historical personages. Religious devotion to sacred texts and saints produces its own form of revisionism since it is contrary to materialism.

But even though appeals to a "pure" communism produce dogmatism (and indeed dogmatic and religious adherence to an imagined communist orthodoxy is a logical outgrowth of the theoretical constellation of, for example, the Trotskyist discourse), it would be disingenuous to pretend as if dogmatism has not affected the anti-revisionist tradition through which Maoism cohered. Thus, while I would like to suggest that Maoism, due to its history of creative theoretical development, is adverse to dogmatism, we still need to confront the fact that Maoism can also fall into dogmatism.

After all, the fact that communism is understood as "science" tends to produce a dogmatic mind-set that is ultimately *anti-scientific* because, being the only revolutionary theory that claims a scientific basis (anarchism scorns science, post-modern approaches claim that the concept of revolutionary science is "totalizing") we often see ourselves as better than those whose practice is "idealist" and intentionally incoherent. Moreover, since this scientific terrain is always compromised (those of us who identify as Marxist-Leninist-Maoist will claim we are "more scientific" than Trotskyists and others who will respond with the inverse claim), waging an ideological struggle to convince others of the scientific necessity of our approach as compared to other tendencies can often devolve into religious mummery. As Tom Clark argued in the preface of *The State and Counter-Revolution*:

A curious phenomenon occurs, however, when intellectuals begin to appreciate the materialist basis of Marxist ideology. They become enamored, not with scientific materialism, but with Marxism; not with a mode of thinking but with a system of beliefs. [...] As in religion, dogmatism is not simply an affliction of a few extremists, but to a varying degree infects the entire congregation. A Marxist intellectual is first and foremost a believer, and like his Christian counterpart, upholds his faith proudly, defends it against attack, and tries to win new converts. The parallel holds true with embarrassing fidelity down to the reverential regard for the class works, study groups, and compilations aimed at reinforcing the faith.[8]

Since I plan to engage with some of Clark's insights in the last chapter of this small book, mainly because *The State and Counter-Revolution* was written in 1983 when the anti-revisionist communist movement had reached an impasse and only some groups could understand this impasse, I will just limit myself to this insight regarding dogmatism. For as much as we want to deny that we Marxists, especially those of us who claim the tradition started by Marxism is a living science, are guilty of dogmatism, the fact that we are trying to accumulate revolutionary forces and agitate for our political line often cannot help but produce a quasi-religious mindset.

Take, for example, the tendency of some Maoists to dismiss left populist phenomena such as the Bolivarian Revolution, sometimes going so far as to label it "social fascism". While I am not suggesting that we uncritically endorse social movements that appear to lack the concrete means to establish socialism, it is undeniable that there is quite often a knee-jerk practice of dogmatic dismissal. Therefore, while I uphold the historical fact that Maoism was initially conceived as a new stage of revolutionary communism by the PCP during the course of its people's war, I also cannot deny the fact that the remnants of this party, most probably because of mistakes made from the very beginning, tend to sound like religious adherents to "Gonzalo Thought" in a matter that is no different in form from an ortho-Trotskyist's adherence to Trotsky. The same can be said of the degenerating RCP-USA and its cultic devotion to Bob Avakian.

Historically, then, there has indeed been a problem with communist organizations declaring slavish devotion to significant revolutionary figures. The construction of a personality cult around Stalin, for example, was a hallmark of a certain period of the international communist movement, a problem that would eventually be enshrined as practice by Enver Hoxha's variant of anti-revisionist Marxist-Leninism. The historical roots of Maoism have also been guilty of this dogmatic practice, and we would be remiss to suggest otherwise: the cult of personality that had developed around Mao Zedong by the time of the Cultural Revolution should not be ignored, especially as it led to a formulaic parroting, amongst anti-revisionist organizations outside of China, of phrases and statements from "the Little Red Book"; and, as noted above, such dogmatism found its way into the People's War of Peru where the PCP eventually raised Abimael Guzman ("Gonzalo") to sainthood, declaring him the "fourth sword of Marxism". Hence, dogmatism has been inherited from the past and should be understood as a problem that needs to be overcome. As Ajith has argued:

Personality cults can never be justified Marxism. But instead of totally rejecting them, Mao limited himself to criticising their extreme manifestations. Though this is sought to be justified by appealing to the complex situation of the class struggle in China, it is unacceptable in principle itself. The issue is not the extent of praise, or even whether somebody deserves to be praised. Such cults foster a consciousness of infallibility of an individual, a leadership and indirectly of that party; something rejected by the Maoist party concept but seen in the Chinese party's adjective, 'always correct'. Contemporary examples of Maoist parties justifying their leadership cults by citing Mao draw attention to the need to achieve clarity in this matter.[9]

What is important to note about the above quotation, made by a significant member of the now-defunct RIM, is that its rejection of dogmatism hinges on a distinction made between *Maoism* and the Communist Party of China led by Mao Zedong. That is, the *Maoist party*, a party of the new type, is not reducible to a political practice based just on the thoughts or practices of Mao Zedong. In order to establish itself as Maoist, rather than an anti-revisionist Marxist-Leninist party that is "Maoist" only insofar as it declares fidelity to the Chinese Revolution led by Mao, such a party must break from the dogmatic practices of the past. And yet, at the same time, Ajith recognizes that emergent Marxist-Leninist-Maoist organizations have inherited this past problem in order to justify themselves. Therefore, recognizing that dogmatism is a problem within the Maoist movement, specifically when it comes to the "cult of leadership", Ajith writes, in another document, "[c]urrent practices... of glorifying the party and the cult of leadership... will reinforce, rather than weaken, a political culture of subservience to power. In a socialist society the danger is amplified because the 'bourgeoisie is right within the party'."[10]

The problem of the leadership cult is thus worth discussing in some detail because it has hampered Marxism-Leninism-Mao Zedong Thought, casting its shadow over the emergence of Marxism-Leninism-Maoism. Aside from the leadership cult built around Mao during the course of the Chinese Revolution, there were also the cults built around leaders of small Mao Zedong Thought parties at the centers of capitalism, such as the RCP-USA's Bob Avakian. More importantly, there was the dogmatic adoption of the leadership cult by the Communist Party of Peru whose most faithful cadre still maintain, decades after the PCP's people's war was defeated, "the application of the principle of Great Leadership and Great Leaders of the revolution".[11]

Although the "great leadership" dogma is generally rejected by the Marxist-Leninist-Maoist organizations that are currently leading the theoretical and revolutionary struggle (i.e. one is hard-pressed to find a personality cult amongst the Maoists leading the people's war in India, or amongst the Afghani Maoists who are spear-heading the rebuilding of the Revolutionary Internationalist Movement), there is still the fact that it affects significant sectors of the Maoist movement. Indeed, a strange Maoist tendency that has emerged in the wake of the RIM's dissolution is a Maoism that, following the defeated PCP, uses the terminology "Marxism-Leninism-Maoism, principally Maoism" and the cultish addendum "Gonzalo Thought". [12]

The fact that Maoism has been adopted as the communist tendency by the most exploited people, most of whom live in semi-feudal, semi-colonial contexts, is one common way to explain the problem of leadership cults but one that I do not find entirely convincing. After all "feudal mystification" does not explain the fact that such cultish behavior existed in the New Communist Movement at the centers of capitalism (specifically in the personality cult developed around the RCP-USA's Bob Avakian) or the fact that it is absent in Maoist organizations in semi-feudal contexts (for example there is no personality cult in the Communist Party of India (Maoist) or the Communist (Maoist) Party of Afghanistan), and so it is hardly a scientific explanation.

Moreover, despite the assumption that Maoism alone is guilty of such cultishness, the dogma of the "great leader" is evident in non-Maoist organizations as well: the Albanian communists built a cult around Enver Hoxha, for example, and the Communist Party of Canada (Marxist-Leninist) built a cult around Hardial

Bains. To this we can add the cult that accrued around Josef Stalin as well as the near cultish devotion some Trotskyists have to their "prophet". While Maoists must indeed reject the deviation of leadership cults, it seems somewhat ahistorical to assume that they are alone in this obvious example of dogmatism.

If anything, the problem of the personality cult is a minoritarian example of the dogmatism that affects communism in general and Maoism in particular: it is just as much of a problem for Maoism as it is for every other tendency; it is only an obvious manifestation of dogmatism, one that is easily dismissed by critical communists because of its obvious religiousness. In other words, the personality cult is not the main dogmatism that Marxism-Leninism-Maoism is primarily guilty of today, the dogmatism that needs to be struggled against; today's leading revolutionary and theoretical Maoist organizations have rejected this obvious manifestation of dogmatism, for obvious reasons, and yet are still hampered by dogmatism. One does not have to adopt the doctrine of "great leadership" to be a dogmatist: as noted above, dogmatism most often emerges in the belief of a "pure" communism—communism as a religious, rather than scientific, doctrine.[13]

Thus, beyond the problem of the personality cult, which is perhaps the most obvious manifestation of dogmatism, there is still the problem of religious behavior that can creep into communist practice even if such a practice aims at rejecting cultish devotion to a "great leader". That is, the elimination of cults of personality does not solve the problem of dogmatism; it is only one symptom of this negative tendency. As noted above, taking specific analyses and statements from the past as beyond criticism, defending a "pure" doctrine in the face of criticism, maintaining a fidelity to what has been written by previous organizations without critical reflection: these are all symptoms of dogmatic behavior.

Although it is true that such dogmatism is symptomatic of

other communist tendencies (i.e. Trotskyism which has almost become paradigmatic for its production of religious cabals), the dogmatism that emerges in Marxism-Leninism-Maoism is significantly different in that it has a concrete basis on which to develop. That is, while the dogmatism of other tendencies is produced to theoretically compensate for a lack of revolutionary practice (lacking any revolutionary experience, they seek bastion in theoretical purity in order to hope and pray for the future irruption of this experience), the dogmatism that develops within the Maoist tendency is due to its confidence in the manifold fact of its historical revolutionary experience. Hence, unlike other communist trajectories, I will argue in this chapter that there is a logical reason for the dogmatism that is expressed by Maoism... Even still, dogmatism is still dogmatism; it can only harm this revolutionary trajectory.

Furthermore, the problem of this dogmatism lies in the movement's historical inability to separate the scientific content meant by the ciphers *Marxism*, *Leninism*, *Maoism* from the nomological form. Again we run into the problem of confusing concepts with names. On the one hand we know that "Marxism" is not reducible to the name of Karl Marx, who was a person and not a prophet; on the other hand, in the course of our fidelity to the science he began, we cannot help but search for proof of this fidelity in his writing, mining it for passages that will authoritatively prove our theory and practice.

This contradiction is a serious philosophical problem and one that haunts the communism we propose as an alternative to other communist tendencies. Furthermore, it cannot be avoided by simply endorsing some sort of empty-headed "critical" Maoism where we uphold *in theory* Marxism-Leninism-Maoism but refuse to critique other tendencies that may indeed be erroneous. A class struggle in ideology is necessary, and we would not have a revolutionary theory if our predecessors had ignored this necessity.

It is worth rephrasing this problem in a clearer manner: i) we grasp that a new stage of revolutionary communism, emerging logically from world-historical revolution and a revolutionary assessment of world-historical revolution, has been theorized and that it is short-handed as *Marxism-Leninism-Maoism*; ii) in the course of accumulating revolutionary forces, necessary for a revolutionary movement, we are forced into ideological line struggle with other competing variants of communism; iii) we often end up suspending a scientific outlook in the course of agitational and revolutionary necessity in order to brand those organizations that, according to a historical-materialist assessment (though, admittedly, sometimes not), are incapable of producing revolution and might even be spreading confusion and opportunism amongst the masses.

Thus, in a somewhat visceral sense, dogmatism is produced by the very practice of revolutionary science, from the desire to be faithful to the revolution and the current stage of theory that revolutionary practice has produced if we are to develop the science further. Perhaps this is a core contradiction to Marxism, especially Marxism-Leninism; as will be clear in the following chapter, Clark indeed thought that the anti-revisionist communism of his day was affected by this contradiction which was why his organization (the Communist Workers Group (Marxist-Leninist)) dissolved after honestly recognizing the limits of that stage of struggle.

But in contradiction to Clark, and also to those who demand a muddle-headed and unprincipled "anything-goes" Marxism, I want to suggest that this dogmatism is a dialectical rather than formal contradiction, a unity of opposites. This does not mean that we should embrace dogmatism *nor* that we should embrace an uncritical "anti-dogmatism" (often proposed as "anti-sectarianism"), but that we should understand the meaning of this supposed core contradiction in order to make sense of our practice.

Militancy in Science

I began this chapter by summarizing the meaning of *revolutionary science*, specifically how and why Maoism, according to what was established in the first chapter, can be grasped as the current culmination of that science. To this we can add that a science, in order to be a science, is distinguished from religion by being open to the future: "truth" is not closed in an absolute, for-all-time set of definitions; truth is a process, science is alive insofar as it understands that it is establishing chains of universal applicability that must necessarily be incomplete... to insist otherwise is to imagine that nothing more can be learned, that we have arrived at the end of human understanding just as Hegel believed that the development of *geist* would terminate in a perfected philosophy. This is why dogmatism needs to be avoided: it can shut down thought, it can prevent investigation, it breeds self-righteous narrow-minded ideology.

And yet, despite this important caveat, we cannot deny that scientists in the various fields of the so-called "hard sciences" have been forced to agitate in act like "religious adherents" to their doctrine in order to develop their respective fields. The emergence of a new scientific theory is never linear, nor have the theories that we accept as scientific ever been predestined, simply waiting for scientists to discover. There is a myth that is generally told about these "hard sciences": the facts are waiting out there in the world just for someone to discover them, some genius like Einstein comes along and figures them out, the rupture in the field of scientific continuity happens with ease because it is obviously correct, but this is not the case.

We need to recognize that the important scientific theories that have developed the fields of biology, chemistry, and physics are most often models to account for phenomena that spilled over the limitations of previous theoretical terrains. What the Newtonian paradigm could not account for produced the necessity of a theoretical rupture, but if history had been different this rupture might not have been accomplished through Einstein's theories of General and Special Relativity.

In those moments where a stage of science has reached its limits, and thus an impasse, various and competing models often emerge and, upon their emergence, an ideological line struggle determines which theory becomes enshrined in the development of the science. Practitioners of a given science will assemble to defend the theories they prefer, debate ensues, scientific practice is mobilized to defend one model over another, journals and entire institutions will be used to promote some models and attack others; scientists momentarily act as adherents to a faith until the rupture is completed through one model achieving hegemony.

Jan Sapp's *Genesis: The Evolution of Biology* is a historiography of these line struggles in science, specifically biology. Not only does he discuss the struggles between the models of DNA that at one point divided the scientific world, he goes back to examine how Darwin and the adherents to the initial theory of evolution were forced to wage a social battle that demanded their absolute fidelity to that theory—here is the space where the scientist becomes a militant agitator, similar but different to the missionary.[14]

Within this context, however, it was practice that was always mobilized: proof was demanded by scientific praxis itself. And though scientific praxis was often broad enough to allow for the defense of various competing models, mediating and emergent secondary concepts (such as "Occam's Razor") were used to weed out abstruse and opaque theories. Just like the history of modes of production, it is possible that the path of the hard sciences could have led in different directions; the problem is that we assume linearity, as must in order to make sense of historical development, after the fact. Before the field of possibilities narrows, there was always the chance things could have gone differently. That is, the necessity for a new theory produces multiple contingencies.

Once we grasp that every science, especially those we often imagine as the "true" sciences, demand these moments of fidelity and ideological struggle, the charge of dogmatism requires a more complex and nuanced understanding. We must ask: were those scientists who acted militantly in fidelity to their chosen model (models that were clearly based on practical results) simply dogmatists? Were the militants who lined up behind Einstein's theories identical to the anti-militants who located their dogmatism in the defense of the Newtonian paradigm? Similarly, are Maoist militants identical to those militants who defend a "pure" form of Marxism, admitting no experimentation or creative development? The former are ideological progressives; the latter are behind the times.

Even still, we need to recognize the "risks", as Robert Biel correctly notes, inherent to the anti-revisionist militancy of the past that may teach us something about the anti-revisionist militancy of the present: "with any movement to uphold orthodoxy", however "relevant to all periods [in which] imperialism exists", there is always, due to this desire to push what is understood as "orthodox", the possibility of "becoming conservative and scared of new ideas".[15] But no struggle emerges without a risk. Moreover, the problem with the most recent expressions of anti-revisionist movements was that, as we shall see in a later chapter, the fact that they were indeed defending the orthodoxy of Marxism-Leninism against "the abandonment of Marx and Lenin's teachings on the inevitability of exploitation, repression, crisis and war under capitalism".[16] In this sense the lapse into dogmatism, due to its attempt to preserve an orthodoxy that was reaching limits that would necessitate a rupture, was unavoidable. The question, then, is whether the militancy dedicated to an emergent stage of revolutionary science is precisely the same as the militancy dedicated to defending revolutionary ideology in the face of revisionism.

Here, perhaps, is another moment of continuity-rupture: the problem of possible dogmatism is preserved, but it is thrust forward into a defense of something new against the orthodoxy of the old as opposed, compared to the previous anti-revisionist period, to defending the old against the opportunism of the new. A militancy dedicated to the scientific past against future mystification is similar to a militancy based on struggling for the scientific future against the limits of the past while, at the same time, completely different. But let us leave this question of anti-revisionism, and a comparison between old and new forms of anti-revisionism, for later chapters. In order to fully understand this difference, and thus key aspects of the problematic of continuity-rupture, we need to first understand: a) the limits of Marxism-Leninism, and thus the concrete differences between these two forms of anti-revisionism; b) anti-revisionism itself, gleaned from the openings produced by a rupture in revolutionary science. Before grasping these aspects, however, we need to fully grasp the threat of dogmatism, inherited from the past, so as to think through how it can be avoided.

Qualifications

We must not forget, however, that the charge of "dogmatism" has often been used to silence principled debate and promote revisionism. Indeed, this charge has historically reified revisionism, transformed it into a common standard of behavior. Thus, as previously noted, dogmatism is often forced upon the militant by the necessities of the historical conjuncture: revisionism becomes the problem, revisionists charge any attack on their theory and practice as *dogmatic* (apparently they themselves are incapable of *dogmatism* despite their religious adherence to their theory and practice that is supposedly "inclusive"), the anti-revisionist militant of a new stage of science is often expected to defend the continuity rather than the rupture of their position. Hence the problem, discussed above, of dogmatism indeed becoming a real danger: forced into a position of defending "orthodoxy", the militant may discover that the charge of dogmatism is a self-fulfilling prophecy, a destiny imposed by revisionism.

Moreover, the charge of "dogmatism" is often leveled at the militant by those who feel that any talk of "science" is tantamount to religiosity. In contexts where a neo-reformist movementism is the norm, and revolutionary parties with a coherent theoretical line are relegated to the past, "dogmatism" is defined as anything that refuses to be a nebulous and unprincipled "anything-goes" ideology. In this context, to even speak of Lenin or Mao is anathema: the militant is dismissed the moment these names leave their mouth. In this context all principled debate is stifled and this stifling, regardless of how it veils itself as *anti-dogmatic*, is as religiously close-minded as the discourse it imagines it has forbidden.[17]

Once more we find a gap between the name and concept of dogmatism. The name is frequently mobilized, applied without conceptual clarity to anything that declares fidelity to a coherent lineage of Marxist science, but it possesses no meaning beyond its name. Those who use it to silence what they feel is a return to the past, even if this return is new in its attempts to also rupture from this past, do so in a manner that precisely demonstrates the meaning of the name they conjure: dogmatism. They have dogmatically forbidden all discussion of the Marxism they despise.

Here we must again mobilize the analogy of the natural sciences and wonder whether those who maintained fidelity to these sciences in periods of despair were as dogmatic as those who sought to remystify reality with spiritualistic categories. For those who sought a return to the past, no matter how critical they pretended they were being, were simply returning to an inchoate and pre-scientific understanding of reality, a spontaneous embrace of reactionary ideology in order to escape from the quandary they had discovered.

The same is true of revolutionary science. Conjunctures of failure are reached that demand reassessment: some refuse to go forward because they are trapped at the boundaries of change; others go backwards because, lacking a revolutionary movement, they are ensnared in confusion; a remainder is capable, following a movement involved in making revolution, of struggling past these boundaries. By a strange reversal of logic, those who remained static or moved backwards invent reasons for their failure and, in this invention, pretend that they are producing an alternate movement: upon justifying their stasis they reject every actual moment of dynamism as backwards and charge everyone who claims otherwise with dogmatism. Take, for example, those scientists who refused to accept the "Big Bang" theory according to its own terms: some tried to pretend it was "religious" because they could only interpret this theory in a religious manner, others went so far as to embrace spiritualistic categories because this theory had shattered their rigid understanding of science. And those who rejected this theory, convinced that their backwardness was scientific, dogmatically charged everyone who was militantly defending the emergence of this theory with dogmatism.[18]

In this context, then, it is no wonder that the militant of Marxism-Leninism-Maoism ends up becoming dogmatic in form even if their theory is heterodox in essence. Often branded without reflection as "dogmatic" and "sectarian" by those who reject an organization based on a coherent theoretical line, the Maoist militant is forced to play a role that they would otherwise reject.

Appreciation of Full Meaning

I would like to suggest the dogmatism that cannot help but affect Maoism is inherited from the militant struggle surrounding the emergence of this stage in revolutionary science. While I believe it is clear that a new stage was forced into emergence through the event and limits of the world-historical revolution in China, the assessment of this revolution's successes and failures is still incomplete. We understand that there was a rupture, and were finally able to articulate this rupture in 1988 and 1994, but now we find ourselves adrift in a new theoretical terrain that, while contingent upon the previous theoretical terrains of the science, demands a development in philosophy.

The terrain remains unexplored, only the bare-bones of the assessment complete, as should be evident in the broad brush-strokes of the RIM statement in 1994: general categories capable of explaining the theoretical rupture were articulated as universal, but the meaning of these moments of universality were left necessarily vague. For at that moment, where there were only emergent revolutionary movements, we were only capable of grasping the world-historical identity of the revolution led by Mao Zedong, just as others before Mao had grasped the world-historical identity of the Bolshevik Revolution. Perhaps our understanding of Marxism-Leninism-Maoism is akin to Stalin's understanding of Marxism-Leninism (in *Foundations of Leninism*) which we now know was ultimately limited: these limitations were proved by the completed understanding of Leninism that was only possible by the time of the Cultural Revolution; the impasse they produced would eventually be explained by critical texts such as Tom Clark's *The State and Counter-Revolution*.

Thus, Marxism-Leninism-Maoism is emergent but incomplete. It is correct insofar as it grasps the general principles of universality based on the assessment of past world-historical revolutions; it requires development and self-recognition insofar as a further world-historical revolution is required to flush out its meaning, just as the revolution in China flushed out the meaning of Marxism-Leninism to correct the vagaries and misunderstandings of Stalin's articulation of Leninism. Here the door was shut on "Stalinism", not that there was really such a thing, just as the door will necessarily be shut on "Gonzalo Thought" or

"Prachanda Path" or any other over-particularist variant of Marxism-Leninism-Maoism that, without a world-historical revolution, is capable only of devolving into dogmatic devotion.

Hence the need for a development in philosophy: there needs to be a critical dialogue over the meaning of this new terrain and what it demands. If we are simply content to speak of Maoism religiously, and dismiss every other tendency as heretical, we might fail to grasp the importance of this development and its requirements. Even worse: by imagining that this terrain has already reached its limits *without a world-historical revolution*, we will end up becoming like members of the RCP-USA and other "post-Maoist" organizations who, despite having once recognized the universality of Marxism-Leninism-Maoism, imagine they have somehow transgressed the limits of this science without having produced a revolutionary movement.

The point, then, is that a real dogmatism emerges when the movement either: a) closes itself off to the future and, still caught in the moment of militant agitation, imagines the questions of the newly opened theoretical terrain are answered; b) turns towards a future that doesn't yet exist by imagining these questions, which are still questions of the recently opened terrain, need to be solved by a new and incoherent terrain. The first problematic locks itself into a pedestrian corner of the emergent scientific stage, contenting itself with religious proclamations based on narrow applications of the general concepts. The second problematic, in order to justify itself in the moment as a new avenue of revolutionary thought, tends to seek religious justification in an especial theory that is believed, for no other reason than superstition, to present an understanding that past world-historical revolutions lacked.

In other words, dogmatism is always a threat because of the nature of the science (just as it is a threat in the other sciences where many scientists refuse to turn towards future developments in their field), and since there are moments where militant fidelity is required this threat is always a danger. I would like to suggest, however, that the danger can be neutralized if we develop the field of this thought which, unlike Trotskyism, is not doomed to a state of dogmatic fidelity: after all, we are speaking of a theory that emerged in the crucible of people's war, that dared to speak of a new stage of communism in the midst of supposed failure, and that has already produced various and exciting avenues of exploration.

When we investigate this field of thought, its still developing constellation, philosophical intervention is indeed required. Dogmatism, perhaps inherited from the necessities of ideological line struggle, should be combatted and placed in context. There was a time when militants devoted to the Copernican Revolution were content only with repeating the axiom that the Earth was not the center of the galaxy; when this revolution achieved hegemony, the full meaning of its theory could be appreciated. Here, then, is an important philosophical point: Marxism-Leninism-Maoism still requires an appreciation of its full meaning.

The Gap between Revolution in Form and Revisionism in Practice

In the RIM's 1994 statement *Long Live Marxism-Leninism-Maoism!* it is suggested that, just as clinging to a "pure" Marxism after the emergence of Marxism-Leninism produced revisionism, clinging to a "pure" Marxism or "pure" Marxism-Leninism after the emergence of Marxism-Leninism-Maoism also produces revisionism. At first glance such a bold claim appears dogmatic. After all, it is the hallmark of religious devotees to assert in a fanatical and sectarian manner that someone is not a "true believer" if they do not adhere to a specific religious faith. Due to the fact that dogmatism does indeed hamper Marxism at each and every stage, it is indeed fair to recognize that such a claim may indeed imply dogmatism: you are a revisionist, a false

Marxist, if you do not believe in Marxism-Leninism-Maoism.

Fair enough: I have already noted how militant fidelity to a developing terrain of a given science often necessitates, especially in this terrain's early and nebulous emergence, a dogmatic attitude and practice. And yet I would also like to suggest that there is a way to read the RIM claim about revisionism in a manner that is expressly scientific rather than dogmatic. I do not believe that the Marxist-Leninist-Maoist movement as a whole has coherently flushed out the full scientific implication of this statement, and I admit that it often falls back unto this statement in a dogmatic manner so as to ignore interventions from other Marxist terrains. At the same time, however, I think it is worth investigating what this statement means for the science as a whole.

Let us examine, for a moment, the field of physics in order to make analogical sense of the RIM's intriguing and bombastic statement. Can we imagine that someone can be a proper physicist if they cling to a purely Newtonian understanding of physics decades after Einstein's theories of General and Special Relativity have transformed the field? The question is obviously rhetorical: we would be inclined to argue that someone militating for a Newtonian worldview is a "revisionist" in this scientific discipline, meaning they are anti-scientific, their ideas undermine the development of science and will lead nowhere.[19]

So in this sense, the RIM statement is scientifically axiomatic rather than dogmatic. It is not that Marxist practitioners who deny the epistemic rupture of Maoism are pseudo-Marxist revisionists. In fact, these practitioners might very well be honest Marxists who oppose revisionism in principle; they might be honest fellow travelers who truly desire class revolution. Rather, the point is that their practice, since it does not recognize new developments in the field of their science, cannot produce what they want it to produce: they occupy a theoretical dead-end, they are caught in a historical moment of theory that has already been surpassed, and thus their insights are limited. They are revisionist in the same sense as the Newtonian who hasn't grasped the rupture produced by Einstein is a revisionist: what new insights will this Newtonian scientist produce when Newtonianism has already been relegated to the past—maybe a few interesting commentaries, maybe some important interventions, but these will always be limited by their failure to understand reality as it has been expounded by a developing field that has passed them by.

We have not yet grasped the full meaning of this RIM insight. Arguing that Marxist theory can only be truly alive within the terrain opened by Maoism demands the development of this field as well as philosophical intervention to make sense of such development. We are still standing at the threshold of this new geography, much as the scientists of the past in another field stood at the threshold of the geography opened by the Copernican Revolution. Since we are still standing at the threshold we are often limited to glancing over our shoulder so that we can remain grounded in the continuity that sometimes feels threatened by the simultaneous rupture in thought. It is only when we have investigated the full meaning of this rupture that we can realize what is and what is not continuous with the previous paradigms of our science. We understand that rupture and continuity are scientific, that they are always in dialectical tension, but we cannot grasp this relationship in its completed sense when we are still only capable of explaining the rupture according to the past patterns of the continuity from Marx to Lenin that is only now, at the moment of *this* rupture, fully understood. So too, returning to our analogy, could the early militant of the Einsteinian rupture only appreciate this rupture by staring back at the continuity of their operating field from Copernicus to the end of Newton, still unaware of the complete sense in which the General and Special Theories of Relativity were continuous with this history.

Thus, due to this backwards-looking glance, RIM's possibly scientific insight can easily be exchanged for dogmatic furor. After all, as noted in the previous section, the early militants of a new scientific stage are always affected by a lamentable dogmatic militancy. It is here that the RIM claim can be treated, even by those who phrased it in a qualified sense based on past moments of continuity-rupture, as a call to fanatical practice. In this distorted manner of recognizing the Maoist rupture in historical materialism, it is all too easy to dismiss everyone who does not expressly proclaim adherence to *Maoism* as anti-communist; we might even go so far as to label other Maoists, whose practice does not resemble our ideas of practice that are often still based on caricature of the most recent world-historical revolution, as also false communists. Indeed, the remnants of the PCP, regardless of its importance in producing the moment of rupture, is wont to disparage every movement and people's war that does not proclaim perfect fidelity to "Gonzalo Thought" as ultimately revisionist.

Perhaps this dogmatic squabbling speaks to the problem of revolutionary struggle, reminding us that the theoretical terrain can only develop through actual revolutions (hence, a revolution that failed is now incapable of any authoritative theoretical insight), but since no revolution since the emergence of Marxism-Leninism-Maoism has gone further than the Chinese Revolution we are still limited to struggling ideologically upon the threshold of this new theoretical terrain. But even here, at the threshold, philosophical intervention might be useful.[20] For philosophy can at least call this militant dogmatism into question, demand that these movements stop looking over their shoulders, and venture further out into the terrain opened by the Maoist rupture. Such venturing will indeed produce new theoretical developments, which further acts of philosophical intervention might explore, because this is now the only terrain that is open as a live option for the field of Marxist science.

Elsewhere it appears that Marxism has turned inwards, is limited by the boundaries of the dead-ends that it has encountered; it might oppose revisionism in theory, but it still amounts to revisionism in practice. At the very least a philosophy tied to the rupture produced by Maoism can explain the gap between revolution in theory and revisionism in practice.

Looking Backwards

When I argued, in the previous section, that those of us who adhere to the Maoist rupture are often still forced to look backwards rather than forwards I meant for this figure of speech to be taken seriously. After all, this backwards-looking glance was examined in the first chapter where I attempted to distance this theoretical terrain from a past era where Maoism was not yet capable of emerging as a new stage of historical materialism. The new terrain opened by this rupture in the field of historical materialism remains hampered by the patterns of the past that still, in the words of Marx, "weigh like a nightmare on the brains of the living". These past behaviors are evident, for example, in the way contemporary Maoists treat Trotskyists: all of the old polemics and insults are mobilized to dismiss Trotskyism as an ideology of "wreckers", a tendency of betrayal that undermined Marxism-Leninism.[21]

But if Trotskyism is properly understood as a historical dead-end, something that we must leave behind, then it must be treated as such rather than as a "wrecking" ideology.[22] Even still, we are pulled back into the past and often cannot resist the temptation to dismiss Trotskyists as "counter-revolutionary" when, in fact, this might not necessarily be the case. At least not in form: while it is important to argue that, like any science, we can only move forward through the paradigm that has proved itself according to the bounds of the specific field of science, and that every other approach can only lead to revisionist dead-ends, it is at least worth noting that there are organizations and individuals who, despite their failure to understand the developing science, are not intentionally revisionist. In some ways these unintentional revisionists may even be allies.

Trotskyism aside, we still have the problem of a dogmatism that is in part culled from our inability to break from previous and unfruitful patterns of behavior. We want everyone to grasp the development of science that we have recognized, to join us in transgressing that threshold, and in our frustration we lapse into past habits of theoretical practice.

We have to ask this important question: is the theoretical rupture of this new stage of Maoism worth investigation and development, or are we simply dressing up the previous period of anti-revisionist communism in the clothes of Marxism-Leninism-Maoism? For Maoism cannot only be continuous with Marxism-Leninism in order to represent a new stage of revolutionary science (if it was simply continuous then it would indeed be the same as the incoherent Maoisms of yesteryear) but must also be a rupture. And in order to recognize the rupture it represents, we have to give up on previous ways of defending Marxism-Leninism, accept Maoism's continuity as self-evident, and move forward to explore the meaning of its rupture.

Rupture as Necessity

In order to explain the meaning of the Maoist rupture, however, we also have to examine the reasons behind its emergence. Theoretical ruptures in the field of any science are not accidentally spontaneous events, though they might appear as such to the casual observer. They do not manifest in a vacuum; rather, they happen for historically significant reasons. To keep with our example from physics, Einstein's theories of General and Special Relativity were not the accidental musings of a genius scientist who just happened to think them up one day because he was bored: these were theories that were intended to transgress the limits reached by Newtonian physics, a rupture made necessary by the questions Newton's theories could not answer. That is, a science had reached the limits of its explanatory potential and theoretical praxis; a new stage had to be theorized if this science was to remain open to the future rather than becoming locked in the contradictions of its limits.

The Maoist rupture, then, happened precisely at the point where Marxism-Leninism had reached its limits. Maoism was not theorized as a new scientific stage for spurious reasons, out of some sense of creative spontaneity, but because those behind its theorization were encountering, in the crucible of class struggle, problems that Marxism-Leninism was incapable of solving. While recognizing that Marxism-Leninism was capable of answering other problems, and was a foundation for revolution, the early militants of Marxism-Leninism-Maoism realized that, by itself, even the most anti-revisionist form of Marxism-Leninism was incomplete. It was not that the figurative wheel needed to be reinvented, but that a transformation of the wheel was demanded: historical necessity forced theoretical rupture.

We only need to examine the period in which Maoism was conceptualized to understand that this was also a period in which the limits of Marxism-Leninism had been reached. At the end of the 1980s and the beginning of the 1990s world capitalism was in the midst of victoriously declaring itself "the end of history": the collapse of the eastern bloc, already thoroughly revisionist, the capitalist road chosen by China, and the disintegration of anti-revisionist communist movements were evidence of the limits of Marxism-Leninism. Any revolutionary movement that emerged in this period would have to make sense of this collapse, fully assess the successes and failures of the past, if it was to even have a chance at surviving.

At the same time, however, the fact that Marxism-Leninism had reached its limits also produced the temptation to abandon this science, go back to the beginning of anti-capitalist struggle, and embrace a different theory. That is, the easiest and most tempting response to the limitations of Marxism-Leninism was to reject Marxism-Leninism altogether, claim that it was a flawed theory from its very inception, and demand a rupture without any continuity: neo-anarchism, Draperism,[23] post-modern praxis. Nebulous movementism was the simplest and laziest solution. These were not new theories, though they imagined that they were, but simply repetitions of historical oubliettes from past epochs of class struggle.

When a science reaches its limits and encounters phenomena it is currently incapable of solving, at the moment of scientific crisis, some scientists do reject the entire scientific project and seek bastion in the past while pretending that the backwards ideas they have embraced are *new* and *critical*. As Althusser once wrote about these moments of scientific crisis and the reactions of some scientists to the questions that their theoretical terrain cannot grasp without a moment of rupture:

> The 'crisis' catches them by surprise, unprepared or, without even knowing it, so prejudiced that their convictions are badly shaken; everything collapses around them and, in their panic, they call into question not simply a given scientific concept or theory so as to rectify or reformulate it, but the validity of their practice itself: the 'value of science'.[24]

But every science always reaches moments of crisis, which are only crises insofar as they are periods where the limits of a theoretical terrain have been reached and a rupture is required. All sciences, by virtue of being *scientific* and thus *open to the future* (where truth is an unfolding process rather than a rigid and dogmatic absolute), must encounter crises. No theory is absolute and each scientific stage is only capable of answering the questions with which it has been presented by history. Other questions, though, will be encountered that cannot be answered by a given stage in theory. The task of a critical scientist is not to accept defeat and abandon the truth process simply because the limits of a given theoretical terrain have been reached but to prove the validity of their practice, the value of the science, by grasping the possibility of theoretical rupture.

Thus, Maoism attempted to answer the impasse reached by Marxism-Leninism not by denying the living science of revolutionary communism that had developed, through world-historical revolution, from Marxism to Leninism, but by theorizing the next moment of rupture. In this context, then, we need to grasp the limits of Marxism-Leninism that necessitated the Maoist rupture.

Notes

1. Again, this was precisely the problem that prompted me to write *Maoism or Trotskyism*.
2. I should note, here, that philosophers of science often *do* use this terminology in order to make sense of the development of a particular scientific field. In *The Structure of Scientific Revolutions*, for example, Thomas Kuhn speaks of "Einsteinian" and "Newtonian" paradigms so as to clarify the meaning of transformation in the field of physics.
3. Laruelle, 50.
4. I have critiqued Laruelle's *Introduction to Non-Marxism* in a review at *Marx & Philosophy Review of Books* (http://marxand-philosophy.org.uk/reviewofbooks/reviews/2016/2209).
5. The relationship between philosophy and theory in general, and Marxist philosophy and science in particular, is a larger discussion than what can be discussed here.
6. See *Reason in Revolt: Marxist Philosophy and Modern Science* by Ted Grant and Alan Woods. Not only is this book somewhat comical in its willful ignorance of science, it is also noteworthy in its mobilization of a reactionary anti-intellectualism (i.e. it mocks "university professors with long strings of letters after their name"—apparently the only thing that

qualifies one to speak of science is not studying it in university but simply being a self-proclaimed expert of *the* science of historical materialism) and racist metaphors (i.e. "the mission [particle physicists] were called upon to carry out puts all the exploits of John Wayne completely in the shade. The most he ever had to do was find some unfortunate women and children carried off by the Indians"), all of which demonstrate an embarrassing level of scientific ignorance.

7. See J. Werner's *Beat Back the Dogmato-Revisionist Attack on Mao Zedong Thought*. Of course, despite the importance of this concept and analysis, this document is still limited by its adherence to a Maoism that is alienated from the current meaning of Maoism. Moreover, the organization responsible for coining this term, the RCP-USA, has devolved into a rather strange and dogmatic organization.

8. Clark, *The State and Counter-Revolution* (Preface), 1.

9. Ajith, *The Maoist Party*.

10. Ajith, *Against Avakianism*. This document is one of the best responses (along with the CmPA's response to the RCP-USA's May 1st letter and the Worker's Dreadnought blog series) to the RCP-USA's claim that it has produced a "new synthesis" of revolutionary theory that all communists ought to adopt. One of the reasons I do not waste much time engaging with Bob Avakian's "new synthesis" is because documents such as this one have already done the work. Otherwise, for reasons expressed in my conceptualization of revolutionary science that foreclose on the possibility of this kind of "new synthesis" even existing, I do not see how an organization, whatever its past merits (its past errors regarding Indigenous self-determination and queer struggle notwithstanding), that has become utterly marginal and cultish imagines it can produce a new theoretical development that we should care about. Since the "new synthesis" is only given a halo of

significance by its adherents (and sadly some Iranian comrades have been hoodwinked by the Avakianites), but in itself is a unremarkable approach to reality that is neither "new" nor a "synthesis", any direct engagement with it is now a waste of time.

11. Communist Party of Peru, "To the Communists...", 16.

12. See, for example, the Communist Party of France (Marxist-Leninist-Maoist) and the Organization of the Workers of Afghanistan (Marxist-Leninist-Maoist, principally Maoist) who, along with similar obscure organizations, promote a cultish variant of Maoism that is more "Gonzaloist" than the Peruvians. It is difficult to know whether these organizations exist in any significant manner outside of the internet, but they still tend to release statements. Many of their statements are aimed at attacking other Maoist groups and promoting needless sectarianism.

13. Ultra-orthodox Trotskyist organizations, for instance, are a good example of this fact. The Spartacist League, despite not openly promoting a leadership cult, still demonstrates a behavior that places it on par with Mormons and Jehovah's Witnesses. Its attempt at doctrinal purity, which results in a theology of theoretical hair-splitting, is a perfect example of dogmato-revisionism.

14. See Jan Sapp's *Genesis: The Evolution of Biology*.

15. Robert Biel, *Eurocentrism and the Communist Movement*, 6.

16. Ibid.

17. I briefly discussed this problem in my previous book. See Moufawad-Paul, 71–72.

18. Here it is again worth noting that some Marxist thinkers are caught up in the wrong side of this debate. Convinced that this theory implied, as both its detractors and its strangest defenders claimed, some form of spiritualism, disappointing theorists such as Ted Grant and Alan Woods would write entire books defending the Newtonian paradigm, ranting

that modern physics was wrong because it was religious, and generally making Marxism appear extremely ignorant. (Once again see Ted Grant and Alan Wood's *Reason in Revolt*.)

19. I recognize, here, that there are indeed some Marxists who, bizarrely imagining that historical materialism qualifies them to speak with expertise in other fields of science, do indeed argue for a Newtonian paradigm over an Einsteinian paradigm. They even go so far as to claim that Einstein and Hawking are "wrong", that the Big Bang theory is "anti-scientific", because they are somehow contrary to historical materialism: as if historical materialism as a science is capable, or at all interested, in intervening in other scientific fields in such a manner. Not to belabor the point, but Grant and Wood's *Reason in Revolt* must again be noted as paradigmatic of this approach: basing itself on discredited physicists and writers of popular science who are not scientists, this book argues against Einstein, Hawking, the Big Bang, Black Holes, dark matter, and a host of other scientific concerns because its authors imagine they are qualified to speak with authority on all sciences simply because they are Marxists. As for physicists who would find such views laughable, Grant and Wood merely dismiss them as apparatchiks of the bourgeoisie with a bunch of fancy degrees. These sorts of books exist to make Marxists look foolish, and are often used as examples as to why we have no right to speak of "science".

20. None of this is to say, of course, that such interventions can and should be performed only by privileged academics, such as myself, who have been trained in "proper" philosophy. Here I mean *philosophy* in a very general sense and I am confident that one does not have to hold a doctorate in philosophy to intervene in a philosophical manner. Moreover, it is also worth pointing out that

philosophy is only capable of intervening in a truth process that is already established and that philosophy is incapable of developing this truth process any further. This process develops through theoretical insights gleaned from class struggle itself, that is *revolutionary practice*, and so philosophy is always forced to tail these movements and attempt to clarify their meaning, a very secondary task. Hence Althusser's claim that philosophy lacks a history, even if it falsely imagines that it is some idealist truth behind history, and can only emerge within the field of a given science or scientific branch.

21. See the Appendix.

22. Which is not to say that Trotskyist groups cannot be wreckers. Many of us, after all, are familiar with the activities of groups such as the Spartacist League that seem to function only to disrupt meetings, act parasitically towards events called by groups they have not supported, and grow only by poaching members from other organizations. And yet I think it is fair to say that there are many Trotskyist-influenced formations that have not behaved in such a reprehensible manner, just as there are many non-Trotskyist organizations that have also acted as "wreckers"—in Canada, the Communist Party of Canada (Marxist-Leninist), which was a Hoxhaite organization, used to go out of its way to physically assault the members of other communist groups.

23. In the final chapter I will discuss this specific phenomenon in more detail.

24. Althusser, *Philosophy and the Spontaneous Philosophy of the Sciences*, 110.

Chapter 3

The General Limits of Marxism-Leninism

...the Cultural Revolution in China, which, having stumbled on the party in the fire of a communist uprising, puts on the agenda the fact that the Leninist party is over. [...] The domain of Leninism makes no real place, when it comes to the party, for the problem of communism as such. Its business is the State, the antagonistic victory. The Cultural Revolution begins the forcing of this uninhabitable place. It invites us to name 'party of the new type' the post-Leninist party, the party for communism, on the basis of which to recast the entire field of Marxist practice.

—Alain Badiou, *Theory of the Subject*

The Impasse of Marxism-Leninism

In the first chapter I discussed the limitations of the "anti-revisionist" Marxism-Leninism that emerged in the 1960s and 1970s. Although this "New Communist Movement", appearing as a necessary response to the "New Left", recentered class revolution by declaring fidelity to the Chinese Revolution instead of the Soviet Union under Khrushchev, it was still incapable of producing a theoretical rupture from a terrain that had nearly reached its limits. By the 1980s China would stumble, its last attempted assault on counter-revolution resulting in failure by 1978, and those movements that had done little more than follow in its wake were eventually forced to concede defeat. Some disbanded honorably, some struggled on into the mid or late 1980s, some collapsed spectacularly, and some succeeded in re-orientating themselves.

Generally speaking, however, the movement as a whole stumbled and turned inwards as it reached an impasse. It is mistaken, as I indicated in the first and second chapters, to assume that this often heterogeneous movement, at that period in time, possessed an understanding of Maoism-qua-Maoism: those organizations that defined themselves as "Maoist" were Maoist only insofar as they declared fidelity to China instead of the Soviet Union; none of them could possibly establish Maoism as a further development of revolutionary science because the world-historical revolution of China had not yet reached its moment of failure: assessment was impossible, and this impossibility conditioned the collapse of that period's anti-revisionist movement.

It is tempting to dismiss those "lost" decades as a general period of failure in which only a few organizations were able to survive by adapting themselves to capitalist triumphalism and, following this adaptation, perhaps embrace the eventual emergence of Maoism in the Peruvian People's War and the foundation of the Revolutionary Internationalist Movement. After all, the RCP-USA survived the New Communist Movement, superseding the vague Maoism of its time in order to temporarily embrace the emergence of Marxism-Leninism-Maoism. And yet this organization would also falter: now it has rejected Maoism and, before this, succeeded in transforming itself into a quasi-religious sect. Furthermore, it is unclear whether the RCP-USA had ever truly appreciated the impasse of the period in which it had risen to prominence, just as it is unclear whether it was still caught up in the logic of this impasse.

So just what was this impasse, and why did this period of anti-revisionism collapse in such a thorough manner? It is difficult to answer this question because many organizations seemed to dissolve almost overnight; many of the significant organizations failed to produce assessments of their dissolution: the WCP, for example, despite being an important anti-revisionist party in Canada, did not make the reasons for its collapse known in a public document at the time of its dissolution. Its legacy is almost forgotten, even though it was once a significant force in the

Canadian revolutionary scene, and the period in which it operated, along with the legacy of other significant NCM organizations such as En Lutte.

It is in this anti-revisionist context that the intervention of a relatively small US organization, the Communist Workers Group (Marxist-Leninist), is worth examining. Although this organization was not as large or influential as other organizations in its time and place, the documents it produced in its dissolution (and, like the Canadian En Lutte, the CWG (Marxist-Leninist) dissolved itself) reveal something important about the movement as a whole.

Tom Clark's book *The State and Counter-Revolution*, which was the CWG (Marxist-Leninist) summation of that period, focuses on what might have been the prime contradiction of anti-revisionist Marxism-Leninism: the boundaries reached by the Leninist stage of revolutionary science that demanded a theoretical rupture. Unfortunately, since Clark and his organization could only grasp Marxism-Leninism (understanding "Maoism" in the older sense of the term) they were incapable of producing anything but an examination of the limits of the movement they had once embraced but eventually found incomplete. They could only interpret this incompleteness as a frightful contradiction at the heart of what they understood to be revolutionary theory, just as past physicists who glimpsed the limitations of the Newtonian paradigm were incapable of grasping the fact that a further rupture in the field of their science might solve the problems they could only understand as contradictions within the science itself.

A Possible Contradiction

It is worth quoting from *The State and Counter-Revolution* at length in order to explain the contradiction that Clark and his organization felt was intrinsic to Marxism-Leninism itself in order to appreciate the full thrust of their assessment, since it is one of the best expressions of the limits of the impasse that cannot be overstepped without rupturing from the Leninist terrain while remaining in continuity with it:

> This contradiction consists in the fact that although communism is formally a political doctrine of the working class, its main theorists and the vast majority of its most active proponents have been drawn from the middle class. Thus despite the fact that according to socialist theory the working class should provide political and organizational leadership to its allies within the petty bourgeoisie, it is in reality ideologists from the petty bourgeoisie that have taken the leading role in politicizing and organizing the working class. [...] [T]his class contradiction is usually dealt with... [through] the logical premise that since the mass of workers does not have a scientific understanding of their actual class position and interests, their spontaneous trade union struggles are necessarily limited to minor reforms and concessions within the framework of capitalism. As Lenin stated, without revolutionary theory there can be no revolutionary movement. [...] But the stultifying conditions of work and life common to most workers prevent them from acquiring academic, scientific and organizational skills necessary to originate sophisticated political theory and the time needed to implement it. The socialist intellectuals conclude from this that political knowledge must therefore be introduced by people, who due to their privileged social status, do have the necessary intellectual training and leisure time, i.e. themselves. [...] Since the advanced workers are initially unfamiliar with the fine points of socialist theory and must rely on the intellectuals for their political education, it is the intellectuals who determine the major principles of the movement and establish guidelines for its practical activity. [...] Although the workers' objective revolutionary potential is a function of their social position as

an oppressed class, their strategic role in production and their socially conditioned collectivity and discipline, the intelligentsia has nothing in the way of material or social conditions to insure a consistent revolutionary outlook. On the contrary, the same social privileges that enable the radical intellectuals to formulate the main principles of socialist theory also engender diverse opportunist views that in the end surround and overwhelm those principles. [...] While separate trends within the socialist movement may admit this of their opponents and in their bitter polemics and mutual recriminations accuse one another of 'petty bourgeois opportunism', none are willing to admit that it is true of the movement as a whole.[1]

Before teasing out the claims made in this long passage so as to appreciate the contradiction it has uncovered at the heart of Marxism-Leninism, it is important to note that Clark saw this as a *contradiction* in the dialectical sense, something that needed to be grasped and overcome, rather than in the positivist sense where contradictions mean irrationality. It would be tempting to read this passage as a simple condemnation of Marxism-Leninism, and its author as a jaded ex-revolutionary who, upon recognizing this problem, believed that Marxism-Leninism should be dismissed entirely. Rather, he saw it as a problem that needed to be overcome but that could not yet be overcome.

So what is Clark claiming if he is not simply dismissing Marxism-Leninism as an erroneous politics and advocating a theoretical reinvention of the wheel? I will simplify the above passage to its most salient points.

1. The working-class caught up in trade unions cannot produce a revolutionary organization by itself because, in this context, it is only capable of producing an economism ("trade-union consciousness"), or a defiant

anarchism, but not a mediating party that produces a revolutionary movement with a coherent and revolutionary theory. Here we must recall Althusser's analysis of the philosophy of Marxism-Leninism where he points out that the working-class, which spends most of its time working, can only conceive of its rebellion according to the ruling ideas of the ruling class.

2. And yet the revolutionary party that approaches the working class tends to be a party composed of petty-bourgeois intellectuals who are only capable of having a thorough appreciation of theory and revolution because, unlike the workers they claim to represent, they possess a measure of social privilege: they have the time to be students or academics. Here we must recall that, in *What Is To Be Done?* Lenin agrees with Kautsky's claim that the party is initiated by the petty-bourgeoisie.

3. The party began by these intellectuals, since it recognizes the proletariat as being the grave-digger of capitalism, must impart revolutionary theory to the workers so that these workers can also be intellectuals. The workers must rely on these intellectuals in order to comprehend revolutionary theory, to understand a revolution that is supposedly about their own interests.

4. A given worker's intellectual development is decided by the petty-bourgeois educator; it is these petty-bourgeois intellectuals who have the privilege of judging whether or not the workers are learning properly, just as they have had the privilege to decide what these workers should learn in the first place—indeed, what counts as *proletarian ideology*. Hence the germ of the contradiction: the petty-bourgeois class becomes the authority on proletarian

ideology when, according to the very ideology they seek to impart, social being should determine social consciousness—how can someone whose class position is petty-bourgeois ever be fully capable of having a proletarian consciousness and thus understanding proletarian ideology?

5. The petty bourgeoisie remains in charge of the movement, its outlook misconceived as *proletarian ideology*, the meter of revolutionary theory, and thus petty-bourgeois ideology becomes sublimated in the movement itself. Counter-revolution happens precisely because there is an unquestioned petty-bourgeois basis to Marxist-Leninist revolutionary movements.

Finally, we can simplify all five of these salient points, as well as the passage itself, to this basic statement of contradiction: on the one hand it is impossible for the proletariat to spontaneously develop a revolutionary party with a revolutionary ideology; on the other hand it is impossible for a party that the workers cannot possibly develop, and thus is developed instead by the petty bourgeoisie, to carry a revolution to its completion. In essence: Marxism-Leninism is correct while, at the same time, Marxism-Leninism is incorrect.

Before examining this contradiction, though, it is worth noting that Jacques Rancière has spent the past couple decades expressing a similar complaint with Marxism-Leninism, particularly the Marxism-Leninism philosophically described by his former teacher Louis Althusser. Worried that Marxism, and particularly a Marxism of the Leninist variant, was "graft[ing] itself onto the voices of working-class protest", and thus an alien presence speaking for the voice of a heterogeneous phenomenon, Rancière has spent much of his career attempting to excavate "a different definition of working-class identity".[2] Inspired by the insights of a germinal Maoism, Rancière's ability to grasp the problem of Marxism-Leninism (admittedly, of the Mao Zedong Thought variety), rather than leading him towards the possibility of Marxism-Leninism-Maoism (which, as we shall see, is the only *productive* way out of this impasse), has caused him to descend into a confused adoption of spontaneism and historical analysis that is more inaccessible than the proletarian subject he hopes to reclaim.[3] Thus, the reason I have chosen to focus on Clark's less popular description of this problematic is because, unlike the critique provided by Rancière, it is more accessible and precise.

The Marxist-Leninist Contradiction as Dialectical

Here it is worth pausing to appreciate the contradiction highlighted by Clark. Since we are often still caught up in the dogmatism inherited from the past epoch of struggle (that I discussed in the previous chapter) it all too easy to dismiss an analysis that serves as a critique of that epoch. After all, there are innumerable and simplistic rejections that could be leveled at Clark's critique: we could point out that the intellectuals who bring revolutionary politics to the proletarian movements are not essentially "petty-bourgeois", but this seems to be a simplistic act of denial; we could even argue that since Clark himself was a petty-bourgeois intellectual his analysis is undermined by his own complaint, but this amounts to a semantic game.

I would like to suggest that the contradiction indicated by Clark is extremely significant, that it serves as a critique of the period of anti-revisionist communism and the limits it reached, and that it even tells us something about the necessity of the Maoist rupture that dialectically unifies this contradiction. Hence, I would like to suggest that Clark has provided us with a philosophical quandary, a contradiction that requires the forcing of meaning, that can only be answered by a philosophical intervention that is produced by the Maoist rupture.

As we pause to appreciate the contradiction revealed by

Clark, it is again worth noting that this quandary cannot be solved by either the denial of its existence or embracing one side of the contradiction. It is a contradiction precisely because *both* the spontaneous development of a revolutionary party on the part of the proletariat *and* the forced implementation of a party by the petty-bourgeois intelligentsia will not produce a proper revolutionary movement: the former is impossible, the latter leads to counter-revolution.

We must also recognize that various [non-Maoist] Marxist organizations have recognized, though incoherently, this contradiction and have attempted to answer it in ways that amount to cunning acts of sophistry. Hal Draper's theory of "socialism from below", for instance, assumes that the party can and will be built spontaneously by the unionized working class through union struggle but, since this has never happened and cannot be pursued as a strategic line aside from vague agitational practices (which might again end up importing ideology from intellectuals to workers, returning us to Clark's contradiction), it is a theory that is in many ways an argument from ignorance. Leaving aside Draperism, for the moment, since I plan to examine it in a later chapter, there are also those "missionary" parties, composed of former intellectuals who imagine they have declassed and who, upon realizing the problem of their privilege, spend all of their time waiting for the working class to realize the "correct line" and gravitate to their slogans and programs. After over half-a-century they are still waiting.

Moreover, although it could be argued that the contradiction highlighted by Clark is not worth examining because Clark's organization was less significant than other organizations in the New Communist Movement, I would counter that this is a dishonest way in which to dodge the charges leveled at anti-revisionist Marxism-Leninism in *The State and Counter-Revolution*. While it might indeed have been the case that the CWG (Marxist-Leninist) was an "insignificant" organization compared to other groups that left their mark in that period of anti-revisionism, it is worth noting that even some of these significant groups recognized the same contradiction but did not have the energy or time to think their way through the problem.

Canada's WCP, for example, noted something akin to Clark's contradiction in a document that summed up its dissolution. Indeed, in *Elements of a Sum Up of the WCP*, the caucus given the responsibility for summing up the reasons for the collapse of the Workers Communist Party noted, among other things, that the "social composition of the party leadership and top cadre" was one of the significant problems leading to the organization's disintegration, especially the fact that this composition was primarily petty-bourgeois.[4] As noted earlier, the WCP was one of the two most significant Marxist-Leninist organizations in Canada during that period of anti-revisionism.

Thus, Clark's contradiction remains salient when it comes to Marxist-Leninist movements of the past period of struggle: none of them are capable of escaping the impasse, of responding to the contradiction highlighted by *The State and Counter-Revolution*. This is why we need to take this contradiction seriously; it should tell us something about the meaning of Maoism, and this is a philosophical question.

Who Decides?

Throughout this book I have attempted to highlight the difference between the *name* and *concept* of "Maoism". I have argued that Maoism did not properly exist as Maoism, despite its prior use, until the end of the 1980s when a revolutionary movement and multiple revolutionary organizations could provide a thorough assessment of the most recent world-historical revolution. Tom Clark's *The State and Counter-Revolution*, which is an analysis of the period of anti-revisionism where multiple groups proclaimed themselves "Maoist", proves that the distinction between *name* and *concept* is important: this is because Clark's organization, though at one point identifying as "Maoist", was incapable of theorizing the meaning of this name.

Indeed, *The State and Counter-Revolution* is forced to concede, still trapped as it is in the final stages of Marxism-Leninism, that the "Maoism" of its time is simply another articulation of Marxism-Leninism; it is singularly incapable of understanding the events of the Chinese Revolution and thus, like so many other organizations, reduces "Maoism" to the principles of the New Democratic Revolution.[5] As discussed in the first chapter, it is precisely this reduction that permits even contemporary Trotskyists, who are unaware of what many of us now mean by Maoism, to reduce this ideology to this theory.

If Clark and his organization were capable of providing a thorough assessment of the Chinese Revolution, rather than reducing it to the New Democratic Revolution, they might have been able to glimpse the elements necessary for the solution of their contradiction. For it was during the Great Proletarian Cultural Revolution [GPCR] where the nascent critique of the petty-bourgeois, if not thoroughly bourgeois, party ideology was begun. The masses were unleashed upon the party, petty-bourgeois intellectuals were "sent down to the countryside", the contradiction noted by Clark was judged as a necessary contradiction of socialism and part of the reason as to why socialism should be conceived as a class society.

For today's Maoists the period of the GPCR possesses a universal significance that greatly overshadows the limited significance of New Democracy. This is not to say that the anti-revisionists of the New Communist Period did not emphasize the importance of the GPCR: to be fair, Clark's book is notable in *not* discussing it since the Cultural Revolution was extremely influential for the post-1968 radical communist movement. Where it begins to become something more than how it was conceived in New Communist Movement is when it is understood as a universal development in revolutionary theory that is not merely a corrective, that overspills the actual event of the GPCR that was reined in by Mao to the point that the capitalist roaders emerged victorious. We should treat the theory of cultural revolution as the recognition of the contradictions of Marxism-Leninism, the necessity that leads to the transgression of this stage of revolutionary science, and in some ways this echoes Clark's critique. For if the party emerges as a revolutionary party through a privileged intelligentsia, and a petty-bourgeois ideology thus remains to hamper the party due to the contradictory way in which it emerged, then the solution is to recognize the period of socialism as one in which a bourgeoisie emerges within the party itself and must be held to account by the masses it claims to represent in order to continue the revolution.

In some ways, the Maoist claim that "class struggle continues under the dictatorship of the proletariat" goes further than Clark by claiming that the problem of bourgeois ideology is not simply limited to the privileged party intellectuals. Rather, petty-bourgeois and bourgeois ideology can and will affect the entire socialist society because it was a "common-sense" ideology prior to socialist revolution and everyone, including workers, has been socialized according to these values. Upon the establishment of socialism, where the economism of "trade-union consciousness" is no longer an issue, the workers need to mobilize against those petty-bourgeois intellectuals who might be standing in their way (for in this period the workers have more autonomy to become "organic intellectuals"), in order to push the revolutionary society towards communism.

But even though Clark appears to ignore the significance of the theory of cultural revolution, the critique of his book is not necessarily defused. Other anti-revisionist groups recognized the importance of the GPCR and were guilty of the very contradiction Clark puts forward. Moreover, we need to ask *who* decides that the theory of cultural revolution is a further development of "proletarian ideology"—is it again the petty bourgeoisie?—not to mention those particular, and sometimes embarrassing, questions for Maoists who, despite their claims of science, still have difficulty delinking *Maoism* from *Mao*. Why was Mao himself not held to account during the GPCR; why did Mao and his most faithful followers, some of whom were indeed privileged, escape the bombardment of the party headquarters? Here we must indeed speak of a Maoism beyond Mao but, in order to do so, we need to recognize the salience of Clark's critique.

Leninism as Rupture

Here it is important to note how Clark's contradiction concerns Marxism-Leninism rather than a Marxism pre-Lenin. In the early chapters of *The State and Counter-Revolution* Clark delineates the Leninist theory of the state from Marx and Engels' insights, arguing that the quintessential Leninist theory of the state (articulated in *State and Revolution*) belonged essentially to the Leninist development of revolutionary theory and was not, despite Lenin's polemic reliance on passages from Engels regarding the Paris Commune, coherently understood by Marx or Engels. Clark argues that Lenin made it appear as if his theory of the state was lifted directly from Marx and Engels; according to Clark, there "is no question that [Lenin] believed this himself".[6] The question then becomes: why do we have a theory of socialist strategy that relies on a concept of a revolutionary state promulgated by middle-class intellectuals? Clark points out that when Lenin cites the opportunists of his time (i.e. Kautsky and his sympathizers) he is utterly ruthless in noting their petty-bourgeois ideology; at the same time, however, Clark claims that Lenin does not apply the same standard of critique to Marx and Engels and instead relies on their "authoritative" insights to attack the opportunists. Thus, perhaps Lenin should have also questioned the class position of Marx and Engels, rather than treating their insights as authoritative, since they were not in the strategic position to provide a proletarian ideology of revolution.

And yet, although it is worth taking Clark's analysis seriously, we must ask why Clark assumes that Lenin believed that his theory of revolutionary strategy regarding the state was lifted directly from Marx and Engels. If anything, Clark appears to assume that the rhetorical form of Lenin's polemic is synonymous with this polemic's conceptual content. Indeed, in the same chapter where Clark accuses Lenin of acting with perfect fidelity to Marx and Engels' conception of the revolutionary state, he also argues that Marx and Engels *did not* have the coherent theory of the state that appears in *State and Revolution*. This dissonance is important: if we assume that Lenin was just as capable as Clark of reading everything Marx and Engels had written about the state, and was thus aware that their theory of the state was not as coherent as the one he would propose, it seems rather simplistic to assume that there "is no question" that he believed his insights were identical to the founders of historical materialism. Indeed, Lenin might have been very aware that he was being selective in what he chose to either highlight or dismiss. If this is the case then it seems more correct to assume that Lenin was using the "authority" of Marx and Engels in the same way that Kautsky or Bernstein used the "authority" of Marx and Engels: to rhetorically defend a potentially heterodox theoretical development.

We should recall that all ruptures must also place themselves in continuity with a science; they mobilize the general concepts of the previous theoretical stage and, in doing so, seek to develop a living theory out of the germinal insights of those thinkers who were incapable of thinking beyond the contradictions of their own time. What Lenin was doing in *State and Revolution* was not simply an act of continuity (nor is it "no question" that he believed he was acting with near-religious fidelity when in fact he was developing something new) but also an act of rupture—but a rupture understood only in retrospect *because it worked.* Otherwise we would have to understand it as a theoretical dead-end, like so many other attempts to produce a theoretical rupture in historical materialism and other scientific fields, rather than a moment that produced a new way of seeing the world and escaping from the boundaries that Marx and Engels themselves could not escape. After all, despite their disorganized critiques and examinations of attempted revolutions in their time, Marx and Engels were incapable of producing a truly coherent revolutionary strategy. We are only able to imagine that they possessed such coherence *because* of Lenin.

Thus, Clark's contradiction should only concern Marxism-Leninism because it is not, as even he points out, inherent to the analysis of Marx and Engels. For this contradiction concerns revolutionary strategy and Marx and Engels, according to Clark, did not present a coherent theorization of revolutionary strategy: those moments that Lenin mobilized to rhetorically defend the theory of *State and Revolution* were contradicted by other moments; Lenin was intentionally selective in how he quoted the first theorists of historical materialism.

So if we place the contradiction within *Marxism-Leninism* rather than a pre-Leninist *Marxism* we should recognize that it is incapable of calling the entire science into question. Marx and Engels might have indeed been "petty-bourgeois" (though even here it is worth noting that Marx lived the last and most significant period of his life as a pauper, subsidized by Engels) but they did not produce a coherent theory of proletarian ideology: that is, a strategy of proletarian revolution. Rather, they produced a science of history that demanded the necessity of proletarian revolution, that grasped that all of history was the history of class struggle, but mainly provided the ideological content of this revolutionary necessity by demonstrating this necessity and forming early variants of communist organizations. This is why the *Manifesto* spends most of its time describing the history that produced the proletariat but stops, just after recognizing the proletarian class as the revolutionary class, short of thoroughly describing this class' ideology content and revolutionary strategy. An examination of the Paris Commune provided them with some incoherent insights regarding this strategy (as noted and systematized by Lenin) but, again as Clark points out, they were singularly incapable of transforming these insights into a general theory.

Therefore, Clark's contradiction belongs in the period of Marxism-Leninism, rather than the period of pre-Leninist Marxism, because it cannot logically apply to Marx and Engels who were never, according to Clark, really theorizing proletarian strategy and proletarian ideology. It is clear they understood ruling-class ideology and how it functioned quite well, but perhaps their privileged social positions—which prevented them from theorizing the strategic content of proletarian revolution—were precisely *why* they were able to provide a concrete analysis of the circumstances of capitalism and capitalist ideology. This foundation of the science is outside of Clark's complaint; its boundaries were defined by different contradictions that, I would argue, Lenin solved (and the proof is in the fact that there was a world-historical revolution in Russia) but that could only produce new contradictions, among them the one that Clark has rightly recognized.

So I do not believe that Lenin was under the impression that he was perfectly representing the theories of Marx and Engels regarding revolutionary strategy. He knew very well that Kautsky, as well-versed in the history of the movement if not more so, was also aware of the same passages and was in fact utilizing other passages to push his ideological position; the entire communist movement, at that period in time, was a confusion of various tendencies, all of which highlighted different aspects of Marx and Engels. Why Lenin chose to highlight certain passages over others tells us more about his object of interest (class revolution and how to achieve class revolution) and his rhetorical ability to find authoritative grounds for his arguments regarding the state.

What Lenin was doing was producing the theoretical work that would eventually affect a rupture in revolutionary theory and, in affecting this rupture, force its continuity through an appeal to possibly germinal insights of Marx and Engels. This rupture was not only continuous because of what it chose to highlight as germinal (what it *decided* was congruent with its heterodoxy) but because it used the very method of Marx and Engels, which does not concern Clark's contradiction, to force the theoretical rupture. And this moment of continuity-rupture could only be proved after the world-historical revolution in Russia.

The Composition of the Leninist Party

Clark's contradiction, then, does not affect the basis of revolutionary science, the theory of historical materialism originated by Marx and Engels, but the first strategic implementation of this science, where it claimed to speak on behalf of the proletarian. And in this speaking it would encounter this contradiction which is a contradiction of revolutionary strategy. For it was Lenin who operationalized Marxism, provided it with a strategy, and in doing so claimed to implement proletarian ideology.

So the question becomes: did Lenin simply implement the petty-bourgeois, though incoherent, reflections of Marx and Engels in regards to revolutionary strategy; was Lenin arguing for a party of petty-bourgeois intellectuals due to the fact that the "trade-union consciousness" of workers was by itself incapable of producing "revolutionary consciousness"; is the final result of Leninism, culled as it was from germinal insights of the originary petty-bourgeois theorists, a contradiction that can only lead to counter-revolution? Leaving aside the larger limitations of the Leninist party, which will be discussed in the final chapter, let us focus only on this potential contradiction.

Clark is correct insofar as the limits of the Marxist-Leninist theoretical moment are concerned. Even if Lenin's theorization of an organized and militant party (the revolutionary advanced guard that could bring revolutionary consciousness to those workers who otherwise were trapped in trade-union consciousness) should not be understood as a party led by petty-bourgeois intellectuals and Marxist academics, we still cannot escape the fact that the concrete circumstances have indeed produced a Marxist-Leninist practice, at least at the centers of world capitalism, where this was the case.

Indeed, Lenin's theory of organization has often been understood as a theory that privileges the revolutionary intelligentsia and their ability, because they have had the time and the means to study revolutionary science and their concrete circumstances, to be the germ of a revolutionary movement. All of the infantile fantasies of petty-bourgeois dreamers are justified by this interpretation of Marxism-Leninism. No wonder there are so many tiny and dogmatic "vanguard" groups proselytizing at universities.

As an aside, to suggest that Lenin was arguing for a party led by privileged intellectuals is something of a misreading of *What Is to Be Done?*: while Lenin agreed with Kautsky that the party was initiated by such intellectuals this is not the same as claiming that it should be led and composed solely by the same social strata. Nor is it accurate to compare the intellectuals and students of Tsarist Russia, many of whom were severely underprivileged (think of the extremely impoverished student characters in Dostoevsky's novels, for example), with the students and intellectuals leading the supposed "vanguard parties" at the modern centers of world capitalism. As some of my comrades who believe in Lenin's theory of the party have pointed out, contemporary first-world academics should indeed be classified as more petty-bourgeois than small-shop owners since the former can easily be bought-off with bourgeois liberal rights whereas the latter might include racialized immigrants who are running small family businesses to feed their families.[7]

Even still, Clark's complaint holds because this interpretation of Lenin's theory of the party vanguard can be found in *What Is to Be Done?* and has been historically maintained by Marxists-Leninists. If revolutionary ideology must be imported *from without*, then we must ask who exists outside of that proletariat that is only capable of understanding an ideology produced by economism—what people compose and define the party that will bring revolutionary ideology to the masses? Rather than trying to make sense of the complexities of party formation, and grasp that this *without* is more of an abstract than concrete principle, it is often natural to assume, along with the Lenin of *What Is to Be Done?*, a party initially led by intellectuals who possessed the privilege to study and comprehend revolutionary science. Nor is this an entirely incorrect assessment of any revolutionary party and project that has existed historically. Marxism-Leninism, at the moment of reaching its historical limits, was indeed affected by this interpretation of the party vanguard.

But if we are to appreciate the force of Clark's contradiction as a *dialectical contradiction*, a unity of opposites, then we have to recognize that there is something within the moment of Marxism-Leninism that is simultaneously revolutionary and counter-revolutionary. We cannot forget that Marxism-Leninism was as much a success as it was a failure, that its completion in the Chinese Revolution was what both demonstrated its limits and provided an opening to a new stage of the science.

So there is indeed something correct, in the Marxist-Leninist moment, about the necessity of the revolutionary party's rational kernel being composed, in a certain sense, by intellectuals. After all, in order for a revolutionary movement to possess a theory capable of unifying its practice, it requires the concrete analysis of concrete circumstances: there needs to be a thorough and precise assessment of what the social circumstances *are*, what the class structure of these circumstances implies, and how to logically proceed based on these facts. Someone incapable of comprehending their social context is not going to provide anything useful for a revolutionary strategy in that context; history should have taught us by now that the lazy application of models from other social contexts, without any attention to the particular problems of the circumstances upon which they are being applied, has only led to immediate failure and/or an inability to move forward.

Hisila Yami, however, encountered the same contradiction discussed by Clark when she wrote *People's War and Women's Liberation in Nepal* during the course of the people's war in Nepal. Although specifically examining the problem of the lack of women cadre, Yami recognized that while revolutionary science developed through the theoretical work of those with the intellectual privilege to provide a concrete analysis of a concrete situation, if the most oppressed and exploited remained incapable of making the same analyses then counter-revolution would remain a significant danger. After all, those who possessed the social privilege to make the initial analyses (in her context, and perhaps in most contexts, *men*) had more to lose and less to gain from a thorough revolution than the more exploited and oppressed; the initial revolutionary theorists might quickly become theorists of the counter-revolution if the masses were not armed with a significant and deep-seeded understanding of revolutionary theory.[8] Hence, Clark's contradiction cannot easily be dismissed: Yami recognized that theory develops through a concrete analysis of a concrete situation, but also recognized that those who make such an analysis occupy privileged social positions—peasant women in a semi-feudal and semi-colonial social formation, after all, do not have the same educational opportunities as their male counterparts.

Problems with Class (I)

Before tying up the various threads in this chapter and attempting to demonstrate how Maoism solves this Marxist-

Leninist contradiction, it is necessary to examine what is at stake with Clark's contradiction: a particular understanding of *class*. In this section I want to argue for the way in which social class should be understood before, in the following section, examining how Clark's implicit understanding (which is actually quite common, and perhaps the way in which classes and their contradictions are treated by many Marxists) leads directly to his impasse.

Clark's contradiction, as we have discussed, manifests according to the claim that the proletarian ultimately finds its meaning, becoming proletarian, according to an agency (i.e. the party) outside of itself so that, rather than being the revolutionary subject in itself it is only the subject through the party. In this sense the party appears to be a substitution for the proletariat that ought to emancipate itself; if the former is *outside* of the proletariat, then how can it know the meaning of proletarian politics; if the latter requires the former in order to become conscious of itself, how will it even be aware of which party expresses a proletarian line? This apparent contradiction, however, is not as confused as it at first appears when we treat class as a social category rather than a nature or essence.

The analysis of capitalism initiated by Marx and Engels noted that the structure of a capitalist mode of production was, in the last instance, determined by the tension between the minority class that owned the means of production and the masses who toiled so that capitalist society could reproduce itself. Whereas the latter produced this society's value, the former was mainly parasitical. A proletarian politics, then, is simply derived from this scientific assessment: those who produce social value should be in command, not the parasites. Any politics that does not pursue a society where those who produce value are in command is not a proletarian politics. From this understanding Marx could derive the social classification of proletariat: those who have nothing left to lose but their chains, and are conscious of this fact, are going to be those who are the most invested in bringing this non-parasitic society into being.

The problem, however, is that this insight is merely an assessment of what is required to transgress the limits of the capitalist mode of production: it does not explain, by itself, how those who have nothing left to lose but their chains will be conscious of this fact; it only explains the social forces necessary for the overthrow of capitalism. A class is an abstract categorization, and though scientific assessments must be abstract if they are to be applied universally, it is a mistake to treat this bare formula of social class in a concrete manner and assume, as many do, that Marx's classification of the proletariat *in itself* means that he was also claiming that the working class will be aware of this historical vocation, scattered as it is throughout society, and that it somehow constitutes a concrete and operationalized meaning as a class (with the requisite consciousness and social meaning) *for itself* and by itself. The hypothesis of a proletarian class is not a hypothesis of an essential meaning to the people who may or may not be part of this class; the proletariat does not exist prior to its hypothesization.

That is, Marx's abstract formulation had nothing to do with importing meaning to the essential lives of the workers, and telling them what their lives mean, as Rancière appears to claim in *Proletarian Nights*. For Rancière, after all, the Marxist (particularly the Marxist-Leninist) project is erroneous because it attempts to educate a working class about the meaning of its lived experience when this working class is quite aware of its meaning, this meaning often defies the Marxist conceptualization of class struggle, and there might not be anything that we can call *the proletariat* but in fact a heterogeneous working class without a singular meaning.[9] But Marx's theorization of class had nothing to do with explaining some intrinsic and essential meaning of workers; it was simply based on the assessment of the limits of capitalism, who produced the value within this mode of production, and how those who produced this value were capable, particularly if they became conscious of the fact that they had nothing to lose through revolution, of transgressing these limits. Therefore, when Marx and Engels speak of *the proletariat* they are not simply speaking of this or that faction of the working class, they are speaking of the position upon which capitalism can be overthrown and a revolutionary classification based on this position.

The reason why it is important to understand that the proletarian classification is the result of a scientific assessment of the capitalist mode of production as a whole, and not at all an attempt to explain the "authentic" identity of a heterogeneous body of workers, is because if we assume that this heterogeneous body of workers will produce a proletarian consciousness spontaneously then we are no longer speaking of the proletarian politics Marx and Engels proposed: "[s]pontaneously, the proletarian consciousness, even in its most radical expression, will not outgrow the spirit of rebellion".[10] Bourgeois ideology is far too compelling and, without being unified according to a common revolutionary project, working-class rebellion is most often limited by economism.

In this context, a party becomes necessary: an organization theoretically unified that brings proletarian politics to the proletariat. How can this party be aware of proletarian politics if it comes from outside? Because this is the politics derived from a scientific assessment of history and society that permits us to understand the meaning of "proletariat" as a social class. It is also a politics that, in its clearest expression, has learned from the history of class struggle, particularly the two great world-historical revolutions in Russia and China, and so can bring the memory of revolution to those who have been taught to forget.

At the same time, however, it would be a mistake to conceive of this party as substituting the very proletariat it attempts to bring into being; we are not speaking, here, of a party of petty-bourgeois intellectuals who will command the proletariat because they alone have had the privilege to study the abstract meaning of this class' hypothetical existence and meaning. We are not arguing that a class of intellectuals (who can easily be bought off with promises of publication, tenured jobs, etc.) are the revolutionary subject, bringing consciousness to the proletariat and remaining in command. Indeed, the very impetus to organize those who have nothing left to lose but their chains is due to the fact that, once this class becomes conscious of itself as a class, only then is revolution possible. That is, if it seeks to become a *vanguard* party, the nascent party must locate and organize the most radical elements of the working class so as to become transformed and held to account by those who, aware of revolutionary theory, will transform this party so that it is a proletarian party: a conscious understanding of capitalism and the necessity of revolution might be imported from outside only so that those who have nothing to lose by supporting a revolution can import *back* a more radical and sustainable politics. The party produces the proletariat; the proletariat produces the party.

With this understanding of the proletariat in mind, it is necessary for a would-be party to begin by concentrating on the strata of the working class where economism is less complete, those most amenable to being conscious of the fact that they have nothing left to lose but their chains, so that the working class as a whole can supersede economism. "For its consciousness to go from rebellion to revolution, the minority of proletarians who already have a revolutionary consciousness—because of their experience, but mainly because they have acquired some theoretical knowledge concerning revolution—must be organized."[11] Organizing these forces first will also discipline those involved in the organizing; the party itself will be organized into a vanguard rather than, had it expended its forces amongst those workers who have a lot to lose in the case of a revolution, becoming inconsequential. To go to the masses with a theory that can explain their lived experience will also mean, once the most revolutionary forces of these masses are encountered and operationalized, that a transformation of the movement will emerge from the masses, but only if it speaks to their lived experience and only if it locates those who are not mesmerized by the phenomenon of economism.

Hence, the proletariat is found according to a process of social investigation in which a unified political movement attempts to locate the exploited basis of revolutionary movement, but the proletariat is also simultaneously *made* into a coherent class as it is gathered into this movement. Furthermore, the movement itself is transformed by this gathering, its own understanding of the proletariat transformed as it learns from, while attempting to lead as a whole, the most exploited. We can thus understand the meaning of *proletarian* only through a movement that is able to conceptualize a particular proletariat based on an organized process of social investigation, but a social investigation that proceeds according to a general understanding of exploitation and is oriented towards ending capitalism. Finally, we can operationalize this understanding of proletariat by making it, while being made by it, the basis of a revolutionary movement.

Problems with Class (II)

Let us assume that Clark is not indicating a contradiction that is *dialectical* but a contradiction in the sense of formal logic, i.e. a contradiction similar to the very simple and banal statement that one cannot literally be a living human and a corpse in a coffin at precisely the same moment in time. If this is the type of contradiction that he is implying—that a proletarian revolutionary movement is impossible because it will always be tainted by the class ideology imported from without—then it rests on a definition of social class that is different from the one outlined in the previous section.

This definition, which was briefly discussed above, holds that

117

the proletariat is a class insofar as it is found as a class empirically rather than a scientific category employed to make sense of the general logic of a given mode of production. Hence the proletariat, if it exists, can be found at point x of the labor process as a very specific and articulated group of people who understand what they are better than those theorizing the proletariat. Here, the divisions of class are material barriers in the crude sense, and more like a caste understanding of reality, where a particular class cannot be understood by those outside of this class because its consciousness properly belongs to its interiority. In other words, only those *within* this empirical proletariat can understand what it means to be proletariat. Those who do not have the empirical characteristics of this class in itself have no business of speaking of class being and class consciousness—this was, as aforementioned, Rancière's argument in *Proletarian Nights*.

Rancière's supposedly left-communist and anti-structuralist insights intersect in an interesting way with the claims made by orthodox Marxists who also think that a particular and empirical conceptualization of the working class (i.e. it is the most organized faction of workers who labor at the point of production) is *the* proletariat that is essentially conscious of its revolutionary destiny. The difference between Rancière's position (as well as Clark's, for that matter) and that of this particular orthodox definition of proletarian is that the latter believes it will be able to dispel the "false consciousness" that inhibits this class from understanding its authentic revolutionary nature; in this sense, and if class is understood in such a way, then Rancière and Clark are correct. For how can someone outside of this found and empirically known proletarian ever hope to dispel false consciousness if it cannot be part of this class? Thus, if we define class in such a positivist manner we will necessarily be faced with Clark's contradiction, and this is why Clark's insights are so important: they show the limits of this crude understanding of class composition.

Such an understanding of class, however, is far from materialist since it is more akin to a theorization of caste or estate, the mystification of social class that Marx and Engels attempted to demolish by theorizing class in the first place. The assumption that class is a social phenomenon that, as E.P. Thompson pointed out, is made rather than found (as we will examine in further detail in the next section), and thus is ultimately contingent on greater social forces, was one of the great insights of Marxism: according to this definition, one's social position is not determined by a law of nature but is ultimately contingent. That is, the lower classes are not lower because nature has determined them as such (as "the great chain of being" of Thomas Aquinas, Confucius' "laws of heaven", and other tributary ideologies of metaphysical alienation would have us believe), but for intensely social reasons: the majority of people are pushed down into subservience, oppression, and exploitation due to the logic of the mode of production; the minority in command were not given their command by nature, but because they happened to be lucky enough or vicious (but also lucky) enough to have clawed their way up a particular social hierarchy.

Therefore, this essentialist notion of class cannot admit the very complexity that the theory of class (as opposed to estate or caste) was meant to express due to its culturalism inherited from a pre-capitalist way of seeing the world. The minority of working-class individuals who are able to become capitalists, thus fulfilling and sanctifying the capitalist ideology of the "self-made man", sometimes take a culture of deprivation with them, believing they are somehow still proletarian, regardless of how wealthy they might become, because they were not educated according to "bourgeois culture". Here we can discover millionaires who speak of the "liberal elite" and imagine they speak for the "common people" because this elitism is defined by literacy. At the same time, intellectuals cast down to the level of proletarian subsistence (a far more common dynamic under capitalism) will be judged as secretly bourgeois, due to their education and regardless of the fact that they find themselves in a social position of exploitation.

Once we define class in such a culturalist manner, then, we cannot accept a party that comes from *outside* because such a party is incapable of ever speaking for the revolutionary subject it seeks to accumulate and consummate. Strategically, this essentialist/culturalist understanding of the proletariat implies some form of spontaneism: it cannot help but produce either a revolution or a party to lead the revolution in the course of its spontaneous struggles against capitalism. And yet, despite implicitly promoting this understanding of class, Clark himself seems to have shut the door on this possibility by implying that: a) this has never been the case historically; and b) Hal Draper's theories regarding the revolutionary state (which imply a limited form of spontaneism) are a dead end.[12] So if there is even a foreclosure on the possibility of the Draperite "socialism from below", and spontaneous proletarian self-organization, then it is possible to interpret Clark as claiming that his contradiction proves that revolution is *logically* impossible.

Based on this understanding of Clark's contradiction, it is impossible to even critique his analysis because doing so would mean, based on his apparent definition of class, that the one making these criticisms is "petty-bourgeois" (for to do so requires a formal, privileged education) and thus incapable of thinking outside of his contradiction. More significantly, all attempts to argue for a way out of his contradiction, since these attempts *also* require a certain level of intellectual training (thus meaning, according to his analysis, that they emerge from a petty-bourgeois position), *also* fall prey to his contradiction. In this sense it is totalizing in a negative sense: if you possess the level of education to make sense of his contradiction and propose an alternative then you are necessarily petty-bourgeois; hence, there is no way to escape his impasse.

We are stuck, then, in a closed circuit of inevitable counter-revolution. If the proletariat has been historically incapable of theorizing its circumstances, and thus a revolutionary ideology, then anyone who attempts to theorize these circumstances and ideology can only be doomed to failure because they are not proletariat and thus are also, due to their non-proletariat class position, incapable of speaking for the class they claim to represent. Here there is a strange simultaneity with post-colonial theory: Gayatry Spivak also wondered whether the subaltern could speak for itself, and whether attempts to speak in its name were impossible.

But Spivak was a privileged intellectual who, in the moment of disputing the right of Marxist intellectuals to speak for the underprivileged, was herself speaking for the same underprivileged. If Clark's analysis is equally all-encompassing then it encounters the same problem: at the very moment that he speaks of the inability of petty-bourgeois intellectuals to speak in the name of the proletariat he is performing the same act: he is also a petty-bourgeois intellectual, based on his own implicit theorization of class, who is deciding the meaning of class contradictions based on his privilege to name and identify these meanings. After all, the proletariat cannot grasp the contradiction indicated by Clark: he is attempting to show it to them as much as he is attempting to show it to all communists; he is deciding what determines *proletariat* and *petty-bourgeois* ideology. His analysis is so thorough that it is possibly undermined by the same contradiction!

The point, here, is that Clark, in indicating what he takes as the prime contradiction of Marxism-Leninism (and in a certain sense, as aforementioned, I believe he is correct), may fall prey to the same problem that he claims to have discovered and that this problem is based on the understanding of class itself. If Clark's contradiction is as thorough and damning as, based on one reading, it seems he believes it is, then it is impossible to talk about this class contradiction in the first place; we *cannot even provide a definition of class* without also being petty-bourgeois intellectuals.

If a revolutionary conception of class can only be provided by the revolutionary class that is found and not made, and this class is not part of the class that provides conceptual definitions (being an intellectual, here, is presumed to be essentially petty-bourgeois), then it is impossible to know what class is in the first place, let alone which class counts as *proletarian* and *revolutionary*. This problem is similar to the problem C.S. Lewis noted in T.S. Eliot's theorization "that poets are the only judges of poetry":

> The first result is that I, not being one of the contemporary poets, cannot judge Mr. Eliot's criticism at all. What then shall I do? Shall I go to the best contemporary poets, who can, and ask them whether Mr. Eliot is right? But in order to go to them I must first know who they are. And this, by hypothesis, I cannot find out; the same lack of poethood which renders my critical opinions... worthless renders my opinions on Mr. Pound or Mr. Auden equally worthless. Shall I then go to Mr. Eliot and ask him who the best contemporary poets are? But this, again, will be useless. I personally may think Mr. Eliot a poet—in fact, I do—but then, as he as explained to me, my thoughts on such a point are worthless. I cannot find out whether Mr. Eliot is a poet or not; and, until I have found out, I cannot know whether his testimony to the poethood of Mr. Pound and Mr. Auden is valid. And for the same reason I cannot find out whether their testimony to his poethood is valid. Poets become on this view an unrecognizable society (an Invisible Church), and their mutual criticism goes on within a closed circle which no outsider can break.[13]

The point, here, is that if we take Clark's analysis of class to its *apparently* logical conclusion then we must accept that it is not only completely damning, we have to accept that we can neither escape the omnipotence of the theoretical boundaries it draws, nor even understand if it is correct. And Clark is also incapable of understanding if it is correct, based on his own inability (due to his petty-bourgeois nature) to understand class. Class itself becomes unrecognizable; anyone who attempts to explain the meaning of class and class consciousness is damned by the inescapable boundaries of this antimony.

In some ways, then, it makes no sense to accept Clark's contradiction since, by the same token, it is equally contradictory: if no one can speak to the meaning of proletarian ideology, then Clark also cannot speak to the same meaning; he is trapped in the very boundaries he has drawn, if this is what his boundaries mean. Therefore, since it seems logically senseless to understand his contradiction in such an extreme manner, it might be worth critiquing the boundaries he has drawn, his implicit definition of class. He himself appears to have an understanding of class, and so if we are to be accused of being equally petty-bourgeois by attempting to explicitly discuss the meaning of class, then we are just as guilty as Clark. And if Clark is guilty, then his entire analysis collapses due to the same contradiction.

Problems with Class (III)

For Clark there appears to be a class essence to the proletariat and the petty bourgeoisie, an inescapable destiny where Marxist intellectuals are always petty-bourgeois and the proletarian are never Marxist intellectuals. In many ways he assumes (perhaps because he is caught within the same Marxist-Leninist moment) the very elitist understanding of Leninism that he has critiqued: intellectuals are petty-bourgeois; the proletariat cannot produce intellectuals without the interference of the petty-bourgeois. We must ask, then, why he has separated *intellectual* from *proletariat* by assuming that the former must always be alienated from the latter, or at best end up as the judge of the educational standards of the latter: this is a possible moment where the concepts of "revolutionary intellectual" and "petty-bourgeois" are simplistically merged.

(Of course, there is a good reason for this merging, and this is why we should take Clark seriously as I have suggested above. In his socio-historical context Marxist intellectuals were generally privileged and petty-bourgeois. If he could not see beyond its boundaries it was because of his social limitations, but limitations we must understand if we are also to understand why Maoism is capable of going beyond Marxism-Leninism.)

But if we understand *class* in the materialist sense rather than mystical sense then we must also understand that it is something that, as discussed above, is *made* and not *found*. One is not born with a class destiny imprinted upon their soul: someone born into a working-class family can possibly become bourgeois, just as someone born into a bourgeois family can possibly sink to the level of the proletariat; class mobility, while not always probable, is often quite possible. After all, capitalism is able to defend its ideology by recourse to the odd *rags-to-riches* story.

So we need to ask, based on the fact that Clark claims that the descent of the petty-bourgeois intellectual deforms revolution, whether the opposite is the case. If someone who is born into a proletarian family ends up joining the petty bourgeoisie, is the petty-bourgeois edifice undermined by the inclusion of someone with a proletarian origin? In this society, after all, where onerous student loans produce the possibility of working-class individuals becoming academic intellectuals (though they definitely have an uphill battle), and where poorer students spend their free time working exploitative jobs to pay their bills, is it the case that proletarian ideology is suddenly imported into the ranks of the petty-bourgeois? (More pointedly, is it even the case that we can define the petty-bourgeois intellectual so easily? A tenured professor might be a petty-bourgeois intellectual, but what about someone working the worst contract teaching jobs, or what of a student who spends most of their time out of class working in a restaurant kitchen? One does not become petty-bourgeois simply by going to university; it is not defined by literacy.)

On the whole, the petty bourgeoisie as a class category is not affected by the intentional inclusion of former proletariats into its ranks, even if they like to dress the part. Everyone who has gone to university knows of at least one professor with a six-figure salary who refers to themselves as "working-class" by virtue of the fact that they came from a working-class family: they are defining class according to a specific conception of culture, an appeal to an authentic essence. Similarly, on a larger scale, the inclusion of former proletarians into the club of the bourgeoisie does not affect the bourgeois class: it is quite happy when people struggle to become wealthy owners of capital; it uses these struggles to defend its pernicious ideology that hard work is the key to class mobility.

Inversely, then, is it impossible to conceive of petty-bourgeois intellectuals sinking to the level of the proletariat? This downwards movement seems to be possible; indeed it seems to be prevalent, due to the fact that losing rather than gaining economic privilege is always more possible under capitalism. Why is it that this descent, whether intentional or unintentional, automatically means the importation of petty-bourgeois ideology into the ranks of the dispossessed? Moreover, what do we make of the scions of the proletariat who have attempted to change their class station through education only to sink back to the level of their family: do they suddenly gain an "alien" class ideology, defined as education, that they bring back to their class origins? These assessments are rather simplistic: we are forced to assume that education, simply because in this society it is inaccessible to many people, is essentially petty-bourgeois. In this context, if we are to resist petty-bourgeois ideology, then we may be forced to adopt a crude anti-intellectualism and demand that the proletarian remain ignorant.

In general, however, we are speaking of *ideology* and so we must return to those limits that are an essential part of Clark's contradiction: it is not that the petty bourgeoisie is changing classes but that it is importing petty-bourgeois ideology into the heart of revolutionary struggle. At the same time, however, Clark pointed out that the proletariat through its economistic struggles, based on Lenin's analysis, is incapable of developing a revolutionary theory. The reason for this incapability, however, is something that Clark never explains although it is explained by Antonio Gramsci, George Lukacs, Louis Althusser, and other Marxist philosophers who were also trying to make sense of the boundaries of their thought: because the ruling ideas of the ruling class become common sense even for the proletariat, because both petty-bourgeois and bourgeois ideology also form the default consciousness of the working class, the victims of the system often attempt to justify their own victimhood based on their acceptance of the values of their exploiters and oppressors. Spontaneity and reformism are ideologically prevalent amongst the proletariat because these are *common-sense* responses to the horrors of capitalist domination: this ideology is just as petty-bourgeois as the values of the intellectuals sinking, intentionally or unintentionally, to the level of the proletariat.

Hence the need for a coherent party, an association that can scientifically sift through the ideological confusion of the current conjuncture. The problem here is not just that petty-bourgeois ideology is being imported by privileged intellectuals (although this is its own problem), but that this ideology is already prevalent amongst the ranks of the working class regardless of these intellectuals; it is a reflection of the values of the ruling class.

Of course, this analysis of class and class consciousness is easily refuted if we take Clark's contradiction to its formal conclusions: all of this is simply a petty-bourgeois analysis of class, due to the fact that it relies on the work of petty-bourgeois intellectuals, and is ultimately meaningless. But again, Clark's analysis itself must be undermined by the same conclusion since he is also speaking in the name of *class* based on his own understanding which also and equally must be understood as privileged. Even still, Clark is correct to point out there is indeed an importation of privileged petty-bourgeois ideology into the heart of any given revolutionary organization. That is, even if a party is required to articulate the meaning of class, making and imposing it through a revolutionary structure organized according to theory and practice, there is still something that an orthodox Leninist party misses: petty-bourgeois consciousness internal to the party is an inescapable problem.

The Mass-Line

In order to grasp the significance of Clark's contradiction, and how it fully explains the boundaries of anti-revisionist Marxism-Leninism, all we have to do is examine how the New Communist Movement of Clark's day was affected by the collapse of revolutionary China. Only a few anti-revisionist Marxist-Leninist organizations were able to recognize that the capitalist roaders were in command; most assumed that the party had necessarily renewed itself, that its intellectuals had the right to speak for the will of the masses, and that any challenge to party authority (based on the party's ultimate right to define what was properly *bourgeois* and *proletariat*) was possibly counter-revolutionary. More than one organization degenerated and eventually collapsed due to an unwillingness to challenge the line of the party under Deng Xiaoping, and those who sided with the Gang of Four sometimes found themselves lost in a new geography where the previous assumptions of anti-revisionism often seemed like a problem of infinite regress: if the prime anti-revisionist force was suddenly revisionist, then would not the emergence of a new anti-revisionism set off an incoherent chain of successive anti-revisionisms? There was no longer a center to anti-revisionist ideology because the center, initially and simply assumed to be built around Mao Zedong and the Chinese party, was now being called into question. In this context, then, new problems emerged: how to make sense of democratic centralism, how to know when a party embarked upon the same revisionism it had initially critiqued, how to make sense of the problem of revisionism itself.

Clark's summation, as discussed above, appeared to argue that revisionism was unavoidable because it was written into the genes of Marxism-Leninism itself. At worse it was a contradiction that could not be resolved; at best (and as I have suggested) it was a dialectical contradiction that necessitated a resolution that could not be conceived at the time. The movement becomes infected with petty-bourgeois ideology (and thus bourgeois ideology) because the party itself is led by the petty-bourgeois who have already decided, based on their class position, the qualifications for revolutionary ideology.

But as I noted earlier, Clark's summation strangely fails to provide an assessment of the Cultural Revolution in China, an event that had tantalized most anti-revisionists of his time and was intrinsic to the germinal conception of what would become Marxism-Leninism-Maoism. Thus, for all his talk of the party hegemony of the petty bourgeoisie, Clark ignores that one moment in history where the petty bourgeoisie was "sent down to the countryside" in droves, where once-privileged Marxist intellectuals were placed under the authority of the masses, and where the authority of the party itself was briefly called into question. Here was a moment that might have allowed Clark to think outside of the confines he was explaining (or at least prove the existence of these confines) but he failed to examine it in a thorough manner.

Clearly, since the Cultural Revolution failed to complete its aim, Clark's contradiction still holds: the party refused to go as far as it should have gone, the resistance of the petty-bourgeoisie to reeducation was significant enough to influence the counter-revolution, Mao himself might have turned his back on the revolution he initially supported. But these are the limits of Marxism-Leninism that were reached, and only temporarily transgressed, by a world-historical revolution that prefigured the emergence of a new stage in revolutionary science that would have to explain these very limits.

During the course of the Chinese Revolution the contradiction noted by Clark was encountered and theorized: the petty-bourgeoisie is indeed within the party, bourgeois ideology leads to party degeneration, and the fact that the party leads the masses while being affected by this ideology is a significant problem. The solution, then, was to unleash the masses upon the party and even upon each other. The problem of the ideological instance was even larger than Clark's analysis grants: the common-sense ideology prior to the dictatorship of the prole-tariat is still a default ideology, is prevalent everywhere in society, and this is why socialism remains a class society.

Leaving aside the absurd notion that to even define the nature of this ideology is in itself an act of privilege (for this leads, as noted in the previous section, to an inability to even make this critique in the first place), we should at least recognize the fact that the GPCR produces a way of moving beyond the contra-diction of Marxism-Leninism. This is because the party does not simply lead the masses; the party also must be held to account by the masses and in this accounting class struggle continues. Those petty-bourgeois intellectuals who once defined the meaning of revolution, if they were indeed petty-bourgeois intellectuals, should be called to account by the very revolution they once claimed to represent. China's failure to complete this revolution simply tells us that it failed to follow this understanding to its logical conclusion, that although it glimpsed a terrain beyond the limits of Marxism-Leninism it was still imprisoned within its historical boundaries.

Only an assessment of the failures and successes of this period could produce the theoretical rupture capable of over-stepping Marxism-Leninism. Hence the emergence of Maoism in the period of 1988–1993 when these contradictions, finally self-evident, demanded a paradigm shift in the field of revolutionary science, guided by the concepts that manifested in the course of the Chinese Revolution. Maoism, then, is precisely that stage that not only recognizes Clark's contradiction but understands it in a properly scientific manner, can explain precisely how it led to counter-revolution, and thus indicates a practice that can pass beyond the boundaries of Leninism.

After all, the Leninist party is completed according to the understanding that the concept of proletarian, as noted above, is consummated in the party itself which preserves the theory of what it means to be proletarian in the first place. And yet, this is not enough: a party that treats itself as the "general staff" of the proletariat, without submerging itself in the class it has conceptualized, must always remain apart. To think of a party that not only conceptualizes the meaning of "proletariat" but submerges itself in the social classes it attempts to mobilize, however, is the province of Maoism. This is what is known as the *mass-line*: the party brings the theory of revolution to the masses, submerges its members in these masses and, by drawing them in, transforms the party itself.

A party formation that functions according to a general theory of the proletariat that is not submerged in the masses, and has not drawn these masses into its organizational structure, is a formation that can never become a vanguard. The reason for this is very simple: if the party cadre are only dispersed intellectuals then they can easily be bought off by capital: a would-be academic, no matter how radical their politics are on paper, might be neutralized by the promise of tenure, freedom of speech, and publishing contracts. Similarly, a party cadre who discovers, through this party, that they have nothing left to lose but their chains will sustain this party, will teach the would-be academics something about party discipline, and will possibly become a party intellectual (for the Maoist turn in Marxism demands that every party member becomes an intellectual) capable of challenging the traditional intellectual apparatus. While a germinal party formation might initiate and preserve itself according to those who have had the privilege to encounter and study revolutionary theory, it will only become more than its germ form by drawing in those who are deeply invested in revolution and, because of this investment, can discipline the party into a fighting force capable of becoming a vanguard.

The mass-line is generally defined as "from the masses and to the masses" and this chronology confuses what is at stake. By placing the *from* in front of the *to* Mao was not defining the temporal order in which revolutionary ideology functioned; he was simply emphasizing the order of importance. Although revolutionary ideology does emerge, in the last instance, from the masses, and though party members have emerged themselves in different ways from the masses, the practice of mass work begins by going to the masses with revolutionary ideology. The participants in a revolutionary movement begin with a revolutionary theory, taken from the history of Marxism, that they plan to take to the masses. If they succeed in taking this theory to the masses, then they emerge from these masses trans-formed, pulling in their wake new cadre that will teach both them and their movement something more about revolution, and demonstrating that the moment of *from* is far more significant than the moment of *to* because it is the mechanism that permits the recognition of a revolutionary politics. For if those with nothing left to lose but their chains do not accept a revolutionary theory (they are not stupid, they are not waiting on some "general staff of the proletariat") then the theory that is being espoused should be questioned.

According to the mass-line, Maoism tells us that any revolutionary theory coming from *outside* must find its limits in the *inside* of the proletariat: if it is rejected by the most radical factions of this class then it should be rethought; if it pulls in new recruits, who will also transform the movement that brings this theory, then it is not some alien affectation imposed on the working classes.

Again: Continuity-Rupture

Those Maoist organizations that have been leading people's wars are not simply organizations led by some privileged petty bourgeoisie. On the one hand, we must recognize that the most revolutionary Marxist-Leninist-Maoist movements have been third-world movements where even the intellectuals are not identical to first-world petty-bourgeois intellectuals. On the other hand, we also have to recognize that many of these movements have doggedly followed the path of *declassing*, have been dismissive of petty-bourgeois intellectuals, and most often are accused of being, by some academic leftists, organizations led by unsophisticated peasants and "lumpen" elements. So we must ask: if one group of academics are claiming that Maoist movements are unsophisticated and backwards, and these petty-bourgeois academics imagine that they represent the standard of proletarian ideology, then it might be the case that Maoism, in its general refusal to play this academic game, has overcome Clark's contradiction.

The overall point, however, is that Clark's contradiction is merely a contradiction of Marxism-Leninism. While Clark might have understood the limitations of Marxism-Leninism, it should be clear from the lacunae discussed above that he was incapable of grasping how the stage of Maoism altered the theoretical terrain of his critique. The concrete praxis of revolutionary organizations devoted to Marxism-Leninism-Maoism has not only been quite aware of the contradiction Clark recognized, but has opened a terrain in which this contradiction is only a lingering problem retained from the past moment of Marxism-Leninism. The fact that *The State and Counter-Revolution* refuses to address the GPCR in any significant detail, going so far as to fail to examine Deng's coup at the end of the 1970s, demonstrates an unwillingness to move very far beyond the limits of Marxism-Leninism.

Even still, regardless of what it ignores, Clark's book is significant insofar as it charts the course of Marxism-Leninism to honestly recognize the limits of an anti-revisionism that has failed to break from this terrain. This critique's inability to transgress these limits, however, is due to the same problem it seeks to explain: it is also caught within the boundaries of Marxism-Leninism and thus can see nothing but the limits it has reached. Hence, Clark's critique is a Marxist-Leninist critique of Marxism-Leninism and must fall prey to the same logic: as indicated earlier in this chapter, if there is a contradiction in party intellectuals deciding what constitutes proletarian consciousness then there must also be a problem, for the very same reason, with a Marxist intellectual making this meta-claim about consciousness and ideology in general. That is, if it is a contradiction for the party to decide what counts as revolutionary ideology, and possess the political right to pass judgment on revolutionary standards, then it must also be a contradiction for Clark to pass judgment on the entire meaning of revolutionary ideology and its possible contradictions.

Again we must return to the claim I made near the beginning of this chapter and understand Clark's contradiction as a *dialectical contradiction*: Marxism-Leninism is correct while at the same time it is incorrect. Here is a contradiction that demands dialectical unity and this unity is located in the opening produced by Maoism: continuity with the universal elements of Marxism-Leninism, grasped in the moment of world-historical revolution, is unified with a rupture from the limits of Marxism-Leninism, grasped in the moment of world-historical failure. Now we find ourselves in a new theoretical terrain that has not yet reached its own limits, that we still must explore, but at the very least we can look back upon Clark's assessment of the last revolutionary gasp of Marxism-Leninism and understand that it was only a sign-post pointing, however vaguely, at a new stage of revolutionary science.

Notes

1. Clark, *The State and Counter-Revolution* (Introduction), 3.
2. Rancière, *Staging the People: the Proletarian and his Double*, 22.
3. See, for example, Rancière's *Proletarian Nights*, which, though beautifully written and useful in its own way, spends most of its time describing the appearance of proletarian experience, rejecting rigor and an examination of any structural principles in order to avoid replicating the Althusserian problematic.
4. *Elements of a Sum Up of the WCP.*
5. Clark, *The State and Counter-Revolution* (Chapter 5), 11.
6. Clark, *The State and Counter-Revolution* (Chapter 2), 2.
7. The party intellectuals who once made this point to me were not academics but were organic intellectuals.
8. Yami, 90–101. Here it is worth noting that, true to Yami's predictions, many of the initial theorists of Nepal's People's War did indeed become revisionists, theorists of the counter-revolution. Ironically, despite her warnings regarding the need to arm the masses with revolutionary theory, Yami herself ended up identifying with the revisionist camp.
9. Rancière, *Proletarian Nights*, 9–10.
10. Revolutionary Communist Party of Canada, *Party Programme.*
11. Ibid.
12. Clark, *The State and Counter-Revolution* (Appendix II).
13. Lewis, *A Preface to Paradise Lost*, 9–10. And though we must

note that Lewis flip-flopped between being an arch-conservative and a [Christian] Fabian Socialist, his analysis of the even-more-conservative Eliot's literary elitism is a perfect analogy for this logical problem.

Chapter 4

Maoist Openings

[Humanity] inevitably sets itself only such tasks as it is able to solve, since closer examination will always show that the problem itself arises when the material conditions for its solution are already present or at least in the course of formation.
—Karl Marx, *A Contribution to the Critique of Political Economy*

New Questions

By transgressing the limits of Marxism-Leninism, the theoretical terrain of Maoism is capable of answering many of the significant questions that hampered the previous period of anti-revisionism. These were questions that hastened the disintegration of numerous Mao Zedong Thought organizations and were often leveled against the theory and practice of revolutionary communism. Despite a few admirable attempts, many of which should form the foundation of our analysis now, these organizations were by-and-large incapable of answering these questions and thus shattered or declined when they encountered this radical criticism. Some groups intentionally dissolved when they realized they could not honestly respond to these new problematics; other groups simply chose the path of denial, often lapsing into vulgar materialism, followed by dishonest back-pedaling, confused responses, and a shabby process of theoretical tinkering.

These questions were those raised by the struggles of minorities, specifically questions regarding race, gender, sexuality, and an entire host of identity-based concerns. Although numerous Marxist-Leninist organizations at the centers of capitalism, specifically in the United States, initially proved themselves capable of answering, in a limited but still important fashion, the question of race and racism (and although world-historical revolutions provided these organizations with a general understanding of the importance of women's liberation) these struggles would still prove to be a stumbling block for the historical materialism of Marxism-Leninism.

The problem of race and racism was most often refracted through the lens of the national question (important when discussing colonialism and perhaps the material basis that was, in the final instance, responsible for racialization and thus racism[1]) but still limited in its application. The problem of women's emancipation was often considered solved by statements made by Marx/Lenin/Mao and institutional practices of revolutionary societies, and though these statements and practices were historically important, they were not enough to allow those anti-revisionists as a whole to grasp the problematic(s) raised by the feminist movement. Indeed, it was quite common for anti-revisionist organizations, along with Trotskyists, to dismiss *feminism* as petty-bourgeois. Most significant in challenging Marxism-Leninism, however, were the questions of sexuality and sex identity, queer and trans demands,[2] that often produced chauvinist practices in organizations that were otherwise revolutionary.

Take, for example, the RCP-USA's inability to understand the queer question (let alone the trans question) and the backwards behavior that this inability produced. Despite the Stonewall Rebellion, despite decades where queer persons were targeted by the forces of reaction, the RCP-USA maintained a chauvinist position when it came to this identity that, despite being veiled in revolutionary language, was no different in practice than the position of bourgeois society: gays and lesbians were treated as aberrant, their sexuality dismissed as "bourgeois decadence", and queer members of the RCP-USA were directed towards bizarre re-education practices that were ultimately the same as fundamentalist Christian anti-gay programs.[3] While it might have been understandable (though not excusable) for a revolutionary organizations in the 1930s (or for revolutionary organizations in semi-feudal contexts) to maintain such an erroneous position, it was extremely bizarre that revolutionary organizations in the USA *after Stonewall and through the Reagan era* were maintaining a position that was lagging behind the revolutionary consciousness of the masses. Moreover, while it might be the case that if the RCP-USA maintained this position now (they do not, though they have also failed to criticize their past practice) we could simply write it off, due this organization's current marginal status, as one weird ideological commitment among many. Unfortunately, the RCP-USA put forward its anti-queer line when it was the most significant communist organization in the US, and it was not alone (both inside and outside of its country) in maintaining such a position.

Hence, emergent anti-systemic struggles were often excluded from even the anti-revisionist movement, a place where they could have flourished, due to aspects of Marxist-Leninist rigidity that had not as a whole been dissolved by the Maoist rupture. In response to this rigidity (where historical materialism reached the limits of Marxism-Leninism and devolved, by virtue of its anti-revisionism, into a dogmatic embrace of certain statements and practices), Marxism was treated as questionable by those who were involved in these identity-based struggles. Why should the nascent queer revolutionary join a movement that rejected their very existence? Why was it that the leadership of many of these groups was comprised of individuals who occupied privileged sites of identity? These were questions raised by struggles that were emerging precisely when Marxism-Leninism was reaching its limits at the centers of capitalism. In Canada, for example, En Lutte dissolved itself willingly because of similar questions: although it understood, as opposed to the RCP-USA, that such questions needed to be both addressed and embraced by a communist movement, it could not theoretically square that period's anti-revisionist Marxism-Leninism with these significant demands.

Thus, since Marxism-Leninism was encountering the end of its theoretical terrain due to those concrete historical facts discussed in the first chapter, and since the anti-revisionist movement was ill-prepared for the contradictions it encountered with the collapse of actually-existing socialism, it was generally incapable of examining the questions raised by struggles partially outside of the traditional Marxist gamut. Dedicated primarily to preserving an anti-revisionist communism, many Marxist-Leninist militants could not thoroughly focus on creatively rearticulating revolutionary theory to account for the aforementioned questions.

Hence the collapse of the Marxist-Leninist movement produced a theoretical void. Into this void rushed post-modernism, post-Marxism, post-colonialism, and a confused constellation of chic academic theory that attempted to make sense of oppressions outside of class exploitation in a manner that was eclectic, speculative, quasi-materialist, or just baldly idealist. If the revolutionary tradition that spoke of a scientific assessment of society and history had reached its end, or so the implicit argument raised by these new radical theories claimed, then explanations that were not tainted with the "totalizing" categories of historical materialism were required. And these new explanations, which claimed to be more radical than a Marxism judged as limited and historically anachronistic, would substitute the concrete categories of *class, mode of production, revolutionary party, historical subject* with speculative concepts such as *intersectionality, oppressive structures, autonomy and solidarity,* and *the decentered subject.* This substitution would also lead to a political practice, at least amongst those radical intelligentsia who rarely practiced much in the way of revolution, premised on radical sites of identity and social movement strategies: identity politics and movementism.

Since I have discussed the problems of identity politics and movementism elsewhere,[4] I will not examine them in significant detail here. I am discussing the emergence of these theories and practices simply to indicate the reasons for their appearance, reasons that cannot be explained by their disparate and nebulous theoretical terrains; this is something that can only be explained by recourse to a historical-materialist approach, the only methodology capable of grasping the concrete movement of history. These theories, whatever their strengths, have only been able to understand the level of appearance and are thus incapable of understanding that: i) they emerged because there was a void in radical theory left by the temporary abdication of Marxism-Leninism in privileged academia; ii) there was a necessity to fill this void since there were phenomena that required theoretical explanation (i.e. race/gender/sexuality/sex/ability oppression); iii) this void only existed because of the temporary defeat of revolutionary communism and the onslaught of counter-revolution. This last point is key because without the era of counter-revolution in which capitalism attempted to name itself as *the end of history*, and thus the temporary decline of revolutionary communist movements, it is doubtful that these new radical theories would have ever gained a measure of hegemony at the centers of capitalism. Therefore, identity politics and the theories behind it, despite the important reasons for their emergence, are now *objectively* the practice and theory of counter-revolution even if they do not understand themselves as such *subjectively*.

Historical Moment of Systematization

The truth is not that revolutionary communism and its supposedly moribund theory vanished (indeed, as noted in the first chapter, it was in the process of reconceptualizing itself as a science by 1988) but that Marxism-Leninism had reached its limits. Thus, what was treated as a void left by communism was in fact the limit reached by the Leninist stage of communism. The interim period in which these anti-oppression movements were primarily being explained and categorized by non-Marxist theories was a period of counter-revolution in which communist movements were forced to reconsolidate, assessing the limits they had reached so they could reemerge with a theoretical understanding that could possibly account for the temporary collapse of communism and the phenomena that emerged during this period of collapse.

Therefore, since Maoism emerged *after* these radical anti-oppression struggles raised their demands, we should now have a theoretical terrain that is capable of explaining these phenomena in a materialist and rigorous manner, one that can provide the explanatory depth these other and speculative approaches sorely lack. A return, then, to revolutionary materialism but a return that is simultaneously a *new return*[5] because, now aware of the existence of a new theoretical terrain, historical materialism should not have to mechanically apply formulaic categories in its attempt to make sense of these questions. After all, those Marxists who did not move past Marxism-Leninism (and especially those trapped in an even more moribund Trotskyism), and who tried to wage ideological line struggle against these other radical theories, often lapsed into crude and formulaic concept-mongering. Maoism allows for a fresher and more creative approach to these problems that is still materialist, but a materialism that is properly materialist in that it is historically relevant and not some fossil theory belonging to the early decades of the 20th-century.

Obviously the germs of a Maoist approach to these problems already existed prior to 1988 in various anti-revisionist texts that claimed some fidelity to the name of Maoism. Frantz Fanon's *The Wretched of the Earth*, the early political economy of Samir Amin, queer anti-revisionists who responded to the chauvinism of the RU/RCP-USA (i.e. the Sojourner Truth Organization and the Los

Angeles Study Group) or the chauvinism of their own social context (i.e. the Gay and Lesbian Caucus of Canada's En Lutte), the theory of the Black Panther Party, the Revolutionary Communist League of Britain's work on eurocentrism, and other Marxist approaches from the historical margins comprise hundreds of seeds for the rich terrain of Maoism. To these we can add subterranean movement texts such as J. Sakai's *Settlers* and Butch Lee and Red Rover's *Night-Vision*, for example, that also contributed to a materialist engagement with the problematic that was emerging just when Marxism-Leninism was waning. Moreover, Mao also produced a body of theory that would be useful in making sense of these problems (specifically and most importantly *On Contradiction*), and some indeed tried to make use of this theory albeit in a patchy and often isolated manner.

The emergence of Maoism as a scientific stage of revolutionary communism, however, means the emergence of a theory that is systematized around key theoretical concepts; it is this systematization that should allow us to understand which attempted past theorizations are useful as well as how and why these theories are affected by the theoretical limits of when they were written. Again it is useful to draw on an analogy from the "hard sciences" in order to explain how *a historical moment of systematization provides retrospective illumination*: as both Jan Sapp and Robert M. Young have pointed out, the emergence of Darwin's *On the Origin of Species*, which was the first systematic account of evolution (and thus provided the term *evolution* with its conceptual content), made sense of previous attempts at understanding the natural and organic development of the human species. Indeed, these previous attempts, which by themselves were limited, were eventually drawn into the orbit of, and validated by, Darwinian theory.[6] We cannot escape the fact that the rupture produced by a scientific paradigm must, by necessity, shed light on the theoretical work that was part of a trajectory that led to this rupture.

In any case, the emergence of a new stage of revolutionary communism can and should permit a thorough materialist engagement with the phenomena that were left unexamined by those Marxist movements and theorists who failed to transgress the limits of Marxism-Leninism. All of the elements necessary to provide scientific assessments of these phenomena exist within the terrain of Maoism, and there is now a small explosion of Maoist theory that seeks to demonstrate this fact.[7]

As noted at the outset of this book, however, I am not interested in *doing theory* but in philosophically engaging with the terrain of theory itself: that is, examining the boundaries in which this theory is possible. Hence, I will not explain *why* or *how* Marxism-Leninism-Maoism can specifically answer the questions raised by these other supposedly "non-Marxist" movements; not only have I indicated elsewhere how this has been done by others, I do not believe it is the job of the philosopher to produce theory.[8] The primary role of philosophy, as I attempted to explain in this book's introduction, is to speak to the question of meaning and thus explain the possibilities (or lack of possibilities) of a given theoretical terrain. Thus, here I simply wish to point out that Maoism is a theoretical terrain that is quite capable of answering those questions that other radical theorists once claimed communist theory was incapable of grasping. Most importantly, I want to explain *why* it is not only capable of answering these questions but is *more capable than other theoretical approaches* of providing thorough and revolutionary solutions.

Materialist Concerns

Since Maoism represents a new return to revolutionary science, the reason it is better equipped to deal with the phenomena that were once considered the purview of post-modern/post-Marxist/post-colonial theory is because it can provide a concrete analysis of a concrete situation. In a word: *materialism*. The failure of these alternative radical theories was their inability to delve beneath the level of appearance and, out of a rejection of totalization, provide a rigorous explanation of their objects of critique. That is, they failed to provide any significant explanatory depth.

The simple way to illustrate this failure on the part of these other radical theories is simply to note the concept of *power* that is common to Michel Foucault, Judith Butler, Gayatry Spivak, Edward Said, and other members of this rebel canon. Here we find a radical rejection of the abstract category of "power" (and often the category of *power-knowledge*) where it is assumed that history is fundamentally a history of oppression and exclusion due to the discursive application of power that ultimately produces the historical subject. Foucault's genealogical approach, which is influential for all of these theories, claims that history is nothing more than the history of power that produces moments of totalization and is murderous in its forcing of meaning.

Since I do not want to waste time explaining this theoretical approach,[9] it is enough to simply indicate that this theory of power is never explained in a materialist sense. That is, none of these theorists can really articulate the origin and meaning of this terrible *power* besides the fact that it exists. Although it is quite easy to claim that any attempt to explain the origin of power is, in-itself, an act of totalization (and thus a discursive power game), and hence that the search for materialist origins is ultimately *murderous*, I would like to suggest that this is a rhetorical attempt to dodge an important question: for if one cannot explain the originary meaning of this power then it is rather difficult to make a value judgment about its deployment: if you cannot explain what power is precisely, then it is somewhat difficult to explain why it is a problem. Most importantly, however, is the idealism behind this concept of *power*: in its lack of material qualification it becomes akin to a Platonic form, an ideal concept of power that supervenes on history, beyond human agency and producing agency, more autonomous than the species that came up with the concept in the first place.

Materialists, however, believe that all concepts are, in the final instance, generated by humans living and producing in historically mediated circumstances. To speak of power outside of this context is to ignore the fact that power is always something material, not just a vague concept, and makes no sense otherwise. Engels made such a point when he was attacking Duhring's similar concept of *power*: he argued that Duhring could not understand that power was not something that existed in and of itself but was always something that was either political or economic, produced by humans in the final instance. The fact that those theorists who follow thinkers such as Foucault are actually reasserting the speculative categories of Eugene Duhring is something I have often thought is worth noting.[10] If anything, it demonstrates that those theories that claimed to transcend Marxism were actually a return to a reactionary past: when materialism falters and temporarily produces a void, idealism always rushes in to fill the vacuum.

The terrain opened by Maoism should be understood, then, as a new return to materialist concerns that are capable of making sense of these phenomena in a way that past Marxisms and these alternative radical theories were generally ill-equipped for. Whereas the latter theories dealt only with the level of appearance, many of the former theories wasted time regurgitating crude materialist categories. If we must speak of the materialist basis of these other oppressions (which in the final instance should have something to do with class struggle) then we cannot simply reject them in favor of a crude notion of *class* that has nothing to do with race or gender or sexuality or etc.

But to speak of the opening of a terrain that demands a return to a materialist analysis, albeit a materialist analysis that can account for this phenomena, is considered offensive by those dedicated to the speculative vicissitudes of this *post-* theory.

Idealists are wont to dismiss every materialist approach as an instance of vulgar materialism since all forms of materialism are dismissed as vulgar by the idealist. Lenin encountered a similar problem when he wrote *Materialism and Empirio-Criticism*, after all, and we should not be surprised that history repeats itself as tragedy.

Thus, any Maoist engagement with these phenomena will necessarily be treated as vulgar materialism, no matter how sophisticated and insightful it might be, by those who have become the academic gate-keepers of these concerns. To speak of material social relations is an act of vulgarity for those who demand the most obscurantist and specialized assessment of reality. In some ways this is the strength of historical materialism; it *should* refuse to be misled by the treacherous currents of specialized academic theory and, against this privileged theorization, assert the demands of the *vulgar* masses.

Proletarian Mass-Line and Class Composition

Since we can and must make sense of those questions raised by the period following the collapse of Marxism-Leninism, questions about other sites of oppression, we will discover that Maoism possesses the tools to answer these questions in a manner that provides revolutionary unification. Those other theories have always rejected unification for fragmentation, necessity for contingency, substance for appearance, and class for identity: the practice resulting from this approach cannot hope to promote revolution because it cannot promote solidarity. Marxism has always held that the only real revolutionary solidarity can come from a movement based on class, a proletarian struggle against bourgeois hegemony, and Maoism is continuous with this insight.

At the same time, however, whereas other Marxisms have been forced to ignore, downplay, subordinate struggles that are supposedly "not about class" in order to emphasize the primary importance of class struggle, or to claim that there are new class subjects that are not the proletariat (i.e. "the multitude"), Maoism possesses the tools to incorporate these concerns within a theory of class struggle. To dismiss these concerns (to subordinate them to an abstract notion of class, to temporarily set them aside, to make up completely new class categories when the majority of the world remains proletarian) is an act of denial; these are *live* concerns because they matter and hence demand a materialist theorization.

As indicated in the previous chapter, the theory of the mass-line (from the masses and to the masses), one of the universal aspects of Maoism, should lead us to the understanding that the revolutionary masses are not simply an abstract and unqualified proletariat. Those who would argue that Maoism tends to replace the category of *proletariat* with the category of *masses* fail to understand that this is not a replacement but a theoretical expansion gleaned through the moment of rupture. It is not that we are replacing *proletariat* with *the masses* but that we are using the latter concept as a substitute for the simplistic *working-class*. The revolutionary masses *are* the proletariat: in one sense they are the working class because, on a global scale, the proletariat is precisely that force that provides the majority of the world's labor; in another sense they are not precisely the working class because the revolutionary proletariat, the so-called "hard core", can be located amongst the most oppressed and exploited elements of the working class, as well as the reserve army of labor: the majority of humanity that has nothing left to lose but its chains.

Once we start examining the proletariat in a *mass* sense, which is what Maoists believe is germinal to Marx's thought, then we are forced to wonder at the composition of the working class in a given particular context. There is a working class at the centers of capitalism that is unionized and possesses certain benefits due to this unionization. At the same time, there are

147

non-unionized laborers and an unemployed reserve army (many of whom perform piece-work acts of production) who are part of the revolutionary masses precisely because they greatly outnumber that fraction of the working class that was once treated, according to tired formulae, as *the* proletariat.

Such an examination must, by necessity, lead us to ask questions about the very composition of the revolutionary class, a problematic discussed in the previous chapter which I will reemphasize here. In racist social contexts, for example, racialized workers are far more proletarianized because they do not, as a whole, possess the privilege of unionization. The composition of the proletariat, then, is over-determined by those sites of oppression that we were told were not unified in the moment of class: we may not find any basis of unity with a revolutionary movement and a bourgeois woman of color, but we cannot deny that women of color make up a minority of the bourgeoisie. Thus, while a revolutionary movement must proceed according to class lines, and any revolutionary movement must not seek allies amongst the bourgeoisie who have a vested interested in counter-revolution, it needs to recognize that the class lines are partially determined by those other sites of oppression. Class is always clothed in the garments of oppression: a racist, heterosexist, and ableist society will always produce a class division that is thoroughly influenced by disparate oppressive moments. In order to properly understand class we must also understand the process of its composition.

Mao had an inkling of this problem when he wrote On Contradiction and argued that the ideological/political superstructure, though in the "final instance" a result of the economic base, always served to obstruct and partially determine the substructure. Ideologies that spring up in one period, generated by material necessity, do not simply disappear, annihilated by some ontological break in the mode of production; they linger, influencing and rearranging the base itself. Capitalism has never been a pure mode of production, in the way that it was (necessarily and for scientific reasons) described in *Capital*, and there are even moments in *Capital* itself (i.e. the sections on primitive accumulation) where Marx recognized that this was the case.

Althusser often argued that *the final instance never arrives*. Inspired by the insights of Mao—and thus a concept of Maoism that had not yet emerged—he meant that, while we can understand the meaning of these other sites of oppression according to the "final instance" of the economic base, there is never an instance of a purely abstract class struggle that is stripped from its ideological trappings. But Althusser, whose critical lens was ultimately aimed at an anti-revisionist Marxism-Leninism, and even then ended up siding with the revisionist orthodoxy of the PCF, was incapable of grasping the full extent of this insight. Now we must take this insight further in order to declare that under capitalism the proletariat and the bourgeoisie are not categories that remain unaffected by race, gender, sex, sexuality, and ability; they are always over-coded by these sites of oppression.

Maoism, then, demands a *mass* understanding of class that can speak to a composition produced by the obstruction of the economic base. At the same time, as a moment that is also continuous with the development of revolutionary science, it rejects an identity politics that refuses to grasp the importance of the "final instance": the final instance might *never arrive* but is always immanent; class might never be an abstract category shorn from these other sites of oppression, but it is still the fundamental category. Let's put it crudely: while the proletariat in, for example, racist and sexist societies might possess a composition that is predominantly racialized and genderized, those persons experiencing racism and sexism in these societies who also own the means of production are not the proletariat.

Hence, those Marxist-Leninist-Maoist theorists who have attempted to deal with these sites of oppression according to this framework have found it useful to use the qualifier of *proletarian* to make sense of their approach. Those Maoists who speak of *proletarian feminism*, for example, have done so for two reasons: i) to distinguish their feminism from a feminism that would recognize the "revolutionary" agency of bourgeois women; ii) to argue that feminist struggle, contrary to identity politics, only makes sense if it is part of a broader proletarian movement.[11] Hopefully we will see the emergence of a new *proletarian anti-racism*, *proletarian anti-heterosexism*, and *proletarian anti-ableism* in the near future. All of these materialist engagements with these other sites of oppression will hopefully undercut the banal "intersectional" approaches of identity politics that cannot, by themselves, produce revolutionary unification. In other words, a proletarian mass-line of class composition.

Vulgar Materialism

And yet the unification in class demanded by Marxism-Leninism-Maoism, despite its unwillingness to ignore those questions addressed by the theory that attempted to replace revolutionary communism, will always be treated as a vulgar materialism by those who are committed to a politics that rejects all materialist analysis. To claim that class struggle is the militant basis of praxis is a claim that is anathema to those who would treat social class as simply another site of oppression, an identity no more or less important than other oppressed identities.

Although the final instance might never arrive, to even claim that the final instance is *social class*, regardless of how Maoism teaches us to understand class, is to be guilty of class reductionism. I would like to argue, though, that we should not fear such reductionism; every science, after all, functions as a science due to its ability to reduce concrete phenomena to abstract categories. According to particle physics, in the final instance all matter is ultimately nothing more than particles moving at high speed; only a physicist completely divorced from reality, however, would claim that reality is completely identical to this necessary reduction. Similarly, although the chemical meaning of water is located in its reduction to H_2O, we do not experience water as this equation.

Hence, to reduce the complexity of social phenomena to the common denominator of class struggle should not mean a rejection of this complexity; rather, the moment of reduction is a method of abstraction that allows us to understand the concrete. Class reductionism only becomes a problem when it cannot properly account for the phenomena it claims to explain, or when it veers into a quasi-Platonic idealism where class is treated as a transhistorical essence rather than a social relation. To dismiss such an approach as vulgar is to dismiss all scientific attempts to make sense of the world and plunge us back into the realm of mystification and superstition. This is why we should not be surprised when some of those theorists who attack Marxism on the grounds of its vulgar materialism also mock the enlightenment, science, and everything upon which their privilege is predicated in a manner that is far more vulgar than the materialism they despise.

None of this is to claim, however, that we should dismiss the charge of vulgar materialism out-of-hand. As I noted in the second chapter, we must guard against a dogmatic behavior that could pull us back into past praxis. Beyond some unquestioned idealism, there is a reason that charges of vulgar materialism are raised against any and all historical-materialist attempts to make sense of problems that were originally treated as outside of the gamut of historical materialism: it is worth recognizing that there have indeed been dismissals of these concerns that even materialists should deem "vulgar", where the class reductionism has veered into a class essentialism, where theoretical violence (most often translating into real-world violence) has been done to the concerns that were once the province of these other non-Marxist radical theories.

Again it is worth noting the RCP-USA's refusal to properly engage with the demands produced by queer resistance. Here a clearly "vulgar" response (sanctified by an appeal to materialist categories) was tendered that was at the same time thoroughly chauvinist: queer persons were categorized as the product of "bourgeois decadence", their sexual identity the supposed result of male supremacy. Although a sophisticated materialist should be quite capable of demonstrating how the RCP-USA's position in this case was more idealist than materialist[12] (because it was little more than a distorted refraction of the ruling ideas of the ruling class through the lens of Marxist categories), the fact that it was put forward as materialist was enough, in the eyes of the critics of Marxism, to spuriously dismiss all materialism as vulgar. Such a dismissal makes sense if you are someone who is concretely affected by a chauvinist analysis that masquerades as materialist; it is enough to taint this revolutionary tradition.

Maoism, however, needs to move beyond the charge of vulgar materialism just as it moves beyond actual vulgar materialism. The theoretical elements for a thorough analysis of these other, and supposedly "non-class", sites of oppression are already in place and have been waiting for a further development in the science to unify them. This is a new opening that should not be held back by the nit-picking of anti-communist theorists who remain trapped on the level of appearance and can offer no revolutionary solutions.

Again: Ideological Hegemony

Here it is worth returning to the problem of *ideological hegemony* raised in the first chapter. Since Marxism-Leninism-Maoism, on an international level, does not yet possess the same level of ideological hegemony that Marxism-Leninism once possessed, it is not surprising that its emergence is often dismissed as a return to the "vulgar materialisms" of the past. The theoretical openings in which it has proven itself capable of operating are openings that it has not yet succeeded in fully claiming from those other radical theories.

The general retreat of revolutionary communism left in its wake a series of phenomena that required theoretical investigation that, without Marxism, were bound to be interpreted as fragmented and disconnected. The radical theories of such thinkers as Michel Foucault, Jacques Derrida, Gayatry Spivak, Homi Bhabha, Jean-Luc Nancy, etc. succeeded in claiming the territory abandoned by this retreat and thus achieved a significant level of theoretical hegemony. But this hegemony was always somewhat contradictory: on the one hand it rejected *totalization*, on the other hand it produced its own totalizing hegemony. That is, this theoretical family's interpretation (and its rejection of the unity that could only be found in the totality of a revolutionary project) was itself total in a complete rejection of any approach that did not recognize the social phenomena in need of explanation. The appearance of fragmentation and disconnection was taken to be an essential fact of nature; the totality of difference was understood as a political virtue.

Therefore, the Maoist rupture has not yet succeeded in overcoming this fragmented ideological terrain on a global level, regardless of its successes on various national levels. This is why it is rather nonsensical to speak of a theoretical conjuncture beyond Maoism when this moment of rupture-continuity has only begun to address the historical problems it has inherited. When a new theoretical paradigm emerges within any science, after all, it is not considered complete if the questions of its time have not yet been fully addressed; such a paradigm is only transgressed when its ability to respond to these questions has reached its limits, when it demonstrates that it lacks the ability to provide the necessary scientific explanation. I think it is fair to argue that Maoism is only beginning to explain the problems of the historical period in which it emerged, nor has it exhausted its ability to make sense of these problems.

But what Maoism demands in the very fact of its proclamation as a concept is the unification of this supposedly disunified constellation of phenomena. It emerges with the claim that it can explain and unify the terrain in which it operates; it possesses the potential to do so due to its basis in historical materialism *and* the fact that it is a moment that is still developing, still open to the future. Indeed, those revolutions which have proclaimed the theory of Marxism-Leninism-Maoism have engaged and are engaging with this phenomenological constellation; this engagement was and is understood as necessary. Most importantly, the revolutionary unity that Maoism brings to these problems is a unity that is found in revolutionary practice and, ultimately, is about changing the circumstances that produce these very problems.

Operationalizing a Praxis

The problem, however, lies in operationalizing a praxis based on the unification of these sites of oppression along revolutionary class lines. Since some of us have come to Maoism after being trained in the theory and practice of identity politics it is difficult to grasp the practice demanded by this new return to revolutionary science: we discovered the limitations of this "anti-oppression" praxis and yearned for the concrete solidarity produced by revolutionary science, and we gravitated towards Maoism because we felt it could answer our questions rather than dismissing them as "petty-bourgeois". Even still, there remains the tendency to import the practices of identity politics into revolutionary organizing.

What Marxism-Leninism-Maoism should teach us, however, is that while we should be able to account for these other sites of oppression and recognize their importance, we should not replace a militant organization pursuing class struggle with some nebulous set of practices that focus primarily on the appearance of identity. It is the political line that matters, and this is always a class question.

While it might be correct to recognize the problems these sites of oppression pose for a revolutionary organization (i.e. the problem of a revolutionary organization whose leadership is predominantly white, straight, cis male, etc.), it is not at all correct to assume that dealing with these problems on the level of identity will provide a solution. Most often, it produces confusion.

Should the viewpoint of a queer woman of color who is also a cop be treated as admissible by a revolutionary organization simply because of her identity?[13] The question is rhetorical because I feel that most radicals, even those who endorse an identitarian approach, would respond with a resounding *no*—and we have to ask *why* they would say no, especially if their praxis should, based on its theoretical commitments, lead them to argue otherwise. We generally understand that the answer to this question is *no* because most of us who endorse some form of anti-capitalism actually do understand, however vaguely, that the political line is more important than the identity of the person espousing this line.

An identity often *does* mediate a given political line, but the latter is decisive. An organization built around a revolutionary political line is more important than a collective in which politics are reduced to the identities of the people involved. Thus, it is entirely possible for an organization consisting mainly of white men to have a more revolutionary analysis of racism and sexism (though it is highly doubtful that they would come to this analysis by themselves) than an organization consisting entirely of women of color. Of course, as Maoists, we would also have to wonder about the composition of the former organization, despite its better analysis, and perhaps locate its failure to grow beyond a white and male membership in a troubling gap between theory and practice.

This disparity between appearance (identity) and substance

(political line) is a significant problem that requires philosophical intervention. On the one hand we should recognize that if someone's identity is determined by a history of oppression or a history of privilege, then it would be anti-materialist to assume that the development of this identity is outside of this history. On the other hand, building a politics primarily (and sometimes *solely*) upon this very simple fact lacks substantial depth. We need to realize that while identity mediates a political line, a political line also mediates identity and that it is the latter mediation that is determinant.

Take, for example, the claim often made by some adherents to identity politics regarding the identity of Karl Marx: since he is a "dead white man" then the content of his work should be treated as thoroughly oppressive and dismissed entirely. Now while it is true that Marx's circumstances, and thus identity, were such that his analysis was often mediated by eurocentrism and, perhaps, a masculinist oversight, to act as if these problems are such that the content of his work is thoroughly tainted is both simplistic and ahistorical.[14] After all, once we examine the history of revolutionary movements, we are forced to recognize that the theory founded by Marx (and Engels) is a theory that has been understood as extremely significant for those masses of people who are not white or male, more than any other theory, and so we are left with two choices: i) recognize that the content of this theory is more important than the identity of the theorist, and that it has been developed beyond its weaknesses by those it might have temporarily excluded; ii) claim that the oppressed identities of those masses who treat this theory as significant are of little importance because these subaltern masses, incapable of speaking for themselves, are being "spoken for" by totalizing communist leaders. This last claim, of course, should be treated as somewhat absurd since those who would discount these masses' ability to speak for themselves in the name of communism are also "speaking for" the same masses.

At the same time, however, it is necessary to recognize the limitations imposed by privileged identity. Such a recognition, however, needs to be grasped according to the basis of political content because often, and especially when it comes to the living science of communism, the content itself can explain the deficiencies in identity.[15] After all, the easiest way to critique Marx's eurocentrism is not to dismiss him altogether but to simply indicate that his own historical-materialist method undermines this eurocentrism in proving that it is an erroneous historical analysis of non-European cultures *and* that "social being determines social consciousness" even in the case of Marx. That is, Marx himself is convicted by his own categories.

And yet it has been a common theoretical practice for Marxists to cling only to the revolutionary content of Marxism without properly noting how this content, though determinant in the final instance, is also mediated by the form. If we are to declare fidelity to the content of a political line, then we must also declare fidelity to what this line is supposed to mean: social circumstances *do* matter, social being determines social consciousness, and a class position is partially composed by these other sites of oppression.

Here Marxism-Leninism-Maoism is significant because, without abandoning historical materialism, it is the only Marxist tendency that has thoroughly attempted in practice, since its germinal stages, to make sense of how appearance mediates substance, identity mediates the content of a political line—how sites of oppression mediate class. Such a nuanced understanding is evident in Mao's early work on social investigation (i.e. *Analysis of the Classes in Chinese Society, Report on an Investigation of the Peasant Movement in Hunan*) as well as his treatise *On Contradiction*. It is also evident in all of the foundational Maoist works up to and after the crystallization of Marxism-Leninism-Maoism. To a lesser, but still important, extent it is evident in those historical-materialist trajectories that were influenced by

Mao and the Chinese Revolution, such as Frantz Fanon's *The Wretched of the Earth*. This rich theoretical history has led many radicals who were once enamored with some form of identity politics (including myself) back to the narrative of historical materialism, and this is why the tendency to import the practices of identity politics into our organizational life is still a practice that needs to be overcome: it is still fresh in our minds.

A Disjunction

The aim of this section has been to investigate how the rupture of Marxism-Leninism-Maoism produces a theoretical opening that is capable of making sense of concerns that are currently treated as the business of non-Marxist theory. I have attempted to demonstrate the philosophical circumstances of this opening, drawing lines of demarcation between Maoism and these other approaches. My general point is that Maoism can provide a more systematic, thorough, and revolutionary answer to these questions. Moreover, these questions also produce an agitational opening where a Maoist analysis and practice can possibly pull more militants into its orbit.

If the limits of Marxism-Leninism have been transgressed by the stage of Maoism, as I have argued in the previous chapters, then Maoist theory can and should be capable of responding to those demands that were raised during the historic retreat of world communism. A science proves its strength when it can provide a concrete analysis of concrete circumstances without nomological danglers.[16] As I have attempted to explain in this chapter, this new stage of revolutionary science is already demonstrating that it possesses the theoretical tools capable of responding to these demands.

The problem, as I have suggested above, lies in the practical operationalization of this politics. As Mao reminds us, it is not enough to have a proper analysis of concrete circumstances; Marxism is about changing these circumstances. And though

Maoism, in the many revolutionary struggles since its inception, has made significant strides in demonstrating how a political line that takes these other problems into account can be operationalized (i.e. the explosion of women's militias in people's armies that aim, though always imperfectly because reality is still messy, to correct the male domination of revolutionary movements), it is still new enough that it is currently struggling to develop its practice.

On the one hand there are Maoists who, while understanding how to make sense of these other questions, are still operating according to the patterns of the previous stage of Marxism-Leninism and are thus unable to synthesize this understanding with their militant praxis. On the other hand, there are Maoists who, while understanding the limits of the anti-communist radical theorization of "identity", are still trapped within the praxis of identity politics and are thus unable to even produce a thoroughly militant praxis. Although this disjunction is historically understandable, it still needs to be overcome. And yet, through Marxism-Leninism-Maoism, this contradiction is being overcome, slowly and painfully, and already lines of demarcation are being drawn.

Cultural Revolution

The aspect of rupture represented by the state of Maoism should be understood as a rupture guided by the theory of cultural revolution. Whereas Leninism was that stage that established the necessity of revolution up to the dictatorship of the proletariat, Maoism is that stage which claims that revolution must continue within the dictatorship of the proletariat and that a socialist movement must be subordinated to a cultural revolution in order to struggle against the counter-revolutionary ideology that is often preserved in the superstructure.

Thus, while it might seem odd to talk about a theoretical opening that is capable of addressing the problems raised by non-Marxist radical theories, and then speak of the necessity of drawing lines of demarcation through and around these problems, this is precisely the concern of the theory of cultural revolution. A struggle in what is often called "the economic base" must be unified with a parallel struggle in the so-called "ideological superstructure"; it is not enough to push these concerns beyond the horizon of a possible socialist revolution and hope that they will be struggled against after another dictatorship of the proletariat has been established: this is what the Chinese Revolution did in the Great Proletarian Cultural Revolution and, though this struggle would produce the theoretical insights necessary for Maoism's emergence, in the context of the Chinese Revolution it was too little and too late.

If Maoism is a stage of revolutionary science that has truly synthesized the insights gained from the most recent world-historical socialist revolution, then it must take the theory of cultural revolution seriously and apply it immediately: this is precisely what the theorization of Maoism demands and what makes it a rupture from Marxism-Leninism that, a few germinal and disorganized insights not-withstanding, was incapable of grasping the necessity of cultural revolution from the very moment of a revolutionary organization's founding.

Mass-line, criticism and self-criticism, cultural revolution: these interlinked aspects of Maoism's claim to be the next stage of science are necessary for building a movement that is capable of addressing the problems facing any revolutionary organization today. Here are some questions worth asking: is an organization building itself according to the will of the revolutionary masses while, at the same time, organizing this will and providing theoretical guidance; is this organization critical of itself and willing to accept that it is wrong; are the movement's cadre serving the people and capable of self-criticism in a way that parallels the "checking of privilege" common in identity politics circles but, unlike these circles, tied to a coherent political line;

does this movement see itself as capable of transcending the ruling ideas of the ruling class, grasping how certain ideological moments distort and over/under-determine the economic base (as Mao pointed out in *On Contradiction*), and constantly reforming itself through the long march of cultural revolution? Failure to answer these questions might in fact be a failure to concretely apply those theoretical insights that are supposed to make the *name* of Maoism into a *concept*.

Notes

1. Frantz Fanon's claim that every settler-colonialist society must also be a racist society due to the fact that colonialism produces the very concept of race was useful in this regard.

2. I realize that the rubric *trans* is often placed under the umbrella term *queer*. I am separating them mainly for the sake of clarity. Moreover, while it is true that *queer* is now a concept that is meant to also embrace trans identity, it is important to recognize that each of the positions in the LGBQT* acronym possess their own unique concerns that cannot easily be homogenized as a singular "queer" experience.

3. For a thorough historiography on the RU/RCP-USA's homophobic political line and practice, see the Kasama Project's pamphlet *Out of the Red Closet*.

4. See, for example, my book *The Communist Necessity*.

5. The concept of *new return* is something I initially discussed in my small book *The Communist Necessity*, something that will be expanded upon in this chapter and the following ones.

6. See Jan Sapp's *Genesis: the evolution of biology* and Robert M. Young's *Darwin's Metaphor*.

7. For instance, Anuradha Gandhy and Hisila Yami's work on "proletarian feminism", which emerges from Maoist movements, is significant in its thorough examination of the history of feminism from a revolutionary perspective.

8. I have attempted to explain the Maoist way of approaching these problems at various points on my blog *MLM Mayhem*.

9. I would draw the interested reader's attention to the fourth chapter of my doctoral thesis, *A Living Colonialism*, where I explain this problem in detail.

10. Again, I examined this in significant detail in *A Living Colonialism*.

11. See Ghandy, 145–209.

12. Such critiques were indeed made, specifically by the Los Angeles Research Group in their polemic *Towards a Scientific Analysis of the Gay Question* that, in their Marxist attack on the RU/RCP-USA's chauvinist line, should be considered useful in developing a proletarian queer theory. Along with this polemic, the various works of En Lutte's Gay and Lesbian Caucus, which are also available at the Encyclopedia of Anti-Revisionism Online, are worth examining.

13. This is not just a hypothetical anecdote. Cops with these oppressed identities do exist and, regardless of their role as guardians of capitalism, have experienced racism, sexism, and homophobia. Whatever chauvinism they have experienced, however, should not outweigh the fact that they are part of an institution that functions according to very clear class logic.

14. For an excellent criticism of eurocentrism in the Marxist movement from Marx and Engels to the 20th-century, interested readers should pick up a copy of Robert Biel's *Eurocentrism and the Communist Movement* which is a historical-materialist analysis of the limits of eurocentrism within the Marxist movement.

15. Hisila Yami's work on proletarian feminism, for example, is useful in this regard. Examining the question as to *why* the formula "Marxism-Leninism-Maoism" is taken from the names of men, she makes the following argument: a) while the concept goes beyond the names, Marx, Lenin, and Mao

were the principle theorists from which it was derived; b) they were the principle theorists because they were the only revolutionary leaders/theorists who provided, in the foundation and the most important moments of the science, a concrete analysis of a concrete situation; c) the fact that such an analysis has hitherto only been provided by men should tell us something about the broader context of oppression—sex/gender oppression prevents women from possessing the autonomy to make these kinds of analyses; d) this exclusion does not undermine Marxism-Leninism-Maoism but teaches us that we need to develop a female cadre who are capable of being significant leaders/theorists.

16. A "nomological dangler", according to J.J.C. Smart, is a phenomenon that cannot be explained by a scientific theory that attempts to explain a constellation of phenomena to which this phenomenon is intrinsically connected. Thus, if a scientific theory of history is incapable of explaining, for example, the historical phenomenon of racism, then it has a significant "nomological dangler".

Chapter 5

A New Anti-Revisionism

Critique and denounce revisionism and its objective allies, the eclecticism of those which believe themselves to be able to dissect what they have announced as the cadaver of Marxism, for fabricating their 'new' theories, their fearful positivism, and their speculative syntheses, far away from class struggle, far away from history... attack the temporary hegemony of the new idealisms that supply the ideological elements of counter-revolution.

—Alain Badiou and Sylvan Lazarus, from the forword to *The Rational Kernel of the Hegelian Dialectic*

Continuity as Rupture & Rupture as Continuity

In the second chapter I discussed the problem of dogmatism inherited from the anti-revisionist past that needs to be overcome. At the same time, throughout this book, I've hinted at the problems of this past that, due to a militant rejection of revisionism, ended up being incapable of addressing those radical concerns that appeared at the end of this anti-revisionist period. Obsessed with defending Marxism-Leninism against a theoretical trend aimed at the liquidation of revolution, this period of communist emergence was primarily concerned with keeping the theoretical boundaries clearly defined: with continuity rather than rupture.

To be clear, I was not arguing against the necessity of anti-revisionism but only against the limits of the past experience of anti-revisionism. First of all, that period's anti-revisionism was necessary because a fidelity with revolutionary communism was indeed required in order to combat the spurious rejections that were being proffered by Khrushchev as well as aspects of the heterogeneous New Left. Secondly, it was impossible for the revolutionary communism of that anti-revisionist period to be anything more than an anti-revisionism of the Marxist-Leninist moment. The point, then, as I argued in *The Communist Necessity*, is to initiate a "new return" to anti-revisionism that locates its theoretical and practical direction in Marxism-Leninism-Maoism. Whereas I ended *The Communist Necessity* with an appeal to this new return, while pointing out some of the aspects it would need to possess, a fuller picture of its meaning should now be apparent based on the previous chapter's discussion. This chapter and the following one, then, will further flesh out the philosophical qualifications of this new return based on the axiom that now there can be no anti-revisionist communism that is not Maoist.

While it is correct to recognize that there are those who deny the significance of the anti-revisionist New Communist Movement of yesteryear,[1] this denial is somewhat bizarre in light of concrete facts. At the centers of capitalism, during this period that spanned the 1970s–80s, we discover the proliferation of militant organizations at both the centers and peripheries of global capitalism that are proclaiming a fidelity to revolution despite the revisionist contraction of traditional communist parties. In the United States, for example, the RU/RCP-USA was large enough to be classified as a principle security threat by the FBI[2] and was embedded in a larger movement that was far more significant than the New Left.[3] More importantly, the anti-revisionist movement in the peripheries provided the basis, though limited, for the most vital Maoist movement today: Charu Majumdar's Communist Party India (Marxist-Leninist), the first Naxal people's war communist organization in India, was the anti-revisionist party that would be the basis of those organizations that would eventually unite to become today's CPI (Maoist). In this peripheral chaos of the New Communist Movement we can also locate the communists in Turkey who would found the TKP/ML and launch their own people's war, as well as the Afghanistan anti-revisionist movement that would serve as a precursor to today's CmPA.

As the RIM statement mentioned frequently in this book implies, any communism that does not accept Maoism is in some shape or form a type of revisionism in that it rejects the unfolding science of revolution. The problem, though, is understanding precisely what this new type of anti-revisionism means due to the very fact that it seems to *revise* this doctrine by adding the stage of Maoism. In other words, if past anti-revisionist communisms defined themselves primarily on the politics of defending the boundaries of Marxism-Leninism (though often qualified, in order to proclaim their anti-revisionism, along the political line of *Mao Zedong Thought*), then how can a new anti-revisionism that *revises* the terrain with the conceptual cipher of *Maoism* be philo-sophically feasible? The point I am re-emphasizing here, then, is that the moment of rupture is also a moment of continuity and that we can only understand these two moments as part of the same dialectical tension: the rupture *is* continuity; the continuity *is* rupture.

When a theoretical rupture emerges in the midst of a revolu-tionary movement then it should be understood as also being a moment of continuity. As I have hopefully made clear by this point, the core of Marxism is concerned with the necessity of class revolution. Thus, it logically follows, based on this foundational premise, that the only way in which Marxism can be developed theoretically is in the crucible of class revolution. Continuity with a practice that amounts to the rejection of concretely making revolution, then, is not at all continuous with the primary axiom of historical materialism: class revolution is the motor of history. Indeed, as the Afghan Maoists have argued:

> rupturing from "elements that are wrong, one-sided and unscientific," and weeding out the previous wrong under-

standings of Marxism... first of all requires emphasizing the foundation of a correct, comprehensive and scientific kernel. Without this axiomatic understanding, Marxism cannot save its scientific kernel. In other words, a firm emphasis on the scientific kernel scientifically means a firm emphasis on the continuation of this science.[4]

Therefore, it is worth emphasizing that we need to understand a significant theoretical rupture in a given science as also a rupture that preserves the science's general continuity. If I have emphasized this point too much, it is because I think it is important to comprehend the dialectical relationship between continuity and rupture so as to understand why Marxism-Leninism-Maoism sees itself as the current synthesis of revolutionary communism: a chain of theoretical ruptures, grasped by assessing world-historical revolutions, that is also a chain of continuity in that each moment of rupture has become such a moment by applying the universal concepts of the previous moments to its particular contexts and, in this application, has maintained a continuity with the revolutionary basis of the science.

It is my contention, then, that the failure to cognize the relationship between rupture and continuity produces theoretical dead-ends. That is, to highlight rupture at the expense of continuity, or vice versa, is to break from the fundamental premise of historical materialism. If Marxism is indeed a science then it must be open to the future; to declare that we know everything about the world, and that science has solved all truths, is not a very scientific assessment. To be open to the future in a scientific manner requires the acceptance of a developmental procedure because no science develops according to transient principles that are invented for spurious reasons. There is a reason why a given scientific paradigm is accepted as *scientific* and why other possible paradigms are not; if such a reason did not exist, then occult explanations of phenomena would be accepted as scientific. Thus, a science that is open to the future, and open to moments of theoretical rupture, is open only according to a concept of scientific continuity that delimits the meaning of this rupture. At the same time, any given rupture sheds light on the meaning of continuity. Again, both rupture and continuity are necessary for understanding the development of Marxism: to focus on one and not the other is to step outside of the boundaries drawn by the science.

To speak of ruptures without continuity, then, is to speak of unscientific and nebulous theorizing that is incapable of developing revolutionary science because it denies that there is anything continuous to develop. After all, the concept of rupture becomes rather banal if one does not accept that there is a continuity that provides this rupture with meaning. That is, outside of rejecting that there is such a thing as continuity, these moments of theoretical rupture are pointless if they do not relate to the problematic of continuity. The logical result of a position that emphasizes rupture at the expense of continuity is the presumption that history lacks clarity and revolutionary moments, all of which are unique ruptures, cannot be rationally understood as revolutionary if there is nothing continuous with which to judge their revolutionary credentials. Emphasizing continuity means emphasizing the fact that every rupture is part of an unfolding science. No science develops according to unqualified ruptures that erupt from a cognitive abyss to annihilate the history to which they belong.

But to speak of continuity without rupture is equally unscientific because every science develops, sometimes in great leaps and bounds, due to moments of theoretical rupture. Hence, to demand a pure continuity that attempts to preserve a tradition where everything the saints of Marxism said or did was and is correct produces a pitiable orthodoxy. A science is only a science insofar as it rejects dogmatism and, in its occasional and great moments of heterodoxy, preserves the very foundations upon which it depends. As noted in the second chapter, this obsessive focus on revolutionary continuity is its own form of revisionism even if it labels itself as anti-revisionist: dogmato-revisionism, the point where dogmatic fidelity to the words and actions of previous revolutionaries undermines the necessity of revolutionary creativity.

Creativity is thus important but creativity should manifest within the boundaries prescribed by history: that is, a creativity understood according to the strictures of the science. While it might be the case that it is creative and "undogmatic" to theorize in a manner that rejects these boundaries and the supposed strictures demanded by historical materialism, such creativity belongs in the fine arts and is rather useless when it comes to the sciences. At best this kind of creativity can pique the imagination and thus spur scientific thought forward; at worst it leads to muddle-headed para-scientific conjectures.[5] The astrologist might be more imaginative than the astronomer, but it is only the creativity of the latter that produces meaning.

Hence, a new return to anti-revisionism will embrace the continuity of revolutionary theory in the very moment of its rupture. For revisionism possesses its own dialectic of continuity-rupture where every "creative" revisionist development declares fidelity to the rational kernel of revisionism: a peaceful co-existence with capitalism. We should thus understand that there is always a tension between revisionism and anti-revisionism and that this contradiction will produce, as symptoms, various dogmatic and eclectic theories on both sides.

Dialectic of Revisionism and Anti-Revisionism

Revolutionary science is thus defined by the principal contradiction of revisionism and anti-revisionism. Marxist theory, then, organically connected to communist movements, will always be affected by this principal contradiction. The anti-revisionist Marxism-Leninism that went by the name "Maoism" has taught us, though in a manner that we now know is incomplete, the importance of this contradiction. As Badiou wrote in his anti-revisionist Marxist-Leninist period:

> The combative Marxist core of the working class is deter-mined by the new revisionist bourgeoisie. This is dialectical determination in the strong sense... In the struggle to purify itself of this, the proletariat *unmasks*... the part of itself that is engaged in revisionism, and posits it as an integral part of the external antagonistic term.[6]

Revisionism is an immanent danger for the revolutionary movement; anti-revisionism is an immanent struggle within this movement so as to constantly redefine the movement's basis. What is meant by "revision" here is a revision of the basis of Marxist theory, that which makes Marxism properly Marxism: the theory of class struggle. When Marxist theory is altered so as to argue that class struggle is no longer necessary, that class revolution is not the motive force of history and that social change can be brought about by a peaceful co-existence between classes (through rational debates, legal reform movements, etc.) then we find ourselves in a theoretical terrain that is no longer Marxist because it is a terrain that already exists, the terrain of liberalism. We will return to the meaning of "revisionist" itself in a later section; what matters at this point is to understand that an opportunistic rejection of the Marxist theory of class struggle that brands itself with the name "Marxist" is always a possibility with each and every creative adaptation of Marxist theory to particular contexts.

Here we have an interesting unity of opposites: to propose an anti-revisionist politics one must be aware of the immanence of revisionism, even within one's own self. Without revisionism there can be no anti-revisionism and vice versa; revolutionary theory develops by constant lines of demarcation, a process

Badiou calls *scission* that "reconvokes—repeats—the space of [revolutionary] placement".[7]

The theory produced by the Maoist rupture is a theory that is conscious of this contradiction, highlighting it as a dialectical tension that mirrors the universal social contradiction of bourgeoisie and proletariat. No theory, after all, is produced "in a vacuum, but [is produced] in a society in which classes exist, and it is possible for bourgeois ideology, the force of old habits and international revisionist trends of thought to affect and poison" the individuals, tendencies, organizations, and parties responsible for theoretical production.[8]

Hence, class struggle will affect even Marxist theory where the ruling ideas of the ruling class will be unconsciously (and sometimes consciously) adopted by some Marxists in a manner that sounds Marxist but is at the same time a rejection of the basis of the science, the necessity of class revolution. Mao often spoke and wrote about the class struggle that existed within the party itself, a "line struggle" between opportunism and revolution. Therefore, within the communist movement as a whole and from the moment it emerged on the historical stage, there has always been a contradiction between revisionism and anti-revisionism: sometimes the former emerges in response to the latter, and sometimes vice versa; the two poles of the contradiction remain locked in an antagonistic struggle that will only be resolved when class struggle is relegated to the past.

In the now-failed socialist societies of Russia and China revisionist trends emerged to eventually reinstate capitalism, and the latter revolutionary context waged a valiant struggle in an attempt to defeat this trend: the Cultural Revolution. Conversely, anti-revisionism at the centers of capitalism emerged in response to a revisionist trend that had consumed the movement. In both instances there was an explosion of theory and practice that was either revisionist or anti-revisionist; in both instances revisionism was victorious. But whatever the outcome

171

this historical insight was clear: just as there can be no proletariat without a bourgeoisie, there can be no revolutionary science without revisionist distortions; just as there can be no bourgeoisie without a proletariat, there can be no revisionist collaboration without the challenge, however small, of anti-revisionism.

This contradiction will produce various dogmatic and eclectic theoretical iterations, rigid orthodoxies and wild heterodoxies that have no concrete basis. While it might at first appear as if dogmatism and eclecticism are themselves a contradiction, they are better understood as characteristic symptoms of the contradiction between revisionism and anti-revisionism. In some ways it is now possible to speak of dogmato-eclecticism and eclecto-dogmatism: there will be those who treat their eclecticism as an unquestioned fact, believing without scientific proof that incoherence is a virtue; there will be those who will incoherently mix-and-match every orthodoxy.

In any case, Maoism has theorized the contradiction between revisionism and anti-revisionism as a significant obstacle to revolution. According to Maoism, the ideas that remain the most compelling within any revolutionary movement will necessarily be the ideas inherited from the ruling classes that such a movement is seeking to combat. That is, since the people engaged in making revolution have been socialized and educated in the society that such a revolution seeks to overthrow, the ideological apparatus of this society (and thus the ideas inherited from the ruling classes of this society) will linger as a "nightmare upon the brain" of a revolutionary movement. We cannot avoid slipping back into the ways of thinking and patterns of behavior that served as props for the society that we seek to overthrow; we will often unconsciously adopt this way of seeing the world, though we might not think so at the time, despite our best intentions to build a new world. This lingering ideology will obstruct any attempt to build socialism even if it is given a "socialist" form (i.e. a defense of the bourgeois division of labor by appealing to the maxim "each according to their abilities").

Revisionism thus emerges due to the inability to overcome bourgeois ideology, which is terribly compelling because we have inherited it from the past, and anti-revisionism simultaneously emerges to combat this trend. Within a given movement, no matter how radical, there will always be a struggle between those who want to shake off the residue of ruling-class ideology and those who do not accept that this residue is distorting the movement. The clash between revisionism and anti-revisionism is inevitable; it is as much of a historical truism as class struggle itself. Indeed, it is a reflection of class struggle.

Hence the Cultural Revolution in China dared to claim that the class struggle was still alive within socialism but not because of external pressure: the class struggle remained because it was sublimated within the superstructure and well-intentioned communists could still be drawn back into the vicissitudes of bourgeois ideology; capitalism could be restored due to the victory of the "capitalist roaders" during the stage of socialist class struggle. Although the GPCR failed to accomplish its aims, and socialism was obviously undermined in China, this is explained by the theory itself, and the attempt to defeat the unavoidable revisionist trend was too little and too late.

Based on the assessment of the successes and failures of the Chinese Revolution, Marxism-Leninism-Maoism theorizes that the struggle against revisionism must be more thorough than what was previously attempted. There must be a cultural revolution, a conscious interior revolution where line struggle is embraced, from the initiation of a revolutionary movement. Thus, there must be a new return to anti-revisionism: a more thorough and comprehensive understanding of revisionism capable of wrenching it from the dogmatism into which it is often ensnared since the possibility of revisionism will remain universal.

Revisionism as a Universal Problem

In order to understand a new return to anti-revisionism (a return that should tell us something about the revolutionary continuity of Maoism) we need to appreciate the importance of anti-revisionist communism in general. Regardless of its dogmatic and/or eclectic lapses, anti-revisionist communism has always been necessary for the preservation of the radical kernel of Marx's theory. So while it is true that there are moments where this revolutionary tendency lapses into dogmatic dead-ends or produces muddle-headed speculation (and while it is true that such lapses should be combated) it is also true that a revolutionary rejection of revisionism is always important and that the main hallmarks of revisionism that must be resisted will never disappear. Indeed, what the history of revolutionary communism has called *revisionism* (that is, something that revises the basis of revolution and, in this revision, undermines revolution) often possesses the same universal applicability, but in a negative aspect, as the positive elements of revolutionary science: just as there is a science of revolution there is, perhaps, a science of revisionism.

Both Luxemburg and Lenin recognized the parliamentarianism of Bernstein and then Kautsky as revisionism. Here was a moment where the ideologues of a significant revolutionary party argued that reform could be the path of revolution, that revolutionary parties could accomplish socialism by participating in bourgeois politics, and that a peaceful co-existence with capitalism was possible to achieve socialism. Communism thus renewed itself as Marxism-Leninism against this trend; it was this trend that produced the collapse of the Second International and the degeneration of Germany's Social Democratic Party that led to the crushing of those working-class rebellions represented by Rosa Luxemburg and Karl Leibknecht. There is no point in going into detail about this significant and originary moment of revisionism that produced the slur of "social democracy" and convicted this type of politics of the revisionism with which it was accused: for the vast majority of communists, history has vindicated the analyses of Luxemburg and Lenin in this regard.

And yet, regardless of this recognition of a theory of revisionism (i.e. parliamentary reform over a party dedicated to revolution), its shibboleth again reared its head during the Khrushchev period of the Soviet Union where a "peaceful co-existence with capitalism" was proclaimed and world revolution denounced. This proclamation was what prompted the Chinese communists to write *Long Live Leninism!* and initiate the "Great Debate" with the Soviet Union. The theory of a "peaceful co-existence" was precisely the same theory as Bernstein's original moment of revisionism: that socialism could be achieved by playing a game defined by capitalist rules without smashing the class basis of these rules.

My aim here is not to provide a thorough philosophical investigation of the meaning of revisionism but simply to indicate its importance as an accepted concept within the international communist movement. One would be hard-pressed to find a self-proclaimed Marxist today who explicitly agrees with Bernstein and Kautsky's articulation of revolution through reformism: even Trotskyists, who generally despise Maoism, side with Luxemburg and Lenin against the Bernsteinian moment of reformist collaboration. If I have gone further and drawn a logical connection between the Soviet Union under Khrushchev and the previous period of revisionism it is simply to point out that the latter took, as its theoretical departing point, the same assumptions as the former and that it was this latter revisionism that defined the emergence of the past anti-revisionist movement.

The point is to demonstrate that what has been historically understood as revisionism possesses a universal continuity, even if there is also something of a rupture between Khrushchev and Bernstein, and that this continuity is based on the liquidation of a revolutionary line: the necessity of breaking with capitalism through a social revolution is replaced with the possibility of peacefully co-existing and producing a social revolution through other (namely *parliamentary*) means. Against this trend it has always been necessary to maintain a revolutionary ideology: the ruling class will not simply abdicate the historical stage because it has been out-maneuvered through elections; it has a class power that needs to be smashed.

This fundamental revisionism emerges, again and again, in each and every epoch. If it was originally a problem in the Second International with Bernstein and Kautsky, it became even more of a problem after the Third International with Khrushchev's denunciation of world revolution. Now we can discover echoes of this problematic: revisionism has not gone away and it can be understood as a problem that has universally affected communist movements. Indeed, the fundamental insight of historical materialism, which has not been and cannot be abandoned through all moments of rupture, is the necessity of class revolution. Thus, revisionism must be understood as that which undermines the very basis of revolutionary science: the necessity of revolution itself.

Revisionism Remains

Revisionism will necessarily remain a problem for every epoch in which class revolution persists. In many ways it is a default ideology, especially at the centers of capitalism, because one of the ruling ideas of the ruling class that has become normative is that peaceful struggles for change are superior to revolution. Revisionism has historically crept into the communist movement when Marxist organizations and individuals have argued that it is possible to accomplish class revolution through the peaceful means of electoral democracy, through pursuing an overall strategy of working within bourgeois parties that are believed to be working class, or even through the economism of union struggles where radicalism tied to one's job and liberal rights for workers ends up undermining the necessity of pursuing an overall revolutionary movement.

The reason we often default to revisionism is because, I would like to suggest, we are socialized to believe that the boundaries drawn by capitalism are eternal and that it is dangerous to transgress them. Hence, though we often speak of revolution, there is a tendency to push the necessity of revolution beyond some distant horizon and focus only on the opportunistic practices of reformism in the meantime.

Such a problem is more widespread at the centers of global imperialism due to the higher level of economic and social privilege that persists in these contexts.[9] Moreover, returning to the problem noted by Clark in the third chapter, since the majority of Marxist and anti-capitalist movements, especially in the global centers, are dominated by students and intellectuals, it does not take very much for this class to be bought off in a manner that allows them to keep their revolutionary politics in theory while advocating revisionist strategies in practice: rights of assembly and speech, book deals, tenure, journalistic positions, etc. are ways in which the radical elements of the petty-bourgeois intelligentsia can be encouraged to adopt an opportunist political line.

I am not interested in proving the historical problem of revisionism in significant detail; I am simply describing what I take to be a given. My concern is not to prove the existence and persistence of revisionism and opportunism (which would be akin to proving the existence and persistence of class struggle, a book in itself) but to examine it as a given problematic in relation to Maoism. So the question, then, is not whether revisionism is a problem but how does Marxism-Leninism-Maoism respond to this problem in a manner that is more thorough than other theoretical trajectories.

Anti-Revisionist Emergence

Maoism emerged as a stage of revolutionary science in the midst of a people's war. That is, it emerged as a theory amidst a large-scale rejection of the reformist road to communism: the PCP boycotted the elections and embarked on the path of class revolution. Maoism was declared Maoism with the understanding that it was theory with a strategic line that was anti-reformist. Thus, while it was a moment of rupture with Marxism-Leninism, it was also a moment of continuity in that it placed itself within the tradition (following Lenin and Mao) of rejecting any strategy of peaceful co-existence. Indeed, the PCP rejected this revisionist strategy in terms that were, admittedly, quite blunt:

> The masses clamor to organize the rebellion and therefore the Party, its leaders, cadre and militants today have a peremptory obligation, a destiny: to organize the disorganized power of the masses, and this can only be done with arms in hand. We must arm the masses bit by bit, part by part, until the general arming of the people. When this goal is reached, there shall be no exploitation on Earth.[10]

Of course we can critique the apparent fetishism of violence in the above statement, a possible problem that may have led to this revolutionary organization's degeneration. I am not trying to defend the position in which the PCP ended up (a tragic failure that resulted in innumerable violent eruptions, purges, and breakdowns of the mass-line), nor trying to defend the reactionary critiques of the PCP (where the Truth and Reconciliation Committee, a dubious organization at best, tried to pin most of the ex-officio killings during the Emergency on the PCP), but simply noting that the above statement seems to cross the line of the necessity of violence to the fetishization of violence by claiming that the mass-line is accomplished, and exploitation

178

is eradicated, the moment the revolutionary masses are armed. At the same time, however, this statement is important because it is a statement that, in the moment of adopting Maoism, is a clear rejection of revisionism. And this rejection is clear when the PCP goes on to assert in the same document:

> Basing himself on Chairman Mao, who generalized revolutionary violence as the universal law for the conquest of power and who established that the principal form of struggle is the armed struggle and the principal form of organization is the armed forces, and that before the outbreak of a war all the struggles and organizations should serve to prepare it, Chairman Gonzalo teaches us that in mass work the struggle for power and the struggle for revindications are two sides of the same coin, with the struggle for Power being the first and foremost demand of the masses. [...] Organize the masses so that they can go beyond what is permitted by the existing legal order, so that they struggle to destroy the old order and not to maintain it. This is accomplished by use of the three instruments of the revolution: the Party where the few converge, the [Revolutionary/People's] Army with more participants, and the new State/Front which is the base which progressively accumulates the masses through leaps. [...] In this way the tradition of electoral fronts, which the revisionists and opportunists apply to channel the struggle of the peasantry and to divert the masses in the cities from not seizing power through war, is destroyed.[11]

Therefore, based on the above quote, Maoism was understood, from the very moment it was theorized, as the next stage of revolutionary science (for this document was written in the same year in which the PCP put forward the first significant theorization of Marxism-Leninism-Maoism), as being a rejection of revisionist practice. Following the PCP, the RIM adopted the same anti-revisionist ideology of prioritizing the strategy of actually making revolution over a strategy of reformism, and, following the RIM, organizations such as the Communist Party of Nepal (Maoist) and the Communist Party of India (Maoist) would embark on their own people's wars.

The point, then, is to understand Maoism as a theory that returns us to the necessity of making revolution, and declares itself in continuity with the past world-historical revolutions, as a fundamental necessity. After all, there are many Marxist tendencies that, when pushed, will agree that class revolution is a goal (they may even provide some formulaic theory, derived from 1917, about revolution) and thus do not openly base themselves upon the revisionist practice of reformism. But there is most often a gap between theory and practice: when the necessity of revolution is pushed beyond the horizon of the foreseeable future, transformed into a fantasy; many organizations have no strategy of pursuing this revolution except to tell us that "it will come when everything is place" and, in the meantime, engage in a generally reformist strategy, it is worth wondering whether revisionism has been accomplished in essence if not in form. If the most important aspect of revolutionary communism now is the strategy required to defeat capitalism, then it is quite telling that this strategy has remained under-theorized by the general Marxist left.

Since Maoism emerged as a theory in the midst of a revolutionary movement, and further developed in successive revolutionary movements, then it should be able to tell us more about what it means to make revolution, and thus to reject revisionist practices, than those tendencies that have never actively pursued revolution in any apparent manner. Here also is a theoretical gauge for those organizations who would now name themselves *Maoist*: if they are not actively attempting to pursue revolution, to strategize a method based on their particular contexts for overcoming capitalism, then it does not appear as if the name, due to its concept, should logically apply. Furthermore, those organizations who name themselves *Maoist* based on their agitation for revolution elsewhere also have no logical reason to adopt this name: at best they are only anti-imperialists; at worst they are refusing to address the necessity that Maoism demands.

The Anti-Revisionist Revision

I want to argue that the necessity for continuity with the revolutionary core of communist science explains the moment of rupture. In order to clear out the dogmatic and reformist tendencies of Marxism (the toothless Marxisms that provide no strategy for making revolution and pursue only reformist methods in the hope of a revolution somewhere and someday beyond the horizon) there needs to be an epistemic break with the previous limits of revolutionary science because they reached their revolutionary limits. To declare fidelity to the revolutionary core of communism demands a new stage that sweeps out the dust of the previous epoch and, in this sweeping, reasserts the demand for revolution in a way that is hopefully fresh and relevant.

Thus, we can speak of a revolutionary revision of communist science, gleaned through class struggle, that is simultaneously anti-revisionism. A revision on one level can simultaneously be an anti-revisionism on another level, and again we need only to look at the history of the "hard" sciences to grasp how this contradiction makes sense. Again, the Einsteinian paradigm revised the terrain once dominated by the Newtonian paradigm but, in doing so, declared fidelity to an anti-revisionist physics. For there was indeed a quandary amongst the physicists of the time regarding the questions the Newtonian worldview could not answer, and all attempts to answer these questions according to spiritualist and mystified categories were attempts that demonstrated a fundamental revisionism because they abandoned the core principles of this living science. The rupture produced by the Einsteinian moment saved the basis of physics from a malaise that was being produced by the boundaries of Newtonianism: it produced a new terrain by revising the boundaries of the previous terrain but, in this moment of production, also saved the basis of the science.

In the unfolding narrative of any living science (what Simone De Beauvoir categorized as *ambiguity* or what Alain Badiou called a *truth procedure*) moments of rupture are simultaneously moments of continuity. The rupture preserves the continuity; simultaneously, the continuity informs the rupture. Sometimes, in order to declare fidelity to the core principles of a science, a rupture is required: on one level theory is rearticulated and revised, and all dogmatisms abandoned, in order to prevent the deeper revision (that is the abandonment) of the basis upon which this science is possible. If a set of problems within a given science cannot be solved then there are two options: an abandonment of this science's trajectory and a rejection of its core premises (i.e. abandon physics for spiritualism in order to seek a solution in superstition), or an abandonment of a specific scientific paradigm in order to reboot the core premises within a new theoretical region.

At the same time, however, the moment of rupture is capable of explaining the failure to maintain continuity with the scientific field. For in the moment of rupture the developing science rearticulates what is necessary, given the requirements of the emergent terrain, to develop the core logic of this science so as to avoid revisionism: if this criteria is not met, then revisionism follows. Thus, if a physicist working on problems within the Einsteinian paradigm decides to return to the errors of the Newtonian paradigm then they are working in discontinuity with the science: the backwards movement is thus foreclosed as an erroneous (that is, revisionist) movement.

So what does this problematic of rupture mean for revolutionary science?

First and fundamentally: a theoretical rupture, when it is historically possible, is necessary in order to declare fidelity to the basis of the science, the primacy of class struggle. Leninism was a rupture from the Marxism of its time, initially appearing as heterodox, that was at the same time more in-line with the foundations of Marxism than those adherents who went to great lengths to find precedence for their revisionism in the collected works of Marx and Engels. A rupture, then, in order to maintain scientific continuity.

Secondly: all failures to pursue the openings produced by these ruptures will result in a failure to achieve continuity with the core principles of the science. To be an anti-Leninist after the science of revolution was renewed by the theoretical rupture produced by the Bolshevik Revolution was to be anti-Marxist. And now, after the assessment of the experience of the Chinese Revolution, to be an anti-Maoist is tantamount to the same revisionism.

Thirdly: all moments of revisionism on the part of those who even go so far as to veil themselves in the name of the rupture can be held to account by the very theory they fail to represent, just as Marx and Engels' flawed insights about the non-European world could be critiqued according to the logic of their own method. This is more than abstract philosophical speculation since it concerns very concrete facts. Some of today's Maoist movements, ever since the concept's emergence as a scientific stage, have indeed faltered and proven their revisionism by their rejection of the Maoist rupture, and such a rejection is simultaneously also a rejection of revolutionary continuity.

The failed people's wars that have veiled themselves as Maoist can be explained according to Maoism; their failure to pursue the very Maoism they adopted explains their failure to remain in continuity with the core principles of the science. Take, for example, the failure of the Maoist movement in Nepal which, in its tragedy, caused innumerable revisionists to gloat: was this failure the fact that they named themselves Maoist or the fact that they refused to pursue and apply Maoism? For Maoism claims there can be no collaboration with imperialism, that there is no peaceful road to communism, and that a line struggle in the party could possibly lead to the enshrinement of opportunistic politics that reject revolution in favor of peaceful co-existence. The failure of the people's war in Nepal is thus a failure to pursue Maoism and, in this failure, the pursuit of a revisionist politics.

Thus, Maoism can explain the failures of even those who adopt its name. It does not inoculate its adherents from revisionism because revisionism is always a problem; it only explains the terms of revisionism and those who abandon its historical assessment will indeed find themselves dislocated from revolutionary continuity.

Thinking Beyond Opportunism

Of course, any critique of revisionism can always be dismissed by revisionists under the rubric of *ultra-leftism*. Revisionists believe that the cardinal sin of communism is not opportunism but "infantile ultra-leftism" and, basing themselves on a selective reading of Lenin's analysis of ultra-leftism, will argue that any criticism of revisionist practice (any open demand for a revolutionary politics that produces militant practice) is the very ultra-leftism that threatens the left. Adventurism, practices that place the masses in danger, and anarchism are seen as the most significant obstacles for the Marxist left, not the more prevalent opportunism that has seeped into the movement.

Although Lenin's *Left-Wing Communism: an Infantile Disorder* has become something of a Bible for the modern revisionists who attempt to veil their opportunism in revolutionary trappings, it is worth noting that even this polemic blamed "ultra-leftism" on the "sin" of opportunism. That is, Lenin did not consider ultra-leftism to be the primary problem facing socialism but only a reactive symptom of the fundamental problematic of revisionism/

opportunism. Thus, it is not "ultra-leftism" that by itself ruins movements, but the practice of revisionism and opportunism that often produces "ultra-leftist" problems as the wages of its original sin.

Moreover, Lenin's screed against ultra-leftism notwithstanding, we need to recognize that even those revisionists who cite Lenin would have to also castigate Lenin and every revolutionary for being the very "ultra-leftists" they despise. The point, here, is that anyone who rejects revolutionary praxis will see the very practice of revolution as "ultra-left" since it is to the left of their rightist commitments. Once a reformist line is misconceived as revolutionary, anything to the left of this line must necessarily be interpreted as ultra-left. Such an interpretation must designate all revolutionaries as ultra-leftist militants because anyone who rejects reformism is necessarily heretical.

Maoism's significance, then, is amplified by the general revisionist malaise that is terrified of anything that openly speaks of making revolution while simultaneously rejecting the practice of reformism. Every successful moment of militant agitation will be dismissed as ultra-leftist, every failed moment of capitulation will be used against Maoism as evidence of its limitations.

Here we discover a moment of rupture that is also a moment of continuity: a rupture with the old practices, and dogmatic ways of citing past revolutionary texts, that have devolved into a lack of revolutionary praxis; a continuity with the necessity of making revolution which has been the main concern of communism since its inception. This is an important philosophical point, implied in the previous section: at certain historical conjunctures theoretical rupture is necessary in order to declare fidelity to revolutionary continuity. (This is why, since the very beginning of this book, I have spoken of rupture and continuity as a contradiction that is also one of dialectical unity; I have attempted to clarify this point since it needs to be grasped in order to understand the necessity of Maoism as part of an unfolding science.) The focus on the necessity of making revolution, which currently is only being pursued in a unified and systematic manner by Maoist parties throughout the world, in a manner that ruptures from the inactive state of revolutionary praxis demonstrated by other Marxist tendencies, is what makes Maoism a live option.

In a context where every attempt to pursue a militant communism is denounced as ultra-leftist, a rupture is indeed required. This denunciation implies that mainstream Marxism has found itself trapped in an opportunism that it is no longer capable of recognizing as opportunism. Indeed, such opportunism is defended as correct praxis by citing Lenin and other past revolutionaries out of historical context and, by relying on the boundaries of previous Marxist paradigms, failing to abide by what is primarily required of Marxism: making revolution.

Maoism, then, challenges us to think beyond the opportunism that has crept into Marxism. Maoism demands, by the very nature of its emergence, a return to the revolutionary core of Marxism; it is a theoretical development based on making revolution. Such a challenge, then, can only be met with hostility on the part of that Marxist tradition which has been conditioned by the limits drawn by capitalism's so-called "end of history" and even many who will define themselves as Maoist will shrink from this challenge. Ironically, and as aforementioned, these Maoists will be held to account by the very theory they claim to endorse.

Notes

1. For example, Don Hammerquist, in his review of *The Communist Necessity*, claims that this worldwide anti-revisionist movement was insignificant.

2. See, for example, Aaron J. Leonard and Conor A. Gallagher's *Heavy Radicals*.

3. See Max Elbaum's *Revolution in the Air*.

4. Communist (Maoist) Party of Afghanistan, *A Response to the RCP-USA's May 1st 2012 Letter*.

5. To be fair to the history and practice of the fine arts, though, it is probably also the case that a creativity that is ignorant of the history of artistic practice results in the production of banal and derivative art.

6. Badiou, *Theory of the Subject*, 9.

7. Ibid.

8. Communist Party of China, 51.

9. This is why Lenin argued that opportunism was the default consciousness of workers at the centers of capitalism due to what he called *a labor aristocracy*. Although the theory of the labor aristocracy has fallen into disrepute amongst Marxist academics at the centers of capitalism, I would argue that it is still a necessary concept and worth grasping.

10. Communist Party of Peru, *The Mass Line*.

11. Ibid.

Chapter 6

Organization and Strategy

Class struggle is not merely an economic struggle, it is a struggle between the oppressed and the oppressor for control over the main means of production and the political life of society. It includes the struggle in economic, political, social and ideological spheres, and the key aspect of revolutionary class struggle is not economic struggle but political struggle—the struggle for the seizure of political power.

—Anuradha Ghandy, *The Caste Question Returns*

Beyond the Fossilized Vanguard

The emergence of Maoism, if it is in continuity and rupture with past moments of revolutionary science, must also mean the (re)emergence of the vanguard party as the primary locus of anti-capitalist organizing, and thus the necessary reconceptualization of revolutionary strategy. Here the point is not that the concept of the party of the advanced guard crystallized by Lenin's *What Is to Be Done?* ever vanished from the historical stage during the disintegration of actually-existing socialist regimes in the 1980s; indeed, there remained parties throughout the world that organized according to the Leninist doctrine of praxis. Rather, the point is that Marxism-Leninism-Maoism promises, as it does with certain theoretical questions, a new return to the question of organization and revolutionary praxis: a *return* because it is in continuity with what was universally established by Leninism; *new* because it is also a rupture from past concepts of the vanguard.

There were glimmers of this new return in past iterations of Maoism, in the germinal period of Mao Zedong Thought, where anti-revisionist organizations and ur-Maoist intellectuals obsessed over the promise of a "party of the new type": that is, a party that remains a vanguard party but is not trapped in the structural monolithism, best represented by the Communist Party of the Soviet Union under Stalin, where party cadre were a disciplined "military staff of the proletariat".[1] In the wake of the collapse of the Soviet Union and the subsequent collapse of anti-revisionism, however, there was a failure to produce such a party, despite promises to the contrary: the moment of rupture had not yet come, the declaration of this party of a new type was premature.

Even those party formations organized according to a conception of the party vanguard *against* some nebulous conception of "Stalinism" were burdened by the very same organizational problems Stalin had operationalized. Hence the infamous declarations, of multiple ortho-Trotskyist parties that had degenerated into cultish sects, that the collapse of socialism in the former Soviet Union was due to a failure to properly appreciate democratic centralism: if we could just tinker with how revolutionary praxis was centralized then we would discover, like the alchemical equation of transforming lead into gold, a perfected vanguard that could avoid all of the errors of "Stalinist bureaucracy". For these parties still resembled, though in a microscopic and inverted manner, precisely the kind of monolithic and top-down formation they sought to avoid. Here there could be no rupture with the existing concept of the party vanguard; it was simply a dogmatic reassertion of a Leninism *before* it was tested and reached its limitations under Stalin.

At the same time, and despite the continuing struggles of those who refused to reject the Leninist conception of the revolutionary party, there was the emergence of a general movementism that was premised on a complete rejection of vanguard-style politics. Since the theory of the vanguard had fossilized under Stalin (and, inversely, under Trotsky), and since capitalism's "end-of-history" discourse had declared a moratorium on this kind of organizing, innumerable anti-capitalists gravitated towards a post-modern and anarchist manner of organizing where revolutionary parties that still appreciated the concept of the vanguard were treated as authoritarian and thus suspect. After all, if one was to interpret the theory of the party vanguard through the lens of Stalin (which was its most popularized articulation) then it was clear that the logical result would be a monolithic and absolutist top-down style of organizing.

We have reached a conjuncture where movementism, which was mainly an organizational trend at the centers of capitalism, has reached its limits and failed to deliver anything useful for an anti-capitalist praxis. It has been well over a decade since Seattle and Quebec City; other first-world movementist struggles were little more than tragic echoes of the demise of anti-globalization. Meanwhile, a decade before Seattle and in the third world, we witnessed the reemergence of people's wars that were directed by revolutionary organizations adhering to a model of the vanguard party inherited from Lenin but somewhat transformed by the Maoist rupture.

Hence, we are now living in an era of people's wars, all of which are premised on the necessary existence of a vanguard party. We were even living in this era when first-world anti-capitalists embraced movementism: the PCP was reaching its moment of decline; the CPN (Maoist) was just beginning its people's war. Something new was happening that was not a movementist surrender but that attempted to rearticulate what it would mean to develop a revolutionary vanguard party now, after the failure of actually-existing socialism, according to the theoretical terrain of an emergent Maoism.

Organization as Strategy

The question of organization leads to the question of strategy.[2] After all, the primary reason the theory of the revolutionary party's viability is examined is due to the problematic of making revolution: by what organizational mechanism can capitalism be overthrown? Although the anarchist or autonomist complaints about the "party vanguard" may often concern hierarchy and authoritarianism, these are part of a larger critique regarding how to supersede capitalism. If vanguard parties lead to bureaucracy, authoritarian socialist states, and totalitarianism, then it makes no strategic sense to embrace an organization that will necessarily produce a general strategy that is hampered by these problems.

These complaints regarding the Leninist party are not entirely misguided; we know that the so-called "Stalinist" party was precisely that monolithic entity, described in *Foundations of Leninism*, which demonstrated those problems that concern anarchists and autonomist Marxists. Since I plan to discuss this problem later in this chapter, I simply wish to indicate that any rejection of the Leninist theory of organization on this basis is, rightly or wrongly, driven by strategic considerations. Hence we only speak and debate how best to organize because we are, at the same time, speaking and debating a general strategy of making revolution.

Clearly, due to the history of these debates on organization and the dogmatism that often emerges on all sides, we often lose sight of the primary reason behind whether this or that form of organization is superior. This is not to say that these debates do not forget the strategic justification for whatever position is being argued, only that they tend to make the question of strategy an abstraction: there is often very little talk on how to use an organizational form so as to concretely operationalize a revolutionary strategy, except in the most general terms.[3]

The anarchist and autonomist approaches to organization, perhaps, are necessarily abstract. Premised only on critiquing the errors of vanguard-style organizing, and treating these errors as the telos of any and all Leninist formations, a proposed counter-strategy can only be vague. Movementism, by its very definition, lacks a concrete theorization of strategy: overdetermined by spontaneity, it is forced to accept that there can be no general strategy beyond an incoherent and multidimensional rebellion that will, in defiance of authoritarian totalization and in respect of heterogeneity, spontaneously develop its own strategy in a utopian manner. While there are, of course, anarchist and autonomist tendencies that desire to provide a more coherent organizational form to this movementism, the rejection of a theoretically and practically unified revolutionary party prevents the implementation of a general strategic theory. For if the masses should not be provided with some form of organized leadership, then we are forced to accept the fact that revolutionary strategy must be a spontaneously generated affair.

And yet many Marxists who continue to endorse the Leninist party formation (who are devoted to *What Is to Be Done?* and *The State and Revolution*) often tend to think of strategy in abstract terms despite mocking the anarchists for this very same fact. It is all well and good to defend the superiority of Leninism by pointing to the October Revolution and arguing that, at the very least, your organizational theory has successfully carried through socialist revolutions, whatever their problems; it is another thing to explain how your Leninist-based organization is providing a strategy for making revolution in your social context. Simply claiming that the Leninist theory of organization has proven successful in the past does not mean that a particular Leninist organization will succeed in making revolution just because it bases itself on the same general theory of organization: this is another form of spontaneism since it assumes that, simply by getting the organizational form correct, revolution will necessarily follow.

Hence, it is necessary to always talk about theories of organization in light of theories of strategy; we should also not assume that a decision on the former will spontaneously answer the particular questions of the latter. The Maoist rupture is significant insofar as it has brought the question of strategy (of what a vanguard party is *for* and how to operationalize this *for*) back into the center of debates regarding organization. According to the Maoist terrain it is not enough to focus on the importance of Lenin's theory of the party, re-realizing it according to the Leninist terms (i.e. trade-union and/or spontaneous consciousness is a failure, so a revolutionary party is necessary) and thus reasserting what was already established in theory by 1917. The point is to think further than the Leninist ossification of Marxism, perhaps even recognizing the importance of some anarchist/autonomist critiques, and begin to conceptualize the long promised "party of a new type" that, in its ability to grasp the contradiction of leadership from above and below, will express a concrete theory of actually making revolution.

Towards the "Party of the New Type"

When it comes to the theoretical terrain of Marxism-Leninism, the boundaries of which were described in the third chapter, we can describe the limits of its theory of organization as being marked by the specter of Stalinism. That is, Stalinism is that historical phenomenon that delivered on the promises of Leninism in the only way, understood in retrospect, that was possible: the formation that accomplished revolution, proved as universal by the very fact that the first socialist revolution was accomplished, was one that could not help but become, based on encountering for the first time new contradictions raised by the dictatorship of the proletariat, a monolithic, disciplinarian, top-down structure. Although Trotskyism is a Marxist tendency that rails against the evils of Stalinism and Stalin's supposed betrayal of the Leninist dream, Trotskyism is also that tendency which, locked within a less complete understanding of the terrain of Leninism, refuses to see the meaning of the limits of this terrain because it refuses to recognize that the terrain even possesses a limit. Moreover, Trotskyism erroneously assumes that Stalinism was a betrayal of Leninism when, in actual fact, it was simply an accomplishment of all of Leninism's universal aspects. Trotskyist parties do not promise anything different when it comes to the theory of organization beyond some tinkering with interior concerns.[4]

Maoism, on the other hand, is that which transgresses the limits marked by Stalinism (limits Stalin did not theoretically recognize) and through the process of continuity-rupture opens up the possibility of new methods of organizational praxis. This is why Maoism-qua-Maoism is different from the little Maoisms of yesteryear: these anti-revisionist Marxism-Leninisms still treated the Leninist terrain, haunted by the apparition of Stalinism, as complete in and of themselves but, due to errors made by Stalin and the revisionism produced by the CPSU under Khrushchev, in need of salvation-through-rearticulation. Hence, due to an inability to actually transgress the limits of the Leninist terrain, past Maoisms ended up being unconsciously haunted by a Stalinist manner of organization regardless of the "party of a new type" discourse.

Even the initial emergence of Maoism, though recognizing the possibility of rupture, could not help but be haunted by some of the problems of Stalinism. The PCP, for example, reinscribed the doctrine of the personality cult upon its people's war; the CPN (Maoist) conceived of "Prachanda Path". Even still, these instances were ruptural openings in that, despite being weighed down by the nightmares of the past, they were consciously aware of the need to overstep the limits marked by Stalin and in some important ways succeeded. Regardless of their problems, proved now by these revolutionary movements' disintegration, the organizational development of the people's wars in Peru and Nepal still demonstrated the emergence of a party of the new type in their application of the theory of the mass-line.

The point, here, is not that the party of the new type has been accomplished but that it is in the process of being accomplished.

More importantly: this accomplishment is only possible if the terrain of Leninism is actually transgressed; otherwise we will be pulled back into a way of building a revolutionary party that accepts as a priori, without any conscious reflection, the theory of organization best conceptualized by Stalin (or, conversely, by Trotsky) that was the only possible result of Leninism without further rupture.

Socialism from Below?

Attempts to transcend the limitations of the Leninist-qua-Leninist party formation, without abandoning Leninism per se, have most often led to theoretical impasses that have had little or no practical or strategic application. Take, for example, Hal Draper's theory of *socialism from below* which is now treated by some post-Trotskyists as a way to square Leninism with the movementist circle. Leaving aside the fact that Draper, like many Trotskyists in the US, was utterly marginal and disconnected from the anti-revisionist movement of the 1960s when he wrote *The Two Souls of Socialism*, even leaving aside the fact of his colonial chauvinism that allowed him to celebrate Zionism as some twisted form of national self-determination, Draper was at least insightful enough to recognize the limitations of Leninist orthodoxy (which he thought of as "Stalinism" or "neo-Stalinism") and thus identify the problem of *socialism from above* or *socialism from outside*:

> The relatively privileged position of managerial, bureaucratic and intellectual-flunky elements in the Russian collectivist system can be pointedly contrasted with the situation in the West, where these same elements are subordinated to the owners of capital and manipulators of wealth. At this point the appeal of the Soviet system of statified [sic] economy coincides with the historic appeal of middle-class socialisms, to disgruntled class-elements of intellectuals, technologists,

scientists and scientific employees, administrative bureaucrats and organization men of various types, who can most easily identify themselves with a new ruling class based on state power rather than on money power and ownership, and therefore visualize themselves as the new men of power in a non-capitalist but elitist set up.[5]

Draper's analysis, though relatively confused due to its separation from the key social struggles of the time, echoes the more concrete analysis made by Tom Clark in the third chapter,[6] and the explanation of the monolithism of the Leninist party made in this chapter. In response to this problem of socialism from above, where socialism is imposed by a party that is the general staff of the proletariat, Draper advocates socialism from below where the working class itself will produce its Leninist party. Anything else would be elitism, bureaucratism, and the imposition of socialism from the outside. Turning Marx and Engels' polemical statements about the "self-emancipation of the proletariat" into a theoretical concept, socialism from below is the theory that the imposition of a party is not required but that, since the working class already possesses its own organized institutions (i.e. mainly trade unions) the trick is to allow these, under the leadership of the grass-roots union leadership, to autonomously and spontaneously develop into a revolutionary organization.

As with most theories that are dislocated from concrete struggle and mass movements, Draper's theory, in its desire to avoid a top-down Leninism, results in the practice of tailism that conceptualizes itself as a bottom-up Leninism where the vanguard will be built by the unionized working class. Moreover, while socialism formally separates itself from the traditional Leninist party formation, it substantially reifies one of the key Leninist orthodoxies: the unionized working class as the most advanced section of the proletariat (due to the fact that they are organized) and thus the theory of insurrection as the strategy for making revolution. Setting aside the orthodoxy of the insurrectionary strategy (or "the October Road") until a later point in this chapter, it is worth briefly noting that Draper's assumption about the unionized working class, and thus much of what he would write in *Marxism and the Trade Unions*,[7] was politically suspect at the time he was writing. One only needs to examine the Civil Rights movement and the height of Black Nationalist struggles to realize that unions could be, and in many cases were, counter-revolutionary in that they were often filled with an economically and racially privileged group of workers; much of the writing around race by groups involved in the New Communist Movement was already attempting to deal with this problem, and thus develop a better understanding of the proletariat in the US, when Draper was advocating a socialism from below that was already out of date.

In any case, the point is not to focus on Draper's numerous short-comings but on the theory he initiated that has become somewhat popular amongst some contemporary (and predominantly first-world) Marxist intellectuals and factions. Draper himself is rather antiquated, and generally uninteresting theoretically, but his conceptualization of socialism from below is utilized by some contemporary Marxist scholars (those associated with the New Socialist Group in Canada, for example, or Solidarity in the US) who take the movementist critique seriously and imagine that a retooled Draperism will allow them to sidestep this problem. While this Draperism retains a quasi-Leninism in theory, in practice it maintains the same spontaneism of movementism. "Socialism from below" and "the self-emancipation of the proletariat" sound nice as phrases but are more rhetorical than theoretical. The problem with this theory is that it runs counter to a materialist theory of class: the heterogeneous body of workers that comprises any social formation does not necessarily function as a social class in a spontaneous sense, not even if and when the workers unionize; this is why the idealist conception of "self emancipation" used by Draper and his contemporary adherents lacks concrete application.

Since I already examined the ways in which we should reinvestigate the meaning of class and the proletariat, it should be clear that "socialism from below" is a theory that fails to make any inroads in this area: the working class will self-emancipate in this sense because there is not a proletarian essence that programs workers' consciousness to be naturally revolutionary. Rather, the ruling ideas of the ruling class partially determine the consciousness of everyone in capitalist society, including workers, which is why revolutionary movements most often erupt at the "weakest links" of global capitalism, semi-feudal and semi-colonial contexts, where capitalist ideology lacks the same hegemony it possesses at the centers of imperialism.

Moreover, and this is extremely important, "socialism-from-below" variants of Leninism actually produce the same kind of elitism they are attempting to escape. By arguing for an idealist "self-emancipation of the working classes", most intellectuals and organizations that support this theory rarely do any mass work, do not attempt to go far and wide amongst the masses, and content themselves with waiting for their idealized proletariat to emancipate themselves rather than trying to participate, learn from, and thus organize *while being organized by* the masses. Many of those parties that supposedly come "from outside", or even possess "top-down" structures of leadership, have sometimes been less elitist than those who follow Draper. Hence the push to *declass* in the New Communist Movement, or the innumerable (and failed) strategies of embedding oneself in working-class organizations in the interest of insurrection. Regardless of the Leninist limits of party orthodoxy, at the very least many of these organizations that were active during the time when Draper was writing learned much more from the proletariat in their "top-down" activities, obvious problems notwithstanding, than someone who engaged with the theory of organization only intellectually, without any social investigation, and no significant immersion in the proletariat. After all, if you immerse yourself in the lowest ranks of the masses in the interest of making revolution then, according to the theory of socialism from below, you are getting in the way of self-emancipation.

Again, we are forced to return to the theory of the mass-line: from the masses and to the masses. The party seeds itself into the masses, trying to pull in those that are most aware of the need to end capitalism, and thus becomes a mass party. Furthermore, the party never abandons its immersion in the masses, always returning to test its ideas and hold itself to account: at times the party headquarters may need to be bombarded by the masses, as they were in the opening stages of the GPCR. Here we have a socialism from below that is simultaneously a socialism from above; the party of the new type is that party, then, that keeps leadership structures, and thus the unity of theory and practice, but understands such leadership as one that will also be led by the masses, seeks to transform everyone in society into leaders, and thus has its "top-down" aspect balanced by a "bottom-up" conception of organization. Such a party will necessarily produce a strategy of revolution that is different from the strategy of a party that has not moved beyond the Leninist limits, even if the latter bases its practice on the theory of socialism from below.

Through the Movementist Critique

So what is this party of the new type if it is not the Draperist solution? Clearly it cannot be this solution for three reasons: i) to assume a Leninist party will build itself spontaneously is an academic abdication of struggle, a religious hope for a party that will build itself without any effort on the part of those who should know better; ii) the party of the new type demands more than the Leninist conception of the party, which leads (as we shall see later) to a particular theory of organization; and iii) the assumption that such a party will manifest within trade-union structures, because they are "the most organized" elements of the working class, is to forget that these structures are organized by capitalism, and thus are quite removed from proletarian consciousness. Draperism is, in the last instance, a movementist economism. That is, according to Draperism, a viable social movement will spontaneously emerge based on the economic struggles of the organized working class.

Contemporary movementism, however, often eschews economism and embraces sites of politicization that generally have to do with oppression: multiple movements against capitalism are realized in struggles against racism, sexism and heterosexism, settler-colonialism, ableism, etc. Contemporary movementism raises questions that speak to the necessity of a rupture from the way in which theories of revolutionary organizing have been understood according to a theoretical terrain that ends with Leninism. Therefore, if Maoism presents an opening in its new return to the theory of the vanguard (a return in which the party, as indicated in the third chapter, is transformed by the mass-line), then the movementist rejection of the paradigmatic Leninist party must be treated as that dialectical counter-pressure which provides the torsion necessary to unravel this problematic.

Take, for example, the autonomist Marxist critique of Leninism that judges the party formation under Stalin as the perfect completion of the Leninist terrain. In some ways this critique is correct because, as aforementioned, the Stalinist party formation is the historical perfection of the Leninist theory of organization.[8] Even Alain Badiou, who was moving towards a theory of the party of the new type but unable to thoroughly grasp the Maoist rupture that erupted in the late 1980s, was forced to grant some legitimacy to this critique and thus ended up endorsing something that was not quite movementist and not quite vanguardist rather than a new return to the theory of the party vanguard: a militant and disciplined organization that is not a revolutionary party.

More salient, perhaps, is Robert Biel's demand for a revolutionary organization and strategy that can respond to the level of complexity that the current conjuncture of senile capitalism has called into being. Since the imperialist stage of capitalism has become more complex since both the times of Lenin and Mao. By sustaining itself through ecological and social "sinks", through appropriating and containing the creativity of resistant movements, and by generating what Biel terms "path dependencies" (bad habits ingrained in the system that, because of the arrow of time, hasten the system's entropic limits), capitalism has become more and more systemically embedded. In the context of this moribund capitalism that often demonstrates an "exterminist" impulse due to its end of history triumphalism, reliance on an organizational form inherited identically from the past cannot respond to the necessities raised by a complex system in catastrophic decay. Biel thus argues that a revolutionary movement must "operate in a new way, because of the issues around linking spaces and the assemblage of components underlying a new mode of production, which can only be emergent. It is necessary to think and act systemically. The Left must relate to a systems-oriented futurology... but must above all do so critically."[9]

While it is correct to recognize that the Leninist party of the past, due to the era in which it was theorized, is incapable of addressing this complexity, Biel's demand for "a process of *assemblage*" that "link[s] contestatory spaces"[10] should not mean a total rejection of everything that the Leninist paradigm generated. There is a way to read Biel's demand for a recognition of the complexity of struggle as a simultaneous demand for a rejection of unified organization where resistant assemblages spontaneously, without any over-arching revolutionary ethos beyond a nebulous anti-capitalism, stumble towards each other and inevitably produce a socialist movement that will naturally work out its strategy, post-capitalist structure, and general ideological hegemony. Since movementism as a whole has failed to come even close to the revolutionary moments produced by Marxist-Leninist methodologies of organizing, this approach should be recognized as revolutionarily bankrupt. But is this simply a case of throwing the clichéd baby out with its bath water or is it something more complex? For maybe the bath water, to continue with this crude proverbial analogy, was indeed connected to the baby itself; maybe a rupture, that is also continuity, needs to conceive of another "baby" that resembles the first one in composition but that is also different. To claim that the Leninist strategy did not solve a significant historical problem is only possible if we deny history; but it would also be a denial of history to pretend that Leninism did not also produce successive problems that we have inherited.

On the one hand we have Leninism and all of the problems the traditional Leninist party, the so-called "general staff of the proletariat", has produced. On the other hand we have a rejection of this organized way of making revolution, what we have called movementism (but is also the influence of the anarchist tradition), that has shown itself to be incapable of even approaching revolution: in *The Communist Necessity* I argued that this was the case; I won't repeat the argument here. To reject Leninism, whatever its problems, will result in a movementist practice, no matter how it might be dressed up, because nothing else can result from a refusal to organize according to something that resembles a party. The inherent deficiency of movementism, then, should lead us to recognize that some type of Leninism is required. At the same time, however, the history of Leninist formalization has indeed led to the enshrinement of a counter-revolutionary bureaucracy within the very structure that was intended to affect revolution. In the context of this dilemma it might seem as if there is no solution: movementism is proven to be a dead-end, Leninism is proven to turn upon itself and stifle the revolution. A diagonal conception is thus required, a rupture with Leninism that is simultaneously a continuation: the Maoist party of the new type that, being a movement of movements structured according to the mass-line, is capable of becoming a comprehensive fighting party.

One of the dismissive reviews of *The Communist Necessity*, which missed the point of that treatise, argued that my critique of movementism "discount[ed] literally hundreds upon hundreds of distinct groups and movements without a more substantive critique".[11] And yet I was never discounting the movements themselves, only the ideology that treated these movements as ends in themselves. The truth, and a truth that I failed to make clear due to the terms of the argument I had constructed, is that these spontaneous movements are not in themselves bad things that should be discounted; rather, they should be treated as implying the *need* for the intervention of a party formation:

> In a certain way, each communist originates from the sponta-
> neous movement; a majority amongst us took their first steps
> towards communism by taking part in the mass
> movements—we shared their aspirations and also their
> fragmentary consciousness. The movement is a sane thing, a
> necessary and universal passage. For some, however, this first
> step becomes the whole thing and is treated as a permanent
> stage: they recognize the spontaneous movements but deny
> the active role of consciousness and its materialization, the
> Communist Party.[12]

The movement possess a political sanity that should not be dismissed simply because it does not express a proper Leninist understanding of making revolution. Movementism is the ideology that treats spontaneous movements as ends in themselves, as capable of producing revolution through the addition of their multiple trajectories, whereas a politics that understands these movements as significant, without accepting an ideology limited by their boundaries, will find a way to bring "the active role of consciousness and its materialization" to these sites of struggle, link them to a party project, and learn from them.

The point, then, is not to "reinvent the wheel" but to replace a wagon wheel with the modern tire: wagon wheels and car wheels might belong to the category of wheels, but in some ways they are also categorically different. Once again: Maoism is not simply an *addition* to Marxism-Leninism, just as Leninism wasn't simply an addition to Marxism, but a transformation. The best way to make sense of this transformation is to accept the movementist critique, to understand that the theory of the party as understood by Lenin reached its limits and completion under Stalin, but to also find a way to transform the Leninist moment of universality from the perspective of Maoism. So, as with every science, we can treat the unfolding of revolutionary theory as a continuous process where universal concepts are in a relationship of successive development. At the same time, though, we have to treat these moments of universalization as paradigm shifts where the truth procedure of science is a series of successive epistemic ruptures.

Biel's "process of assemblage" and the necessity of linking spaces of struggle was indeed about a new return to the concept of a revolutionary party, one altered by the Maoist moment of rupture-continuity:

The whole key will be the relationship between the organised radical contingent and the wider movement. The generalised, endemic level of struggle never ceases, and it still very strongly encompasses [...] those marginalised not only just through racist oppression but in other, often superposed ways, particularly gender, and all the forms of super-exclusion characteristic of the globalisation era—informality, various forms of indentured service, lack of status, lack of papers. Here, too, the Maoist tradition fully retains its relevance: it always critiqued the labour movement tendency to perceive only those segments of the working population who fall under the limelight of official recognition. [...] The creativity of the wider mass movement can supply resources not just for the struggle against the current order, but for the building of a new one.[13]

On the one hand the organized and radical contingent, the germ of a developing revolutionary party. On the other hand, the mass movements that it encourages and develops, as well as the already-existing mass movements that it supports and invests itself in (here we must recall the mass-line metaphor of the party-as-fish immersed in the masses-as-sea). The germ of the party is incubated within these mass movements, extending its sphere of hegemony if and when it learns to grow.

Deviations

The Leninist theory of the party that is still caught within the Leninist terrain is by itself is no longer open to future developments. Such a party generally leans towards a theory of insurrection as its revolutionary strategy, though there are exceptions. There are, after all, the traditional "right" and "left" strategic "deviations": variants of social-democratic reformism, which are most often some form of electoral legalism or entryism, on the right; variants of adventurism, such as Che Guevara's focoist strategy, on the left. But if the Leninist party formation is the norm, then the classification of any possible deviation becomes rather formulaic.

We know that the Leninist party emerged in response to the

revisionism of Bernstein and Kautsky and was thus founded upon building a party to actually make revolution, overthrow the state rather than collaborate with the state, and establish the dictatorship of the proletariat. We also know that the Leninist party intends to be a party that is recognized as the vanguard by the proletariat rather than an anarchist organization devoted to the propaganda of the deed. Based upon this understanding of the Leninist party formation, one can classify "right" and "left" deviations by whether or not they resemble those strategic approaches that the Leninist party was meant to reject. Moreover, such classifications should lead us to appreciate the Bolshevik strategy of insurrection: on the one hand, it ultimately rejects collaboration with the state since it seeks to build towards a moment where the state can be overwhelmed, seized, and smashed by insurrection and civil war; on the other hand, it seeks to accomplish revolution with the participation of the class it claims to represent and not leave this class behind in the spectacle of militant adventurism.

These calculations, of course, are only simple on an abstract level; simultaneously, the "deviations" are the logical result of a precarious, but important, dialectic between an opportunism and ultra-leftism that are intimately related to the strategy of insurrection. Indeed, these "deviations" are, in the last instance, logical expressions generated by the contradiction of Marxism-Leninism that is insurmountable within the terrain of Leninism. That is, in some ways it might be inaccurate to use the word *deviation* when, at the end of the day, it is difficult to prove whether these failed avenues of revolutionary strategy are really deviating from Leninism in the abstract. There is a point, perhaps, in which these deviations do not treat themselves as such and may have grounds, culled from the terrain of Leninist theory, to defend what we should be able to classify as opportunist or ultra-leftist. Leninism by itself lacks the analytic tools to make such a qualification since these supposed deviations are part of its interior momentum; something external, another Archimedian point, is required—just as Leninism was that Archimedian point that could decide upon the contradictions encountered by Marxism.

This is why, lacking that Archimedian point, some Leninist parties can submit themselves to electoral politics while claiming that they are only doing so in order to build towards insurrection. Lenin's *Left-Wing Communism: an Infantile Disorder* is cited, for example, as a defense of entryism: this is a cynical form of opportunism treated as tactically correct since it is conceived as part of a general strategy of insurrection where the party is built by participating in building a bourgeois party, splitting the ranks of this party, and slowly pushing for the grounds of a general strike and civil war. The same text, as well as the October Revolution, is cited as proof for every participation and collaboration with social-democratic politics, every support for the "lesser-evil" bourgeois party, and every set politics that confines itself only within trade-union boundaries. This kind of practice, which is purely concerned with legal agitation for social reform (in the hope that this agitation spontaneously produces revolutionary consciousness) imagines that it has made contact with the proletariat even though it tends to circulate, if it even circulates at all, amongst the most privileged strata of workers. In these cases, all forms of militancy are treated as suspect instances of ultra-leftism, and innumerable Leninist and quasi-Leninist arguments about the perils of adventurism and ultra-leftism are mobilized to support a practice that might in fact be opportunist.

Similarly, those who embraced a Guevarist strategy of focoism did so because they believed that the Leninist party of the avant-garde could be the "grin without a cat" (to use Chris Marker's metaphor) that could appear before the body of the masses in revolt and in fact encourage this revolt. Although Che Guevara apparently claimed that his theory of focoism was a tactical implementation of Mao's theory of people's war, it is more accurate to understand it as a tactical implementation of the theory of insurrection. A small cabal, a germinal party, embarks on military adventurism so as to produce the context for insurrection: the state reveals itself as reactionary and ramps up its suppression, the masses are radicalized, insurrection becomes inevitable. Those who embrace this strategy would most probably conceive of the above category of "deviating" Leninists as opportunists and would be justified in doing so: many of the supposed "adventurists" were betrayed or abandoned by their Leninist inversion.

Strategic Lines

Rejecting the premise that Maoism is not a new return to the theory of organization, and that Leninism was a complete theory in and of itself, leads precisely to a revolutionary strategy lifted uncritically from the Bolshevik Revolution and noted in the previous section: insurrection. This is the logical destiny of the purely Leninist party of the advanced guard; it follows precisely, with philosophical clarity, from the assumption that the revolutionary party is a "general staff" of elite managers who are the perfect stand-in for the proletariat.

How does the perfect Leninist party make revolution? The answer is rather straight-forward: circulate amongst the masses and involve oneself in a protracted legal struggle designed to push traditional workers' organizations (i.e. trade unions) towards the moment of general strike; use every possible economic struggle, every strike, to teach those with "trade-union consciousness" to move towards "revolutionary consciousness" (decided, as Clark has reminded us, by the privileged cadre who already possess this consciousness); eventually, if the protracted legal struggle is successful, when the moment of the general strike arrives the party cadre can strike and affect a break from trade-union consciousness, forcing a civil war; the army and police will be split, the party that was most disciplined and organized will grow exponentially so as to lead the masses in insurrection.

The above formula for revolution, which is cited as the way in which the Bolsheviks achieved power, follows directly from the theory of the Leninist party. Since the purely Leninist party lacks a coherent theory of the mass-line, and is often conceived (or misconceived) as an elitist party with the consciousness of a religious elect, the theory of insurrection makes the most sense. This is Vanguardism 101, the moment of *Leninism* endorsed by Trotskyists and Stalinists alike: the fundamental theory of organization, the party formation, receives its ultimate meaning in the field of revolutionary strategy.

But here is where the strategy of people's war appears as the result of an opening produced by the emergence of Maoism. Both the PCP and the RIM (at least in its 1993 statement) argued that protracted people's war (PPW) was the revolutionary strategy of the proletariat: the emergence of Marxism-Leninism-Maoism suggested this strategy as one of the "universal" insights that could be gleaned from the experience of the Chinese Revolution. Unfortunately, aside from simply suggesting and stating the supposed universality of this strategic theory, the claim still requires further development. Indeed, some Maoist groups leading revolutionary struggles today do not recognize this insight (and generally agree that whereas PPW is the way to carry out revolution in the global peripheries, the strategy of insurrection still holds at the imperialist metropoles) and those who do agree that PPW is universal, but are also in a situation where the strategy of people's war is already treated as acceptable, are not compelled to argue about its application to the global centers because they are not trying to carry out revolution in these centers. Since the early 1990s, then, the only organizations that have attempted to significantly elaborate on this claim about the potential universality of people's war—by theorizing how it applies to the centers of global capitalism—have been Canada's

PCR-RCP and Italy's nPCI, and they have done so in somewhat different manners.

Thus, my interest in talking about the strategy of PPW must necessarily be limited by the fact that there is still a lacuna of theorization in this area. Moreover, since contemporary Maoist currents do not agree on this proposal (and I am not about to argue that an organization involved in PPW in its context is *not* Maoist because it rejects the possible universality of this strategy[14]) I do not want to waste time explaining theories of how this strategy can be applied universally. At best we can argue that the theory of insurrection is *not* universal because, following the October Revolution, it has met with quick obliteration everywhere it was faithfully applied.[15] To recognize the false universality of this purely Leninist theory of strategy, however, does not allow us to derive the axiom that PPW is universal; it remains a hypothesis. But I want to explore how and why this strategic theory is a compelling hypothesis, though still only that, because of the way in which the Leninist thesis of the vanguard party is transformed by the Maoist moment of continuity-rupture. For if the purely Leninist party vanguard necessarily produces, as aforementioned, the strategy of insurrection, the Maoist party of the new type would necessarily develop another strategic approach because of the way in which it is organizationally articulated.

That is, a transformed theory of the party formation can only lead to a transformed theory of strategy that will initially appear as *heterodox* to those who are invested in the strategic theory that belongs solely to the Leninist terrain. What strategic theory would the Maoist "party of the new type" produce, based on its method of organization? A movement of movements that seeks to embed itself everywhere in society, deployed through every progressive counter-hegemonic movement, will necessarily have a different strategic approach than a party formation that does not invest itself in these movements, maintaining an agitational distance in the hope that the radical elements of these movements will just gravitate towards its orbit. A party that seeks to locate a dispersed proletariat, rather than imagining that a ready-made revolutionary agent can be found at the traditional "point of production" organized according to trade-union consciousness, will also develop a strategy of dispersal. A party that employs the mass-line, and believes it is important to locate the most radical elements of these masses, will find itself confronting a complexity that the traditional Leninist appreciation of proletarian identity cannot grasp. In this sense, the theory of PPW is at least one theory that fulfills the demands produced by a party that understands reality in a manner that transgresses the boundaries of traditional Leninist thought while also reaffirming the crucial aspects of Leninism: rupture and continuity.

The theory of PPW, therefore, is not simply a theory of strategy that is divergent from insurrectionism any more than Maoism is divergent from Leninism; rather, the strategy of PPW is the transformation of strategy, grasped at the moment of Maoism's continuity-rupture, just as Maoism is a transformation of Leninism. In this way it not only incorporates what was particularly applicable during the October Revolution in the theory of insurrection but also, as part of a scientific truth procedure, transgresses the limits of that strategic theory.

As opposed to the strategy of focoism, the theory of PPW should not be confused with an adventurist articulation of the theory of insurrection. This theory is not about turning a party into an armed cabal that is forced to operate only clandestinely and divorced from the masses, but is about building a mass party that will develop in its ability to challenge state power without having to agitate and take hold of an insurrection. After all, the modern state is trained to crush insurrections, and the masses involved in these insurrections (along with the party circulating in these mass uprisings) will be ill-prepared to fight the state machinery that exists precisely to prevent insurrection: a protracted process is necessary. Nor should the universal aspects of protracted people's war be confused with the particular tactical aspects of the theory (i.e. the countryside surrounding the cities), except perhaps metaphorically, that apply primarily to semi-feudal and semi-colonial contexts.

If PPW is universal, then its aspects that apply to every social context are actually quite simple: develop the embryo of a people's army while building the party; connect with the masses and develop so as to intervene at their behest in a way that draws them into the party's orbit; figure out how to build a fighting movement deeply embedded in the masses so as to move through the axiomatic stages of protracted war. These stages are: the accumulation of forces, strategic defensive (where a guerrilla war becomes normative), strategic equilibrium (where dual power is approached and warfare becomes mixed), strategic offensive (frontal war where the establishment of the dictatorship of the proletariat is possible and where insurrections may happen as part of the protracted process). What we have here is a strategy that is ultimately more complex than the strategy of insurrection and that requires the development of a party that can spread throughout the masses and prove itself, by its actions and inter-actions, as the vanguard. Any revolutionary party is a process; the Maoist theory of strategy, which emerges from the mass-line, is simply the conscious recognition of this fact: the revolutionary party is a protracted process that should make people's war.[16]

People's War?

Although I generally agree with the claim that PPW is a signif-icant insight of Maoism-qua-Maoism, its controversy amongst contemporary Maoists should still be recognized. I want to suggest that this controversy, though, might also be a result of a lingering confusion between the name and concept of Maoism. After all, the anti-revisionist Marxist-Leninist movement of yesteryear that aligned itself with the Communist Party of China under Mao Zedong, *did* maintain that PPW only applied to semi-feudal/semi-colonial (i.e. globally peripheral) contexts, whereas "the October Road" remained the strategy of revolution at the centers of capitalism. We could even argue, and not without evidence, that Mao himself believed that his strategy of making revolution in China did not qualify as a universal development of revolutionary science.

My contention here is that if the Leninist party vanguard is transformed by Maoism due to the theory of the mass-line, then so also is the strategic theory that is dependent on the former transformed by the emergence of the latter. In the last section we observed how insurrection was the only strategic theory that could be conceptualized based on the limits of a purely Leninist terrain; once that terrain is transgressed and transformed so is its strategic theory. Therefore, I think it is fair to assert that those who would deny the universality of people's war without providing another alternative to insurrection could be led, if they wish to be consistent, to deny the fact that Maoism has anything to say about the party formation; this would imply the denial of a key aspect of Maoism's universality.

Moreover, even though all of the elements necessary to produce a universal strategy of people's war can be found in the strategic-theoretical writings of Mao Zedong, these elements need to be organized in retrospect and delinked from what Mao himself, being a consummate Marxist-Leninist unaware that he was producing the germ of a new theoretical break (any more than Lenin was aware), might have thought at the time. The particular aspects of the theory of people's war (i.e. surrounding the cities from the countryside) must be rearticulated according to the universal aspect understood only at a historical point beyond Mao. When read back on his theoretical strategy, the claim to universality causes these previously Marxist-Leninist insights to resonate with a meaning that spills beyond their initial intention. We find much of the same retrospective historical reading when Lenin looks back at some disorganized claims of Marx and Engels so as to produce the theory of the dictatorship of the proletariat, or when Mao looks back at some disorganized claims of Lenin so as to theorize the mass-line.

The initial Maoist rupture located in the 1988–1993 process indeed treats people's war as universal. As the PCP argues in its 1988 document *On Marxism-Leninism-Maoism*:

> A key and decisive question is the understanding of the universal validity of people's war and its subsequent application taking into account the different types of revolution and the specific conditions of each revolution. To clarify this key issue it is important to consider that no insurrection like that of Petrograd, the anti-fascist resistance, or the European guerrilla movements in the Second World War have been repeated, as well as considering the armed struggles that are presently being waged in Europe. In the final analysis, the October Revolution was not only an insurrection but a revolutionary [people's] war that lasted for several years. Consequently, in the imperialist countries the revolution can only be conceived as a revolutionary war which today is simply people's war.[17]

Moreover, RIM's *Long Live Marxism-Leninism-Maoism!* document, though arguing that there were indeed particular aspects to Mao's theory of people's war that clarified how to make revolution in "countries oppressed by imperialism", still claimed that the "theory of People's War is universally applicable in all countries, although this must be applied to the concrete conditions in each country and, in particular, take into account the revolutionary paths in the two general types of countries— imperialist countries and oppressed countries—that exist in the world today".[18]

I cite these two threshold moments not as arguments from authority but simply to point out that this theory of revolutionary strategy was considered universal by the very process that originated the theory of Marxism-Leninism-Maoism. Thus, controversy within the worldwide contemporary Maoist movement regarding PPW might in fact be a controversy inherited from the clash between Mao Zedong Thought and Maoism or, more accurately, an anti-revisionist Marxism-Leninism and Marxism-Leninism-Maoism. Thus, the desire to hold onto the theory of insurrection at the centers of global capitalism while locating the strategy of PPW at the peripheries is an anti-revisionist Marxist-Leninist gambit that is largely disinterested with the process that produced Maoism-qua-Maoism with which this book is concerned.

The fundamental argument that should lead us to think about the potential universality of people's war was already apparent: if the party formation is transformed by Maoism, then so is its strategic theory. For there is something that emerges from a vanguard party with a mass-line, the party of the new type, that transgresses the limits of the simple and limited formula of insurrection. When the party goes to the masses in order to reinvigorate itself, and structures itself based on a non-antagonistic dialectical relationship of bottom-up and top-down (that is, it is neither commandist nor tailist), then a strategy that is more complex than insurrection is produced, just as the game of Go is more complex than chess. The latter game's strategy is dependent on arithmetical lines of force; the former game relies on a strategy of fields that are always in flux.

The Civil War Already Exists

The Maoist party of the new type is a revolutionary party that, in continuity with the Leninist paradigm, seeks to be the militant and disciplined vanguard capable of leading the proletarian revolution and its multiple movements. Simultaneously, rupturing from this paradigm's limits (delimited by the cipher of Stalin), the Maoist party will also be an organization that, learning from the critiques of Leninist monolithism, can become a party that develops according to the mass-line, where the top-down discipline is balanced by a bottom-up creativity. We have already witnessed glimmers of this party in the historical experience of the Chinese Revolution, particularly in the Cultural Revolution, and Mao Zedong's theoretical writing that encouraged the party cadre to immerse themselves in the revolutionary masses so as to rejuvenate the party by holding it to account.

Such a party, however, will necessarily produce a theory of strategy that reflects this rearticulated structure. As aforementioned, the strategy of insurrection is particular to the Leninist-qua-Leninist party because it is precisely that strategy which is derived from an organizational structure that, after legal agitation, is able to strike at the moment of mass unrest, force an insurrection, and as the most coherent and disciplined revolutionary organization take control of the spontaneous elements of rebellion. Such a strategy worked in 1917 (if we are to reduce the Bolshevik Revolution to this moment and what it understood as the *how* of making revolution), but it has never been repeated with any level of measurable success. Hence the need for a more sophisticated strategy of revolution, one produced by a party formation that has developed beyond the Leninist limits.

Interestingly enough, the need for a sophisticated strategy of proletarian revolution was grasped in 1906 by Karl Liebknecht in a manner that questioned the theory of insurrection eleven years before the moment of its historical origin. Arguing that a military strategy was "almost lacking in the case of proletarian revolution",[19] Liebknecht's examination of capitalist militarism led him to assert that:

> the superiority of the army to the unarmed people, the proletariat, is far greater today than it was ever before on account

of the highly developed military arts and strategy, the enormous size of the armies, the unfavorable local distribution of the various classes and the relative economic strength of proletariat and bourgeoisie which shows the proletariat in a particularly disadvantageous position, wherefore alone a future proletarian revolution will be far more difficult than any revolution that has taken place hitherto.[20]

Did the strategic theory gleaned from the October Revolution provide a proper response to this problem? No: at best it was an incidental theory that applied only to the particular circumstances of Russia in the early 20th-century that could not be universally applied. Hence the historic inability of replicating its success. Moreover, the fact that Liebknecht, writing this treatise on *Militarism* eleven years before the Bolshevik insurrection and civil war, saw that the solution to this problem might be developed out of "[t]he tactics of the urban guerrilla method, splendidly developed in Moscow [in 1905]", and that such a development would be "epochal" and thus universal, suggests that the problem of proletarian military strategy he grasped could not easily be solved by the theory of insurrection.[21] If anything, the forces arrayed against the contemporary proletariat are even more enormous and organized than they were in 1906; to imagine that we can solve this problem of strategy in the same way it was solved in Russia in 1917, where the enemy's military strength was already in shambles and the semi-feudal army not even the same kind of fully developed capitalist army (that Liebknecht also describes in the same text), is the result of lazy thinking.

Similarly, if we were to reduce the Chinese Revolution to the most tactical components of PPW, where the cities are surrounded by the peasant countryside, then we would also sacrifice universality upon the altar of the semi-feudal and semi-colonial particularity that could only be found in regions such as

1949 China. In order to answer Liebknecht's problematic, then, we need to locate the universal elements in both the Russian and Chinese experience, less conceptually articulate in the former, that are only unlocked by the emergence of Maoism and its mass-line party's strategic possibilities.

For it is only the party that immerses itself in the masses that can develop a coherent strategy that is one step beyond the theory of insurrection. This party of the new type, by aiming to diffuse itself amongst the masses, ought to begin the process of making revolution in its diffusion rather than planning for a revolution within the sphere of disciplined monolithism. Such an organization spreads its tentacles into every struggle, through innumerable fronts, so as to accumulate advanced forces that will become the germinal sites of military opposition. Every PPW to date has followed this process and has struck before the clichéd iron was hot: building its military experience and spreading slowly, accumulating cells and the seeds of dual power, so as to begin the moment of strategic defensive. When the PCP boycotted the 1981 Peruvian elections and went so far as to set the voting booths on fire, it was little more than a tiny organization emerging from the majority faction of the former PCP that, until this point, was in decline. But its willingness to build a party through an explicit participation in class struggle is what allowed it to grow and find its roots in the masses.

The civil war already exists; the class struggle, which results in so many massacres even when the proletariat is not consciously fighting the bourgeoisie, needs to be engaged and, in this engagement, made visible.

Notes

1. Stalin, 107. Stalin's conception of the party as a "general" or "military" staff, though in many ways understandable in its time (and no different from the way in which Trotsky understood it), is significantly different from the conception of the

party that would start to be developed in the foundational process of the Chinese Revolution. Although some try to argue that Mao's conception of the "mass-line" is not unique because Stalin mentions the need for the party to be "connected with the non-Party masses" (107), this mention of the masses is about as conceptually relevant as Lenin's throwaway lines about "cultural revolution": these are terms in search of a theory, not theoretical conceptualizations. Indeed, in the same passage where the necessity of being connected to the masses is proclaimed, Stalin describes this connection in a top-down manner, with the Party conceived as the "moral and political authority of the masses", rather than something that can ever be held to account by these masses (107). Such a conception of the party, where line struggle is forbidden because "the existence of factions is incompatible with Party unity and its iron discipline" (117), would forbid the masses from "bombarding the headquarters". The point that the political process that produced Maoism raises, however, is that factions cannot be forbidden because they will necessarily exist, just as bourgeois and petty-bourgeois ideology will also exist within the Party. Not because "petty-bourgeois somehow or other penetrate into the Party into which they introduce an element of hesitancy and opportunism" (119), but because even the most faithful cadre will carry with them the ideology of capitalist social relations.

2. It is important to note, however, that the question of organization and the question of strategy, though connected, are not identical. Due to the fact that these questions are connected, it is quite common to find that the question of strategy is under-theorized because it is conflated with the question of organization. I have examined this problematic, and the way in which insurrectionism is treated as normative, in my article "Quartermasters of Stadiums and

Cemeteries" (*Socialist Studies,* Winter 2016). Some of this chapter was previously published in that article.

3. See, for instance, the issue of *Socialist Register* that was devoted to "the question of strategy" (Volume 49). There is not one article in this issue that thinks through a strategy of making revolution according to a concrete analysis of a concrete situation. Focused mainly on the question of organization—whether Leninism, quasi-Leninism, or anti-Leninism is the best—it simply assumes that the problem of strategy will be answered all by itself once the problem of "what type of organization is the best" is solved.

4. These "tinkerings" are generally ahistorical and idealist: a promise to avoid "bureaucracy", a focus on the "permanent revolution", and other claims that have no historical basis since they have not and cannot be implemented. Again, the Appendix is relevant in this regard.

5. Draper, *Two Souls of Socialism.*

6. Here it is worth noting that, in one of *The State and Counter-Revolution*'s appendices, Clark actually dismisses Draper as an unremarkable Marxist thinker.

7. Draper, *Marxism and the Trade Unions.*

8. Again, the Trotskyist inversion of the Stalinist party formation does not succeed in escaping this critique: in its most orthodox form it resembles all of the problems of Leninism, indicated by the autonomists, that if implemented, though that historical opening is now closed, would result in something quite similar to the party under Stalin.

9. Biel, *The Entropy of Capitalism,* 332.

10. Ibid., 328.

11. André Moncourt, *In Defense of Strawmen* (http://kersplebedeb.com/posts/andre-moncourt-in-defence-of-strawmen-seventy-three-questions-for-j-moufawad-paul-and-then-a-brief-statement/).

12. Revolutionary Communist Party of Canada, *It's Right to*

Rebel: Maoist Manual for Serving the Struggle of the Masses.

13. Biel, *Eurocentrism and the Communist Movement*, 199–200.

14. This would be a foolish claim because, for example, the CPI (Maoist), despite carrying out a people's war, does not believe that the strategy applies to the imperialist metropoles.

15. Derbent, 19.

16. For more specific analyses of the theory of protracted people's war and its universal aspects, the interested reader should examine two important documents produced by the PCR-RCP: *Protracted People's War is the Only Way to Make Revolution* (http://www.pcr-rcp.ca/old/en/pwd/1e.php) and *More on the Question of Waging Revolutionary War in the Imperialist Countries* (http://www.pcr-rcp.ca/old/en/pwd/2a.php).

17. Communist Party of Peru, *On Marxism-Leninism-Maoism.*

18. Revolutionary Internationalist Movement, *Long Live Marxism-Leninism-Maoism!*

19. Liebknecht, 15.

20. Ibid., 177–178.

21. Ibid., 15.

Epilogue
The Maoist Necessity

Slavoj Žižek once argued that "there is no 'authentic Marx' that can be approached directly, bypassing Lenin".[1] But we need to go further than Žižek and declare that there can be no authentic Marx *or Lenin* that can be directly apprehended, bypassing Mao. That is, just as Marx could only be understood through the "Leninist ossification",[2] now there is the further "Maoist ossification" that must be projected backwards unto our understanding of Marxism as a whole. The science that bears Marx's name, and thus even our understanding of Marx himself, must necessarily be refracted through those theoretical instances in which this science developed with great leaps. These are indeed the moments of rupture that, at the same time, are part of a larger continuity.

In this book I have intervened on behalf of Maoism based on the dialectic of continuity-rupture and my assumption, which should now be clear, that Maoism is the most recent theoretical terrain in this unfolding science of history and society. Moreover, I have also implied that it is necessary to accept this dialectic in order to appreciate Marxism as a living science: continuity is just as important as rupture, and vice versa, and to argue otherwise is to undermine the basis of revolutionary science itself. This is indeed a philosophical point in that it draws a line of demarcation precisely at the level of meaning, at that metapolitical point that seeks to answer the second-order questions regarding the veracity of Maoism. After all, to ask *why Maoism?* in the terrain of revolutionary struggle where a people's war has claimed the field is not a philosophical question; the answer is provided by the very fact that there *is* a people's war that veils itself as Maoist.

In any case, my implication that the moments of continuity

and rupture must be understood as terms that are intimately related is worthy of some reflection. There will be those who reject the moment of rupture in favor of the moment of continuity; there will be those who reject the moment of continuity in favor of the moment of rupture. Both tendencies lead nowhere.

Those who reject *rupture* and instead demand a "pure" conceptualization of Marxism that is unbroken from Marx to the present will become imprisoned by nostalgia: everything Marx and Engels wrote was correct, everything their most faithful adherents wrote (depending on the tendency, the faithful will differ) was also correct, and it thus becomes necessary to find a way to dismiss all moments of contradiction and all errors. Under this interpretation the search for an "original" and "pure" Marx becomes an act of dogmatism that will simultaneously be revisionist because it denies the necessity of revolutionary change that is intrinsic to the very doctrine it seeks to defend.

Those who reject continuity to instead fetishize rupture will become enraptured by an imaginary future. Believing that there is nothing beyond disconnected moments of revolutionary ferment, each one entirely unique, it is easy to become lost in an endless search for a new method that does not have to place itself within the frameworks inherited from the past. Although the past does indeed weigh upon us "like a nightmare", when we pretend that this weight does not exist we are in danger of reinventing all of the mistakes, dead-ends, and revisionist denouements from previous epochs.

And yet the dialectic of continuity-rupture cannot be suppressed by those who cling to either side of the contradiction; the opposing moment will always be expressed, an unrelenting return of the repressed. Indeed, the absolutist rejection of rupture results in the worst form of rupture: if Marxism is a living science, open to the future, then seeking only continuity with its past is a rupture from Marxism itself. Simultaneously, the fetishization of rupture will result in its own form of continuity: a continuity, often unconscious, with every previous attempt to ignore history, to produce a new revolutionary strategy without any scientific attention to the past, and thus a continuity of failure.

Therefore, both continuity and rupture need to be actively grasped as moments belonging to a relational whole: there is revolutionary continuity that links Marxism to Maoism; there are significant ruptures between Marxism, Leninism, Maoism. Moreover, it is always the most recent moment of rupture that will wrench continuity from the jaws of the past. At one point we could not approach Marxism directly except through the door of Leninism, now we must understand that Marxism and Leninism are realized through the lens of Maoism.

Most important, however, is the fact that continuity with the revolutionary tradition theoretically initiated by Marx and Engels demands, regardless of its successive ruptures, fidelity to the necessity of revolution. That is, bringing communism into being should be the main focus of any movement that dares to name itself *communist*: all theory and practice needs to be filtered through this necessity, all failures to pursue this necessity should be treated as suspect. We are not communists because communism is an academic exercise; we are communists because we want to end capitalism. If this maxim is the case, then we require a communism that is devoted to concretely making communism.

The most significant Maoist movements to date have tended to center their theory on the locus of revolutionary strategy, attempting to make communism in particular circumstances through people's war. This focus has set Maoism apart from other communist tendencies which are most often content to agitate, participate in incoherent movementist strategies, and do not appear to consider the pursuit of a revolutionary military strategy.

By claiming that the *time is not yet right*, and pushing revolution beyond a nebulous future horizon, some tendencies are satisfied with low-level agitation, participation in reformist politics, and waiting for some coming insurrection where the masses will succeed against professionalized state armies due to their spontaneous revolutionary potential. Other tendencies, even if they label themselves with the name Maoism, wait for the most oppressed sectors of the global masses to do their work for them; they feel there is no reason to strategize since their job is simply to wait for revolutionaries in other social contexts to make a global revolution.

Here it is important to consider T. Derbent's thoughts on this matter:

> Every social revolutionary project must think ahead to the question of armed confrontation with the forces of power and reaction. To put off making such a study because "the time is not right yet" for armed confrontation amounts to making choices... which risk, at that point when "the time will be right" for armed confrontation, leaving the revolutionary forces powerless, vulnerable, with characteristics that will be totally inadequate. [...] Organizations that claim to be revolutionary but which refuse to develop a military policy, disqualify themselves as revolutionary forces. They are already acting as gravediggers of revolution, the quartermasters of stadiums and cemeteries.[3]

Although it would be incorrect to argue that the development of a military policy is the yardstick of revolutionary theory (after all, reactionaries can also develop successful military policy), it is important to note that such a development is necessary for any tendency that seeks to concretely implement its political line. Without such a focus, after all, there is no point in talking about communism: it needs to be brought into existence through revolution, its emergence must be strategized. The enemy, after all, has strategized how to prevent such an emergence.

The historical experience of Maoism, however, has broken from the refusal to strategize revolution and, aligning itself with the necessity of concretely making communism, has produced various comprehensive party formations that take the question of revolutionary strategy seriously. Not only has the emergence of Maoism been inseparable from people's war, Maoism has produced strategic insights regarding this practice.

While there are indeed those Marxist critics who will argue that there is no need to talk about the strategic operationalization of communism, it is worth asking how such arguments are in any way part of the larger continuity of revolutionary science. For if Marx argued for the necessity of class revolution, then anyone who places themselves within this tradition must logically accept that such a necessity must be taken seriously: it cannot simply be treated as a foregone conclusion, as something that history just *does*, and thus cannot be left to chance. Here, then, is the final aspect of continuity-rupture that contemporary Maoism represents: continuity with the necessity of bringing communism into being; rupture with the refusal to concretely make revolution. The entire problematic of continuity-rupture is unified by this focus.

History is a mausoleum of those revolutionary movements that failed to strategically implement their politics. Our duty as communists is to escape this crypt and return to the necessity of actually making revolution. And this necessity is the practical basis of Marxism-Leninism-Maoism.

Notes

1. Žižek, 2.
2. Ibid.
3. Derbent, 1–2.

Appendix
Maoism or Trotskyism

The question "Maoism or Trotskyism?" might seem absurd to ask now, over a decade into the 21st-century. Such an ideological debate might at first glance appear to belong to a period of struggle before the collapse of actually-existing socialism. After all, the last gasp of anti-revisionist Marxism-Leninism in the 1960s–80s was marked by sustained polemics against Trotskyism as well as counter-polemics by various Trotskyist organizations. Innumerable tracts and books either asked the question "Leninism or Trotskyism?" or argued that Trotskyism *was* Leninism and that everything else was simply some variant of "Stalinism". And those communist organizations that attempted to wage ideological struggle against both Trotskyism and the revisionism of the Soviet Union were often organizations that veiled themselves as "Maoist" because they identified with the so-called "Chinese path" rather than the "Soviet path".

Now we are living in a period where the Soviet Union has long since collapsed and China has itself embarked on the capitalist road, a period that spelled doom for an anti-revisionist Marxism-Leninism that had pinned its hopes on China as the center of world revolution in the Cold-War period of imperialism, a movement that was doomed to fail because it was unable at the time to systematize the successes and failures of the second world-historical socialist revolution. This is a period where capitalism has proclaimed its triumph, claimed "the end of history" for itself, and countless communist movements have disintegrated. This is also a period marked by the rise of anarchism, post-modernism, and left-communist movements that openly disavow Marxism-Leninism and any type of communism that bases itself on a "party of the vanguard" organized to establish the dictatorship of the proletariat.

And yet this is a period where Trotskyism and Maoism still exist, sometimes thriving, both claiming to authentically represent and even supersede the tradition of Marxism-Leninism that was supposed to have died in the 1980s. This is also a period where the anti-Leninist leftist currents are beginning to reach the impasse that was always present in their ideology, leading to disaffection and a renewed interest in the communist tradition that was supposed to have died when capitalism declared itself victorious over communism.

Furthermore, Trotskyism never went away and, despite sectarian splits and critical openings, has still maintained a consistent influence at the centers of capitalism, especially amongst Marxist intellectuals living in North America and Britain, even when it was not openly proclaiming itself as "Trotskyist". Here we can speak of the "post-Trotskyist" groups (such as those influenced by Hal Draper or Raya Dunayevskaya) who might more resemble anarchists in practice but who still declare a certain level of fidelity to Trotskyism in their under-standing of history and key moments of theory. We can also examine the renewal of old Trotskyisms such as the International Marxist Tendency that, regardless of their possibly moribund approach to political action, temporarily attract young leftists who are fed up with the post-modern "movementism" that has now revealed its lack of revolutionary focus. In this context Trotskyism has a history of waging a somewhat successful ideological struggle within academia at the centers of imperi-alism and thus exerting a significant level of control over the intelligentsia's discourse of Marxism.

At the same time, however, Maoism only emerged as Maoism proper at the end of the 1980s and beginning of the 1990s when capitalism was declaring communism extinct: first with the people's war carried out by the Communist Party of Peru (PCP), followed by the emergence of the Revolutionary Internationalist Movement (RIM) with its 1993 statement *Long Live Marxism-*

Leninism-Maoism!. It was in this context that the experience of the Chinese Revolution was systematically examined and "Maoism" was declared the third stage of revolutionary science. For the first time, then, "Maoism" was theorized as an ideological development of Marxism rather than just a "thought" that had replaced Stalin's thought as the interlocutor of Marxism-Leninism; the PCP and the RIM argued for *Maoism-qua-Maoism* rather than *Maoism-qua-Mao Zedong Thought*, claiming that what they called "Maoism" was a theoretical development of scientific communism, a continuity and rupture from Marxism-Leninism, because it possessed tenets that were universally applicable. Hence, the RIM would argue that Maoism is the latest encapsulation of Marxism and Leninism, and Marxism-Leninism as it was is no longer sufficient.[1]

The birth of Maoism would signify an explosion of revolutionary development and people's wars in the peripheries of global capitalism, what Mao called "the storm centers" and Lenin called "the weak links", where Trotskyism was generally seen as an alien ideology. But the fact that Trotskyism has historically been treated as an alien ideology in the so-called "third world" does not necessarily mean it is theoretically bankrupt. Indeed, it is not enough to point out that a theory has failed to make any head-way in certain regions to relegate it to Trotsky's "dustbin of history": various cultural nationalisms, some of which are quite reactionary, have often eclipsed Maoism in the global peripheries and yet we would not argue that this makes them properly anti-capitalist and anti-imperialist; and Maoism's failure to claim ideological hegemony amongst Marxists at the centers of capitalism, regardless of some significant transformations here and there, should not mean that Maoism, as some have argued (even some who fancy themselves "Maoist"!), is only applicable to third-world revolutions.

Moreover, the question "Maoism or Trotskyism?" should not be confused, as it sometimes is, with the older question of

"Leninism or Trotskyism?" asked by anti-revisionists or rugged orthodox Stalinists. The latter was a question that was often asked in bad faith because it began by presupposing that, true to the Stalinist narrative of Trotsky's expulsion from the Soviet Union, Trotsky was an arch anti-Leninist, a "wrecker", and possibly even an agent for imperialist reactionaries. The standard Trotskyist response to this polemical question was simply to cast itself in the mold of Lenin and, without using these words, declare itself Marxist-Leninist-Trotskyist. Whether or not Trotskyists theorized "Leninism" correctly might be an important issue, and one we will examine tangentially in some detail below, but the accusation that Trotskyism was the express enemy of Marxism-Leninism was most often a rhetorical stance and semantic game: since Stalin theorized "Leninism", the argument went, Trotskyism must be anti-Leninist and thus anti-Lenin since it is also anti-Stalin.

Therefore, to ask the question "Maoism or Trotskyism?" as a Maoist is to try to investigate Trotskyism as a competing ideological current and to perform this investigation not to make sectarian points because of some religious adherence to the signifier "Maoist" but in order to point out why Maoism rather than Trotskyism is a necessary theoretical rallying point if we want to make revolution. Indeed, if Trotskyism was able to demonstrate that it was such a rallying point, that it was kick-starting Bolshevik-style insurrections the world over which, even in their failures, were providing a significant communist challenge to capitalism, then we would have to question the validity of Maoism. Since anything is possible, maybe this will happen in the future (and if it does we should all become Trotskyists and accept that this is the correct path to revolution) but maybe also the "movementist" post-modern approach will prove itself successful, or maybe capitalism really is the end of history, and so these multiple possibilities are not enough to prevent an ideological engagement with a theoretical tradition that has so far proven itself incapable of being a revolutionary science. For if we are taught by history and are communists, then we should also recognize that the only way to understand history scientifically is to theoretically systematize the lessons gleaned from history's motor: class revolution. Since ideologies are historically mediated, we also have to examine whether or not they are viable in connection with class revolution.

Nor can we simply fall back on the old adage of anti-Trotskyism that marked the anti-revisionist Marxism-Leninisms of yesteryear. In those days it was enough to call Trotskyists "revisionists" (or worse, "social fascists" and "wreckers") and then attempt to ignore them, except when their more orthodox adherents showed up at an event they hadn't helped organize to chastise everyone for being fake communists. Therefore, it is also important to recognize that Trotskyism is not simply "revisionism",[2] that Trotsky was not an anti-communist renegade, and that Trotskyists are not dyed-in-the-wool "wreckers" who are committed to ruining communism. Even more importantly, it is necessary to recognize that Trotsky was a significant revolutionary during the Russian Revolution and that some Trotskyist theorists have even contributed to the Marxist theoretical canon. Indeed, the fact that Trotskyist intellectuals were able to wage a somewhat successful ideological struggle in the imperialist academic sphere is cause for celebration: it is due in a large part to their efforts that Marx and Marxism remain as valid academic pursuits.

In any case, the current demise of the people's war in Nepal proves that Maoists also can be revisionists. The behavior of the RCP-USA in the RIM might prove that Maoists can also be wreckers. These are charges that can be made of communists in every Marxist tradition; they are not some original sin attributable only to Trotskyism. If we are to properly ask the question "Maoism or Trotskyism?" we have to climb out of this rhetorical swamp.

We also must honestly ask "Maoism or Trotskyism?" as Maoists, rather than ignore this question altogether and go about our work, because Trotskyists are asking the same question. Ever since the emergence of Marxism-Leninism-Maoism and the people's wars that have blossomed in the storm centers of imperialism, ever since vital organizations at the centers of capitalism have started to gravitate towards this coherent form of Maoism, Trotskyist ideologues and intellectuals influenced by the narrative of Trotskyism have been writing theoretical engagements with Maoism.

Generally, these theoretical engagements have been quite poor. Loren Goldner's *Notes Towards a Critique of Maoism* is a recent example of these attempts to combat Maoism from a communist tradition that, though not Maoist, takes its analysis of the Maoism and the Chinese Revolution from Trotskyism. Jairus Banaji's critiques of Indian Maoism or Chris Cutrone's dismissal of Maoism altogether are other salient examples. These critiques most often venerate Trotsky over Mao, denigrate Maoism as "Stalinism", and indeed demonstrate the same understanding of Maoism possessed by the most orthodox Trotskyist groups like the Spartacist League and the International Bolshevik Tendency: that Maoism is simply "bourgeois revolution with red flags" because Mao's theory of New Democracy (which every Trotskyist assumes, having apparently never read the RIM statement or any of the theoretical expressions of Marxism-Leninism-Maoism, is the prime definition of Maoism) is erroneously understood as "class collaboration". In none of these critiques is there any recognition that Maoism-qua-Maoism finally crystallized as a revolutionary theory only in 1993 and that a sustained engagement with the "Maoisms" of the 1960s and 1970s is off the mark.[3]

These extremely flawed theoretical engagements, however, demonstrate the necessity to ask the question "Maoism or Trotskyism?" from a Maoist perspective. On the one hand they show that some Trotskyists and/or post-Trotskyists are taking Maoism seriously (indeed, they cannot deny that it is currently the only variant of communism successfully mobilizing the masses at the storm centers of imperialism); on the other hand, it demonstrates a certain level of panic amongst orthodox Trotskyists (who, like all orthodox communists, are angry that people are choosing a communism other than their own), and amongst non-orthodox Trotskyists and post-Trotskyists who are confused by a communism that, at first glance, does not resemble the kind of communism they believed was *proper* communism.

Most importantly, though, these theoretical engagements with Maoism demonstrate the emergence of an ideological line struggle where those committed to a communism that, to whatever degree, is influenced by Trotskyism are trying to prevent people gravitating towards communism from committing what they see as an ideological error. They want young communists to back away from the temptation of Maoism, to adhere to a more respectable Marxist tradition, and they want this because they believe their tradition is the only tradition capable of bringing about communism. Since we Maoists believe the same, we should at least recognize that this attitude is laudable. The problem, though, is that we are making the inverse claim.

The point here is that Trotskyism and the communism inspired by Trotskyism cannot be dismissed as "revisionism" but should rather be understood as a theoretical dead-end. History has many dead-ends and blind alleys, after all, and it is our contention that Trotskyism is ultimately another theoretical anachronism that is incapable of developing a path to revolution; it lacks the theoretical tools necessary for providing ideological and practical unity to a revolutionary movement. So in this engagement we will demonstrate this failure on the part of Trotskyism by examining: a) its theory of "permanent revolution", which is *the* theory that defines Trotskyism; b) its complaints about "Stalinism" and the failure of actually-existing socialism; c) its inability to be anything other than a dead-end when it comes to actually making revolution.

Permanent Revolution

If Trotskyism can be boiled down to a key theory then it is the theory of "permanent revolution, best exemplified in *The Permanent Revolution* (1931) but also expressed in germ form in earlier documents such as *Results and Prospects* (1906). It is this theory that determines Trotskyism's theoretical engagement with Maoism; it even explains why Trotskyism chooses to misunderstand Maoism. All Trotskyist organizations declare fidelity to this theory, even if they spend a lot of time arguing about what it means or attempting to modernize its theoretical terrain (i.e. Tony Cliff of the Socialist Workers Party attempted to do so and was called a "revisionist" by the orthodox Trotskyists), and so it is their theoretical linchpin.

To give credit where credit is due, the theory of permanent revolution is actually the result of Trotsky asking correct questions: how does one sustain and carry forward a revolution in a country that has not had a bourgeois revolution; how can socialism be built at the global peripheries where the political context and productive forces that are produced by a bourgeois revolution are absent? Clearly Trotsky asked this question because of his experience in the Russian Revolution and the inescapable fact that Russia seemed to lack the necessary elements, directly following the Bolshevik seizure of power, for socialism: the persistence of the peasant masses who were themselves stratified and outnumbered the working class, the supposed "grave-diggers of capitalism"; the absence of the forces of production that would have allowed for a predominant working class *and* the foundations for socialization, an absence that led to numerous economic plans on the part of Lenin and the Bolshevik leadership; and, perhaps most importantly for what would become the theory of permanent revolution, the lack of an infrastructure necessary to prevent socialism from degenerating since it would always be under attack by the more economically advanced capitalist nations. Moreover, since Trotsky was an important participant in the Russian Revolution, he wanted to argue, correctly and contrary to a very strong revisionist Marxist current at the time, that revolutionaries in underdeveloped countries (such as Russia) do not have to wait for an articulate bourgeois class to appear in these countries and have their revolution first.

Borrowing the terminology "permanent revolution" from Marx and Engels, Trotsky tried to make sense of the problems that confronted the revolution in Russia and summed up his understanding in the following manner:

> The Perspective of permanent revolution may be summarized in the following way: the complete victory of the democratic revolution in Russia is conceivable only in the form of the dictatorship of the proletariat, leaning on the peasantry. The dictatorship of the proletariat, which would inevitably place on the order of the day not only democratic but socialistic tasks as well, would at the same time give a powerful impetus to the international socialist revolution. Only the victory of the proletariat in the West could protect Russia from bourgeois resoration and assure it the possibility of rounding out the establishment of socialism.[4]

So far so good: some Trotskyists would be surprised to discover that Maoists agree with most of this statement. Where we differ, however, is in how Trotsky fully theorizes his perspective on permanent revolution, the problem of which is contained in the last sentence of this summary where the final responsibility of socialist victory is accorded to the proletariat at the centers of world capitalism (in Trotsky's day this was the "West" meaning

"West of Russia", i.e. central Europe, predominantly Britain and Germany). We'll return to this later.

Furthermore, the main part of Trotsky's revolutionary strategy in the context of peripheral countries is dedicated to a very specific analysis of the peasantry that sets it apart from the Maoist understanding. As noted above, Trotsky claims that the dictatorship of the proletariat must lean on the peasantry, but what he means by this is not that the peasantry in peripheral nations might be a revolutionary class but that, rather, they must be submitted to the discipline of the more advanced but minority proletariat class. Indeed, in *The Permanent Revolution* Trotsky accuses Lenin of "overestimating the independent role of the peasantry" and says that Lenin accused him of "underestimating the revolutionary role of the peasantry".[5] Hence he can speak of how the peasantry does not possess a revolutionary consciousness, that it will actually be counter-revolutionary (following Marx's analysis of the French peasantry in *The 18th Brumaire of Louis Bonaparte*), and that the proletariat will necessarily come into "collision" with the peasantry when it is consolidating the dictatorship of the proletariat.

Thus, Trotsky's claim that the dictatorship of the proletariat must lean on the peasantry seems to be rhetorical; he is rather confused by the peasantry and its position within a revolution that emerges in a semi-feudal context. On the one hand he wants to think beyond the crude "stagism" (a charge Trotskyists will later apply to any theory of revolution that tries to answer the same question but that isn't the theory of permanent revolution) inherent in the revisionist Marxisms that consistently focused on a bourgeois revolution happening first; on the other hand he is still caught within the same positivist categories of class where, following very dogmatic readings of Marx, the proletariat must look like the proletariat in western Europe and the peasantry must eventually and always be like the peasantry in the France of the *18th Brumaire*. There is a tension here between the desire to break away from dogmatic applications of historical materialism and the gut reaction to stay within the safe territory of a "pure" Marxism.

Ultimately Trotsky's commitment to Marxist orthodoxy would defeat his desire for Marxist creativity, the form of Marxism overwhelming its methodological essence. That is, Trotsky would prove incapable of particularizing the universality of Marxism within a given social context: he understood the importance of the peasantry in semi-feudal countries but, by also seeing them as a counter-revolutionary force in the final instance, believed that the nascent working classes in these countries, as we shall see below, needed to hold the revolution in permanence and discipline a most probably reactionary peasantry.

Generally Trotsky thought the peasantry would support a democratic revolution led by the proletariat but, because of their feudal consciousness, would cease supporting this revolution when it became socialist. Hence his reason for assuming the possibility of a "civil war" between the peasantry and the industrial working class in *The Permanent Revolution*, a civil war that could only be avoided if there was an international revolution led by the working classes in the more developed regions of global capitalism. Again we are led to his emphasis about the "victory of the proletariat in the West" as the necessary mechanism to prevent bourgeois restoration.

But before we get into this international dimension of the theory, we should examine how Trotsky's views of the peasantry were articulated within the semi-feudal context that gave rise to Maoism: the Chinese Revolution. In 1925 the Trotskyist current in the initial Chinese Party of China (CPC), represented by Chen Duxiu, opposed Mao's argument, following rigorous social investigation, that the party needed to embed itself within a peasantry that was already engaged in revolutionary action. Chen did not think that the party should embed itself within the peasantry because he felt, following Trotsky's line, that the peasantry would ultimately prove to be a reactionary force when it came to the struggle for socialism; instead he advocated remaining within the ranks of the Kuomintang and trying to win over the working class so that the party would have the necessary class forces to command the already-revolting peasantry. Here, it is interesting to note that the representative of Stalin in the initial CPC, Li Lisan, advocated the identical practice but for different reasons (Li's erroneous argument was that the Kuomintang was a bourgeois revolutionary force) and so, at the end of the day, both Trotskyist and Stalinist ideological lines resulted in the same dead-end practice: while Mao split from this configuration of the CPC and rebooted the party in the revolutionary peasantry, those loyal to the political lines of Chen and Li were liquidated by the Kuomintang under Cheng Kaishek in 1927.

Furthermore, one only has to have a conversation with an orthodox Trotskyist about revolutions outside of the developed imperialist centers to understand what a nearly-religious adherence to the theory of permanent revolution means for an understanding of the peasantry. They will tell you that peasants have either a reactionary or "petty-bourgeois" consciousness because they are fully embedded in feudalism and that any revolution that bases itself on this peasantry, even if they are the most numerous and value-creating class with nothing to lose but their chains, is not properly Marxist. The industrial working class is the only class capable of being the back-bone for a revolution, is the argument, and if this class does not exist (and sometimes *cannot exist as a revolutionary class in a capitalist formation that will remain underdeveloped under imperialist oppression*) then there is no point in doing anything but holding the revolution in permanence and waiting for the more developed working class at the centers of capitalism to lead the world revolution.

This is because Trotsky, in some ways intersecting with Lenin, understood that while revolutionary movements happened at the weakest links of global imperialism, the fact that the centers of world capitalism still possessed the economic power to crush these peripheral revolutions was something that needed to be understood. Unfortunately, rather than trying to make sense of the dialectic between center and periphery, Trotsky placed the onus of revolutionary responsibility on the shoulders of the proletariat at the centers of global capitalism. This was, after all, a proper proletariat that should have a proper proletarian consciousness. As he argues in *Results and Prospects*:

Without the direct State support of the European proletariat the working class of Russia cannot remain in power and convert its temporary domination into a lasting socialistic dictatorship. Of this there cannot for one moment be any doubt. But on the other hand there cannot be any doubt that a socialist revolution in the West will enable us directly to convert the temporary domination of the working class into a socialist dictatorship.[6]

In fact, Trotsky goes on to approvingly cite Kautsky's claim that "[s]ociety as a whole cannot artificially skip any stages of its development, but it is possible for constituent parts of society to hasten their retarded development by imitating the more advanced countries and, thanks to this, even to take their stand in the forefront of development".[7] So much for Trotsky's avoidance of "stagism": instead of it being possible for there to be socialist revolutions in the global peripheries, at best there can only be "artificial" socialist institutions[8] that can influence the more advanced nations to take the lead in producing authentic global socialism. One must wonder, then, what makes a socialism "artificial" as opposed to "authentic" when, according to Lenin, socialism is a process, a transitionary stage where the bourgeoisie is placed under the dictatorship of the proletariat, and thus as heterogeneous as the period of mercantile capitalism, where there were various attempts to place the aristocracy under bourgeois dictatorship, that preceded the emergence of capitalism. But we shall return to this point about the Trotskyist understanding of socialism in the following section.

Trotsky's theory of "combined and uneven development" was fundamental to his understanding of the theory of permanent revolution's international meaning. Here we have a theory that seems to imply that capitalism is a global mode of production that develops in a combined and uneven manner, rather than a theory (as those influenced by what would become the Maoist tradition have argued) of a world system of capitalism where capitalist modes of production form the centers of capitalism, and impose/control global capitalism through imperialism, and capitalist social formations on the periphery that are still economically defined, internally, as pre-capitalist modes of production.[9]

If the world is a single mode of production, then it makes sense for there to be a single world socialist revolution determined in the final instance, obviously, by those who are at the correct international point of production, i.e. the industrial proletariat at the centers of imperialism. For if capitalism is a global mode of production, then its point of production must also be global and it makes sense to speak of a global proletarian class rather than various proletarian classes in various social contexts which might not have a nation ideologically but still exist within a national economic framework materially. In this context the nascent industrial working class in the economically "backward" regions must not only place the most probably counter-revolutionary peasantry under their advanced discipline but also, due to the inability of building socialism in a particular region without a world revolution, hold the revolution in permanence and wait for the lead of their more advanced counterparts in the more economically "advanced" parts of the global mode of production, much like the workers at a small factory in a small town waiting for the workers in the massive factories in the big cities to have a general strike and start the insurrection.

We can locate this eurocentric understanding of worldwide revolution in the earlier theoretical work of Trotsky, particularly in his draft of the Manifesto for the First Congress of the Third International:

> The workers and peasants not only of Annam, Algiers and Bengal, but also of Persia and Armenia will gain their opportunity of independent existence only in that hour when the workers of England and France, having overthrown Lloyd George and Clemenceau, will have taken state power into their own hands. Colonial slaves of Africa and Asia! The hour of proletarian dictatorship in Europe will strike for you as the hour of your own emancipation![10]

The chauvinism of this claim was only more apparent when Trotsky went on to write that the "smaller peoples" in colonial and semi-colonial contexts (i.e. the people directly oppressed by imperialism and engaged in some significant revolutionary struggles) will discover their freedom in the proletarian revolutions of the imperial centers that would "free the productive forces of all countries from the tentacles of the national states". Hence the oppressed nations were ordered to carry out their struggles "without any detriment to the unified and centralised European world economy".[11]

This erroneous line was struggled against in the Second Congress of the Third International, and eventually overthrown with the position taken on the "national question", emerging through a dialectical argument between Lenin and Roy, though it is clear that it has lingered in various forms to the detriment of revolutionary movements. What is interesting to note, however, is that while the majority of the Third International succeeded, at least formally, in rejecting the position put forward by Trotsky in the First Congress, Trotsky, and hence Trotskyism, continued to maintain this line. As a side note, this speaks to the overall static nature of Trotskyism and may perhaps tell us something about how the staunchest Trotskyists tend to demand a return to the theoretical thinking of the early 19th-century.

Returning to the problematic of the internationalization of the capitalist mode of production, however, we find an impulse, amongst multiple strands of Trotskyism, to also internationalize the revolutionary party. While we Maoists must agree with our Trotskyist counterparts about the necessity of internationalism, we also hold that it is a false internationalism to establish an international communist party. This is because we Maoists believe that every nation has its own unique class composition,[12] its own particular version of a universal mode of production, and one cannot simply impose the analysis of class and class struggle that was developed in Western Europe or the United States on regions as diverse as Pakistan, Vietnam, etc. Most often this type of "internationalism" ends up being a rearticulation of imperialist chauvinism where the "more advanced" elements of these international parties (i.e. the party members in the US or Britain) dictate the theoretical analysis and behavior to their party counterparts in a third-world country, failing to realize that a revolutionary movement in these regions can only proceed from a concrete analysis of a concrete situation rather than the imposition of an alien analysis connected to other regions.

Hence the failure of Trotskyist parties to launch even the beginning stages of a revolution anywhere, particularly at the peripheries of global capitalism; even in those rare instances where they had significant membership (i.e. in Vietnam before the rise of Ho Chi Minh's party), they could not initiate a revolutionary process and were quickly eclipsed by those movements that had developed organically, however flawed the theory of these movements might have been, in these particular contexts. Thus, if communism is ultimately about making revolution, we have to question a theory that has been unsuccessful in launching a revolutionary struggle anywhere. And though it is true that Trotskyists claim that other revolutionary struggles failed because they did not take into account Trotsky's theory of permanent revolution, the fact is that these ultimately-failed revolutions were still more successful than any revolutionary movement guided by Trotskyism. The theory of permanent revolution is an originary failure that has proved itself incapable of even launching a revolution, but I will talk more about this problem in the final section of this polemic.

If I am spending a significant amount of time trying to describe the ins-and-outs of the theory of permanent revolution, it is because a Maoist response to the core theory of Trotskyism requires an adequate summary. Moreover, as noted above, the Trotskyist understanding of Maoism can be traced to the fact that this is the foundational theory for the former ideology; thus, anything that appears to contradict this theory on the part of the latter must be treated, I would assume, as that theory's most important facet.

Here, of course, we are speaking of the theory of New Democracy that was another way to answer the same question. Since the Chinese Revolution happened in a semi-feudal/semi-colonial context, the CPC under Mao was also interested in theorizing how socialism could be built and thus there are moments where the theory of New Democracy and Permanent Revolution, at least in this sense, intersect. The divergences, though, are crucial: the CPC, unlike any Trotskyist organization, actually succeeded in answering the question and building socialism in China.

The theory of New Democracy is generally about how to build the forces of production necessary to produce socialism (i.e. the industrial infrastructure that normally would have emerged under capitalism but is often largely absent in a semi-feudal social formation) since the centralization of productive forces that is the hallmark of socialism is only possible if these productive forces exist in the first place. Rather than wait for a bourgeois revolution to produce the capitalist groundwork for socialism, though, the theory of New Democracy argues that: a) such a revolution is generally impossible in a country that is dominated by imperialism, and unnecessary since global capitalism means that every country is in some sense a capitalist formation; b) the economic infrastructure necessary for socialism will be built under the direction of the communist party, thus the productive forces will be submitted to socialist productive relations and politics will be in command; c) under the direction of the communist party there can be an alliance between the "revolutionary classes" in this period, an alliance necessary to achieve (b) that will consist of a worker-peasant alliance with the participation, to a certain degree, of the national bourgeoisie that would remain under the guidance of the party.[13]

It is important to note that Trotskyists focus obsessively on point (c), while dismissing the other points as "stagist" (ironic because the theory of permanent revolution also has its "stages" with artificial socialist institutions in the peripheries first, true socialist revolution led by the proletariat at the centers later), because they feel it is tantamount to "class collaboration" and that this, more than anything else, proves that Maoism (which they reduce only to this theory) is a theory of "bourgeois revolution with red flags". They will often use examples that have nothing to do with New Democracy as it was practiced in China, and as it has been understood by Maoists now, to prove the class-collaborative aspect of this theory. Indeed, Trotskyists will often cite the failure of Indonesian communism in the early 1960s as an example of the failures of New Democracy (and by extension "Maoism") even though Sukarno's theory of "Guided Democracy" was not identical to Mao's theory of "New Democracy" and, in any case, the event that would generate the theoretical core of Maoist theory (the Great Proletarian Cultural Revolution) had not happened when Sukarno proposed his approach to revolutionary nationalism in 1957. Nor was the Indonesian Communist Party behaving according to the theory of New Democracy; contrary to Mao's theory noted above, this party had placed itself within the framework of a national bourgeois structure, and thus was under the command of the national bourgeoisie rather than vice versa. New Democracy, therefore, is only possible if the revolution is being led and completed by the communist party: communist politics must be in command; the relations of production politically necessary for socialism must direct the building of the forces of production economically necessary for socialism.[14]

Moreover, the reason the theory of New Democracy claimed that the national bourgeoisie in a semi-feudal and semi-colonial context could be a "revolutionary class" (but only to a certain extent and always under the direction of the party) was because this class, unlike the *comprador bourgeoisie* (that is, the bourgeois who represented imperialist interests), often had a vested interest in getting rid of imperialist interference and semi-feudal ideology. In the framework of building socialism in a semi-feudal/semi-colonial country, this consciousness was objectively revolutionary. "Being a bourgeoisie in a colonial and semi-colonial country and oppressed by imperialism", writes Mao in *On New Democracy*, "the Chinese national bourgeoisie retains a certain revolutionary quality *at certain periods and to a certain degree*... in its opposition to the foreign imperialists and the domestic government of bureaucrats and warlords".[15] Note that Mao qualifies that this "revolutionary quality" is only possible "at certain periods and to a certain degree"; indeed, he would qualify the limits of this quality just a few paragraphs later which demonstrates why the theory of New Democracy has nothing to do with class collaboration and tailing the national bourgeoisie:

> At the same time, however, being a bourgeois class in a colonial and semi-colonial country and so being extremely

flabby economically and politically, the Chinese national bourgeoisie also has another quality, namely, a proneness to conciliation with the enemies of the revolution. Even when it takes part in the revolution, it is unwilling to break with imperialism completely and, moreover, it is closely associated with the exploitation of the rural areas through land rent; thus it is neither willing nor able to overthrow imperialism, and much less the feudal forces, in a thorough way.[16]

This does not sound like class collaboration. In fact, the way Mao understands the national bourgeoisie in a semi-feudal/semi-colonial context (which is a bourgeoisie, he would argue, that is different from the bourgeoisie at the centers of capitalism) is similar to how Trotsky understands the peasantry: a useful force to draw upon at a certain stage of revolution, but a stumbling block to revolution later on. Hence the reason to place the national bourgeoisie under the command of the party during the period of New Democracy and the complaints, on the part of reactionary historians even today, of how these poor bourgeois people were tricked into collaborating with communism only to have their bourgeois "rights" taken away.

Indeed, and this is extremely important when it comes to the question of "Maoism or Trotskyism?", the period of New Democracy was over by the end of the Great Leap Forward (despite some of the latter's significant failures which, it should be noted, were not as tragic as bourgeois reactionary historians claim), and the conclusion of this period was openly declared by the faction of the party united under Mao, and socialism was finally emergent. In this context the problem was no longer how to build the context necessary for the dictatorship of the proletariat, but how to maintain the dictatorship of the proletariat and produce the social relations necessary for communism. Here it is significant to note that there was a political line in the party that did not want to go beyond New Democracy, that confused this period with socialism, and did not want to carry forth the struggle to consolidate the dictatorship of the proletariat. Thus, during the Great Proletarian Cultural Revolution, there emerged a critique of the theory of "productive forces", a theory arguing that we should only concentrate on building the productive forces necessary for socialism, rather than dealing with the political question of relations of production, and thus continue only with New Democracy and mistake this period as socialism.

The recent events in Nepal are a good example of this problem. The CPN (Maoist) launched a successful people's war and was able to establish something akin to a period of New Democracy when it became the UCPN (Maoist). Since Nepal was also a semi-feudal/semi-colonial country it needed to establish New Democracy in order to produce the necessary context for socialism but the bourgeois line within the party triumphed earlier than it did in China and even New Democracy was abandoned as the revolution degenerated into what could accurately be called, but only at this moment of degeneration, a "bourgeois revolution with red flags".

However, since Maoists argue that a line struggle will always manifest within a revolutionary context (a struggle between those who do not want to go further down the socialist path and those who want to complete the revolution), this line struggle will happen whether or not there is a New Democratic revolution. Indeed, in China the line struggle existed before, during, and after the period of New Democracy; the bourgeois line did not attain victory until the end of the Cultural Revolution where the forces gathered around Deng Xiaoping emerged victorious and capitalist restoration, originally envisioned as a return to the period of New Democracy, began. Thus, the problem with the restoration of capitalism has nothing specifically to do with the theory of New Democracy: it is always, for Maoists, a possibility under socialism because socialism is also a period of class struggle; this is a key theoretical component, universally applicable, of Marxism-Leninism-Maoism.

Therefore, it is important to note that the theory of New Democracy, even if understood properly, is only a theory, according to Maoism, that is applicable to revolutions that emerge at the peripheries of global capitalism. Revolutionary movements at the centers of global capitalism (that is, movements that manifest within completed capitalist modes of production) will not pursue New Democracy since the problem New Democracy is meant to address has nothing to do with the capitalist mode of production where the economic infrastructure necessary for building socialism already exists. This is why Maoism, which has been promoted as a new theoretical stage of revolutionary communism, is not primarily defined by the theory of New Democracy since a new stage of communism should exhibit universal aspects that are applicable in every particular context. Marxism-Leninism-Maoism's crucial point is what was noted above, and this point connects to further points about how the party should function, how the super-structure obstructs the base at given moments of historical development, how the party can be held to account by the masses, how to act towards people, and an entire host of concepts that not only take into account the importance of third-world revolutions (and agree along with Lenin that these tend to happen more frequently because these are the "weak links" of the capitalist world system) but also teach us something about making revolution in the first world and the problems we will necessarily encounter.

Indeed, the fact that there is no significant peasantry or a national bourgeoisie with some sort of "revolutionary quality" at the centers of capitalism means that the entire possibility of New Democracy in these regions is patently absurd. Rather, the fact that building socialism will mean the mobilization of the masses and a possible united front between communists, various sectors of the proletariat, some conscious elements of the petty bourgeoisie (i.e. students and intellectuals), and (in contexts like the US and Canada) oppressed nationalities struggling for self-determination against settler-colonialism is something worth considering. Moreover, the fact that any possible establishment of socialism will also mean a class struggle between those who want to push socialism forward and those who want to cling to bourgeois ideology (that is, that class struggle continues under the dictatorship of the proletariat) is the key element in understanding Maoism across regions. We will examine this point in more detail in the following sections.

Maoism is Stalinism?

A significant problem we encounter when we engage with Trotskyism is the charge that any form of communism that accepts the basics of Leninism but that is not-Trotskyism is, ipso facto, "Stalinism". Thus, after Lenin, there can only be Trotskyism or Stalinism and nothing else. Maoism, then, is treated as a variant of Stalinism for rather simplistic reasons.

Generally, Maoism is Stalinism according to Trotskyists because it supposedly accords to Stalin's theory of "socialism in one country". Here it is worth noting that Trotskyists are primarily responsible for defining "Stalinism" which they see as the only ideological option competing with Trotskyism in the Leninist terrain. The fact that Stalin argued that it was possible for a single country to build socialism (but not necessarily *communism* by itself, and this is important) not only rubs up against the Trotskyist theory of permanent revolution but is sometimes interpreted, by the most uncritical Trotskyists, to mean that Stalin only cared about the revolution in Russia at the expense of all other revolutions.

Well it is true that the Chinese Revolution under Mao did attempt to build socialism in China without a world revolution and so I suppose this, if such is the qualification for "Stalinism", might make them guilty of the Trotskyist charge. At the same time, though, the Maoist understanding of the Chinese Revolution is such that it accords with a very important theoretical distinction between *socialism* and *communism*, a distinction made by Lenin in *The State and Revolution* but lacking in Trotsky's writings on permanent revolution. And this understanding is that socialism, the dictatorship of the proletariat, is possible in a single country and is the transition to communism, but that full communism, since it would necessarily be stateless, requires the entire world to also be socialist. But just because most of the world isn't socialist does not mean that a single country cannot establish a dictatorship of the proletariat; most significantly, the more storm centers that enter this transitionary phase, the more likely world communism becomes.[17]

But Trotskyists are under the impression, because of the theory of permanent revolution and the fact that the world is conceived as a single "combined and uneven" mode of production, that the entire world must have a socialist revolution and that particular socialist revolutions are impossible. Nations in the periphery embarking on socialist revolutions, under this interpretation, can therefore hope for nothing more than a democratic revolution with "artificial socialist institutions" and will eventually run up against a civil war with their peasantry *unless* the revolution isn't commanded by the more developed proletariat at the centers of global capitalism. Once again we have a tension between the creativity Trotskyism desires to express and its inability to escape a dogmatic adherence to orthodox Marxist categories. The socialist revolution at the peripheries must be permanent, we are told, must not submit to the trap of waiting for a bourgeois revolution; at the same time, however, this revolution is impossible, and can only be a *democratic* revolution (a bourgeois revolution?), without the revolutionary intervention of the more economically developed nations.

So just as Trotsky conflates the categories of the capitalist mode of production and the capitalist world system, he also

conflates the categories of socialism and communism. His justification for arguing that only a global socialist revolution is
possible, and that socialism cannot just emerge in particular
countries, is to be found in those passages where Marx and
Engels also claim that only a world socialist revolution is
possible, and Trotskyists are keen to remind us of this fact. The
problem, though, is that Marx and Engels often used the terms
socialism and *communism* synonymously and that it was not until
Lenin wrote *The State and Revolution* that further semantic clarity
was added to these categories. That is, Lenin went to great
lengths to point out the moments in the work of Marx and Engels
where the concept of *socialism* (i.e. a centralized state where the
bourgeoisie was placed under the dictatorship of the proletariat)
was treated as a progenerative category for *communism* (i.e. a
classless society).[18] Under the Leninist clarification and
concretization of these concepts, then, it is quite possible that
socialism, or a dictatorship of the proletariat, can exist in
particular countries while other countries remain
capitalist—though, admittedly, the existence of such a socialism
will be affected by external imperialist pressure. At the same
time Lenin argued, following Marx and Engels but without the
semantic confusion, that communism was only possible globally;
after all, in a very pragmatic sense, the state has to wither away
in order for communism to exist and, in the context of the
capitalist world system, if a state was ever to wither away then it
would seem that the imperialist nations would immediately
crush this emergent communism. Trotsky, however, did not seem
to accept Lenin's conceptual categories here and was led by the
way he understood world capitalism to simply argue that
socialist revolution was possible only with a world revolution.

Therefore, there has really never been any actually-existing
socialism according to Trotskyism, just degenerated/deformed
workers' states and "Bonapartist" regimes. When capitalism is
restored in these contexts, then, the Trotskyist response is to

proclaim that this is simply because they were never socialist to begin with! Maoists, however, take a different tack: they claim these regions *were* socialist, or even on the socialist road, but that they failed to carry the socialist struggle through to communism because, and this is a key insight of Marxism-Leninism-Maoism mentioned above, *class struggle continues under the dictatorship of the proletariat.* That is, capitalist restoration can happen because socialism is also a class society: the bourgeoisie, after all, is being held under the dictatorship of the proletariat and so it can always defeat this dictatorship and return to power. Significantly, bourgeois ideology lingers in the superstructure, becomes a compelling force in socialist society, and this is because most of us were born and raised in a context where bourgeois ideology was hegemonic (it is hard to simply break from this because we arrive, after a revolution, seeped in the filth of the past mode of production) and this ideology remains compelling *even for people within the communist party.*

And yet Trotskyists have a different story to tell about the restoration of capitalism in formerly socialist contexts. Their story is rather simplistic and, as such, cannot account for very much: Stalin and the bureaucracy he produced ruined the Russian Revolution, mainly because Stalin and his bureaucracy wouldn't recognize permanent revolution. The solution to this problem, then, is to have Trotsky instead of Stalin lead the Russian Revolution post-Lenin; it breaks down to a problem of great figures of history. But we Maoists assert that Trotsky's leadership of the Russian Revolution wouldn't have made things significantly different: for one thing, he clearly wasn't capable of realizing that class struggle continued under socialism and even within the party, and his theory of permanent revolution predicts his failure: how he would have been able to command a global socialist revolution from a Russia that was being attacked by the forces of reaction is rather impossible to surmise. Thus, even according to Trotskyism, the Russian Revolution was destined to fail with or without Trotsky.

Again, we Maoists argue that the failure of any socialist revolution is *always* a possibility because socialism is a transitionary stage and thus still a period of class struggle where a revolutionary class is attempting to complete its hegemony. We understand that revolutions can always fail, even before socialism, not because the revolutionaries involved lack some pure understanding of Bolshevism and a party with the magical ingredients of *true* democratic centralism, but because capitalist restoration is always immanent during socialist revolutions. There are line struggles in the party itself and sometimes the line that best represents the capitalist road will triumph.

Returning to the general question of Stalin and Stalinism, which is often the main concern of Trotskyism (since it defines itself as the only Leninism that is not-Stalinist), we should at least agree that it is important to correctly critique Stalin and the phenomenon that Trotskyists call "Stalinism". Unlike Marxist-Leninists who declare complete fidelity to Stalin as *the* successor of Lenin, who argue that any revolutionary movement that critiques Stalin to any degree is not properly "Marxist-Leninist", we Maoists think that every positionality within the communist movement (even Mao's) should be subjected to a concrete and thorough critique. This is why we do not imagine that Stalin is beyond reproach, nor that criticizing Stalin is tantamount to counter-revolutionary behavior as Hoxhaite tradition would have us believe.[19]

However, simply focusing on Stalin as some sort of evil dictator who ruined the Bolshevik Revolution smacks of bourgeois moralism and retains some of the worst elements of reactionary propaganda regarding the Russian Revolution. Moreover, this perspective is unable to explain what happened to the Soviet Union *following* the Stalin period when Khrushchev denounced Stalin and the "Stalinist" period. Indeed, Trotskyists at this time praised Khrushchev because they felt he was proving the correctness of Trotsky's theories regarding the Soviet Union. But if this was true, then the intentional revisionism embraced by Khrushchev (his theory of peaceful co-existence with capitalism), which was the reason for his denunciation of the Stalin period, would have to be treated as also correct.

So, if Khrushchev was clearly embracing revisionism and was not-Stalin, and clearly rejected anything that could be called "Stalinism", then would this not make the Stalin period something more than just a "deformed/degenerated workers' state" in that Khrushchev's break from this period was the hallmark of revisionism (i.e. the peaceful co-existence thesis being precisely what was argued, in a smaller context, by Eduard Bernstein)? Even Trotskyist critiques of Khrushchev are unable to make correct distinctions between this period of the Soviet Union and the Stalin period, seeing it as the same thing (because there was a bureaucracy!) and refusing to recognize that Khrushchev's rupture from this period was a serious epistemic break in the Soviet Union's theory and practice; indeed, it shook the world, disaffected innumerable communist movements worldwide, led to the failed Bandung project, and cannot simply be treated as another variant of "Stalinism" or, even worse, a revolutionary rejection of "Stalinism" that proved Trotsky correct. At the most Trotskyists try to claim that Khrushchev was just another "Stalinist", as were Gorbachev and Yeltsin, a homogenization that is clumsy at best, idealist at worst.[20]

Rather than examine the failure of the Soviet Union as the result of an evil individual who possessed the power to produce a bureaucracy devoted to his nefarious plans (the kind of analysis that belongs in fairy tales and fantasy fiction), Maoists try to make sense of the failures of the Soviet Union in a historical-materialist manner. We do not dismiss Stalin as an evil figure; rather we see him as someone who, at one point in time and for whatever reason, was leading a revolutionary state (if history had been different, and Trotsky had won the line struggle and Stalin was in exile, we would have said the same about Trotsky) and, in attempting to lead, committed various errors.[21] But we see the approach to building socialism under Stalin as the error that produces revisionism and the failure of the Russian Revolution or any revolution for that matter.

Again: the theory that class struggle continues under the dictatorship of the proletariat explains both the failures of the Stalinist period and the revisionism of the Khrushchev period. Stalin did not understand the possibility of capitalist restoration as a natural part of socialism (that is, that socialism is still a class society) and that counter-revolutionary political lines come from the inheritance of bourgeois (and even semi-feudal) ideology, preserved in the super-structure. Thus, rather than seeing people who might or might not have adopted bourgeois political lines within the party and Soviet society as something that would necessarily happen under socialism, the forces assembled around Stalin (the so-called "Stalinist bureaucracy" as Trotskyists put it) simply acted as if these individuals and groups and ideas were the result of foreign interference or intentional treason. Moreover, they failed to understand that the party itself would be host to an organic line struggle that would be a reflection of the predominance of class struggle under socialism and that the party's leadership would often preserve bourgeois ideology. And this theory, more than anything else, can explain why Stalin's chosen successor, Khruschev, who was initially quite happy to carry out policies of liquidation and political policing in the Stalin period, could also be a revisionist. Not because he was a foreign agent (as "Stalinism" would assume) and not because he was a bureaucrat (as Trotskyism would assume) but because bourgeois ideology and thus revisionism is always compelling, *especially* to people in positions of party leadership.

The Trotskyist analysis of "Stalinism", however, tells us nothing about how and why socialism can fail other than "it wasn't socialism to begin with", or "just because some bad man was leading socialism", or "if only there was not that cold bureaucracy then things would have been different". None of these explanations can show how to build socialism properly except, perhaps, to hold the revolution in permanence and wait until everyone in the world builds socialism together. But would such a scenario prevent "bad men" from coming to power and ruining everything or would we need to have some sort of magical democratic centralism mechanism that would forever prevent such evil people from gaining totalitarian power? The solution is to just get a Trotsky in there, a solution based on personality types. Moreover, to assume that a bureaucracy (which, by definition, is an organized structure of adminis-tration) would not emerge in even the imaginary context of a single global socialist revolution is itself a fantasy: how would socialism be developed and consolidated in this context, sponta-neously and without any struggle over administration? Bureaucracies can and will emerge despite any anti-bureaucratic attempts on the part of revolutionaries. Rather than pretend that they won't because of some supernatural anti-bureaucratic powers on the part of pure revolutionaries, therefore, we should see them as spaces for class struggle under socialism: structures that will emerge but must be opened to the masses and placed under the control of the masses. Yet again, the Maoist theory of class struggle continuing under the dictatorship of the proletariat tells us something about building socialism and the struggles that will necessarily happen in this period; this is the main reason why Maoism is applicable in every context, is a development following Marxism-Leninism, and is not simply reducible to a communism only for third-world peasants.

Ultimately, there is no such thing as "Stalinism" beyond what Trotskyists say it is, and what they say it is really has no scientific meaning beyond "socialism in one country", a theory that only Trotskyists obsess about. We Maoists do not recognize that there is anything worthy of being called "Stalinism" and think that those who bother identifying as "Stalinist" are also adopting a dead-end communism that is no more scientifically relevant than Trotskyism.

Making Revolution

As noted in the section about permanent revolution, Trotskyism has been singularly incapable of even embarking on the revolutionary path. This problem is generally the result of the failure of this theory's revolutionary strategy *politically* and *militarily*. Its political strategy was discussed above in reference to the theory of permanent revolution and the focus on world socialist revolution. Its military strategy is basically the Bolshevik strategy of insurrection, the so-called "October Road", where a mass strike and armed insurrection will follow after a period of protracted legal struggle.

It is important to note that all attempts to make revolution following the insurrectionist strategy have failed since the October Revolution and this, in large part, is why some Maoists speak of the universality of people's war as a military strategy for making revolution. Since this theory is still a subject of debate amongst the international Maoist movement, however, I will not spend time comparing it to the military strategy of insurrection in order to say why Maoism is superior to Trotskyism in this regard. After all, some Maoists and other non-Trotskyists (even some anarcho-communists) uphold the theory of insurrection.

The point here, though, is that none of these failed attempts to make revolution through insurrection were even Trotskyist; that is, Trotskyism has proved itself singularly incapable of even sparking an insurrectionary moment, though it likes to claim other insurrectionary moments as its own—either asserting that the Bolshevik insurrection was all due to Trotsky's work and he was leading the Bolsheviks in the October Revolution (a claim that ignores the period of guerrilla war that began in 1905 or the fact that Trotsky's contributions to the revolution were *tactical* rather than *strategic* and that the revolutionary strategy that produced the so-called "October Road" was due to Lenin), or naming themselves after an uprising performed by a group whose leading members did not like Trotsky.[22] Every failed insurrectionary attempt has been led by: a) Luxemburgists; b) Marxist-Leninists who often declared fidelity to the Soviet Union under Stalin; c) even anarchists, but only once, in the case of the Spanish Revolution.

Thus, there is not a single example of a Trotskyist attempt to actually make revolution and this is due, primarily, to the general *political* strategy of Trotskyism, the theory of permanent revolution. Indeed, if a socialist revolution cannot hope to succeed unless it is led by the advanced working class at the centers of capitalism, and this revolution must ultimately be a *global* revolution in order to be properly called "socialist", then what Trotskyists are really advocating is holding the revolution in permanence until everyone is ready to go at it all together, everywhere in the world, which of course means they have been waiting since the Fourth International and performing only a long and protracted legal struggle.[23]

Sometimes Trotskyists will defend their practice by claiming they are protecting a "true" Marxism and, in (with)holding the revolution in permanence, are simply preparing for the time when the working-class will realize, through decades of propaganda and entering trade unions, that this or that Trotskyist sect's approach is correct and, like a sudden spark igniting, a proper Trotskyist revolution will erupt. Here we have another version of the tired "the-time-is-not-right" refrain that some Marxists, and not just Trotskyists, like to repeat ad infinitum. And yet this "time-is-not-right" approach is intrinsic to the Trotskyist strategy of revolution: for the time has never been right across the entire world at the same time. The time for revolution, contrary to the Trotskyist assumption, will only be right if those whose "time is right" (or who make the time right) in specific contexts embark on protracted revolutions that are capable of disarticulating imperialism by pursuing the socialist path rather than waiting until everyone pursues it all at once. Thus, despite the Trotskyist claim that it is avoiding economic determinism by theorizing its version of permanent revolution, its strategy in actual practice ends up reasserting a productive-forces approach, holding the revolution in abeyance until the global "combined-and-uneven" mode of production is at a balanced point where everyone can make a go of it altogether.

No one, however, is really gravitating towards the sectarian Trotskyist guardians of "pure Marxism" because, though they are probably the best examples of Trotskyist theory due to their orthodoxy, most people find their sectarianism, dogmatism, and missionary-Marxism annoying, offensive, and generally cultish. More important, then, are those influenced by the Trotskyist tradition but correctly wary of the productive-forces approach (those who we generally refer to as "critical-Trotskyist" or "post-Trotskyist"), who still cannot break from the theory that produces a strategy incapable of making revolution. These groups often base themselves on Hal Draper's "socialism from below" theory and end up, in practice, tailing mass movements. Others become little more than clubs for university students, intellectuals, and trade-union bureaucrats (this despite Trotskyism's toothless critiques of bureaucracy). Still others imagine that entering social-democratic bourgeois parties and embarking on a reformist project, perhaps because its lack of militancy allows them to be respectable communists, will eventually allow socialism to emerge. In all of these cases, though, as with above, Trotskyism and those strands of Marxism highly influenced by Trotskyism have never seriously approached revolution in actual practice.

Since this is *the* most important facet of communism, *making revolution and overthrowing capitalism*, it is extremely telling that the Trotskyist tradition has no revolutionary experience to speak of unless we count the Bolshevik Revolution in which Trotsky *participated* as a revolutionary. But this was not a "Trotskyist" revolution; Stalin also participated in the Bolshevik Revolution (and to such a degree that he had an entire underground apparatus surrounding him and this, more than anything else, allowed him to push Trotsky out of the Comintern) but your average Trotskyist would have a conniption fit if you called the Bolshevik Revolution "Stalinist"!

So, unlike Maoism which, even before it was fully theorized, has inspired significant people's wars throughout the world, Trotskyism has no revolutionary experience to call its own, has proven itself incapable of producing a revolutionary experience of its own, and thus cannot learn from its successes and failures when it comes to revolutionary strategy. Indeed, all Trotskyism can do is critique other revolutionary movements from a position of nowhere, a stand-point based only on its understanding of the Bolshevik Revolution and its belief that everything must be precisely as it imagines the Bolshevik Revolution to have been although, as an ideology, it has failed to replicate this instance and, more importantly, the world is not the same, spatially or temporally, as Russia in 1917. And though Trotskyists have participated in insurrectionary moments like mining strikes and factory take-overs throughout Latin America, in all of these cases they were simply tailing a larger mass movement rather than organizing and leading these struggles towards a revolutionary moment.

Of course, the way Trotskyism has traditionally rejected this charge, as I noted in the section on permanent revolution, is by pointing out that all of these other revolutionary movements have failed and that maybe they wouldn't have failed had they followed the theory of permanent revolution. This is an easy charge to make because Trotskyists are able to claim a "pure Marxism" by the very fact that they have never had a chance, as their theory prevents them from ever having a chance in the first place, to lead a revolution and thus encounter all of the messiness revolutions tend to generate, as well as the two-line struggle we Maoists say (based on our historical experience) is bound to happen; Trotskyism has not made any mistakes because it hasn't done anything that would allow it to fail or be successful. It's a bit like someone who has never gone to school claiming they have never failed a test: it's an absurd and fallacious position but most importantly it demonstrates an idealist conception of Marxism, where a pure communism is like a Platonic form, existing outside of space and time, and that all we have to do is correctly reflect on its essence in order to produce a truly perfect revolution.

But we Maoists assert, along with Marx, that it is only possible to know something through practice; thus, it is only possible to understand revolution through revolutionary praxis, through trying and sometimes failing at revolution. We are taught by history, but not in circumstances we choose, and we can only solve those questions, as Marx was keen on reminding his readers, that are presented to us by history if we solve them at all. Trotskyism, it must be said, has not even tried to solve the problem, in practice, of how to make revolution: it has only theorized this problem and relied on a theory that projects revolution far into the future, thus escaping the hard work of building an actual revolutionary movement.

Indeed, the obsessive need to argue that Maoism is pseudo-communism seems more a product of an ideology concerned with a pure Marxism (i.e. a Marxism that exists beyond class struggle, that can be discovered only by reading the precise words of Marx, Engels, Lenin, and Trotsky as if these words are sacred) as well as an ideology that feels threatened when other Marxisms, unlike the supposed apex of communist theory (Trotskyism), actually succeed in building movements capable of launching revolutions. So rather than examine why these other communisms are successful and what their theories are actually saying, rather than question its own absence of revolutionary praxis, Trotskyism instead contents itself by arguing that these are fake revolutions and then, when these revolutions fail (because no revolution is determined to succeed and success is extremely difficult), some Trotskyists chuckle knowingly and argue that their theories can explain this failure when the truth is that the theories of those who failed actually do a better job, as noted in the previous section, of making sense of revolutionary failure.

In fact, some of the more orthodox Trotskyist groups try to argue that this lack of revolutionary history is a virtue: "the faction fights that have taken place since the inception of Trotsky's Fourth International over 50 years ago have been struggles to preserve for the cause of the proletariat internationally the principles and revolutionary traditions that were brought to bear by Lenin's Bolshevik Party in leading the toiling masses of the former tsarist empire to victory".[24] Meaning, then, that the principle duty of a revolutionary is to preserve the traditions of the past, gleaned through a very particular social and historical context, and that such a pursuit justifies a factionalism and sectarianism that only exists because Trotskyist group x thinks that Trotskyist group y has the wrong ideological interpretation of very specific and rarified theoretical positions held by Trotsky.

Thankfully, these ultra-orthodox variants of Trotskyism are seen as ludicrous caricatures of Marxism by the majority of the left (including the majority of other Trotskyists and leftists influenced by Trotskyism), and the only reason they manage to persist is for the same reasons that cults manage to persist. We only mention this ortho-Trotskyist defense of preserving history at the expense of revolutionary action to indicate that some Trotskyists are quite aware of Trotskyism's inability to produce or lead a revolutionary movement. Moreover, this orthodox sectarianism should teach us that the only reason to engage in ideological line struggle with other variants of communism is not, as some would have it, to promote banal sectarianisms and static factionalisms, but to clarify the theoretical grounds necessary for making revolution. Obsessing over these theoretical grounds without attempting to implement them in revolutionary practice—and thus being unable to learn how to articulate them creatively in a given social-historical context—is the antithesis of communism.

Theory and Practice

Thus, as discussed at the outset of this polemic, the question "Maoism or Trotskyism?" has nothing to do with an abstract sectarian squabble; it is a question about concrete circumstances, about the theoretical grounds necessary to make revolution. Moreover, it is a question that emerges from a tradition of communism that has actually been attempting to make revolution and understand what this means since the significant but ultimately failed people's war in Peru. After Peru there was Nepal that went further but still ran up against the problem of revisionism that emerged, as Maoism tells us, through the party's two-line struggle. After Nepal there was the renewal of the people's war in India which is still growing and throwing the country into a civil war. And in a few years the Maoists in Afghanistan might end up launching their people's war, proving that the 21st-century will be one of revolutions. In the centers of global capitalism new Marxist-Leninist-Maoist formations are emerging and trying to understand how to make revolution at the centers of capitalism, a question that has not been thoroughly examined for a very long time and that, most often, is answered with entryist and/or insurrectionist theories that have never been successful.[25]

This is why we are not interested in repeating the stale refrains that past Marxist-Leninist movements sang about

Trotskyism. We think it is possible to recognize Trotskyism as one interpretation of the Marxist-Leninist tradition (we even think it is worth admitting that there are many Trotskyist individuals and groups who have provided useful contributions to theory and who have tirelessly sided with the masses); we just do not think that this interpretation, according to its theoretical foundations, is capable of being anything more than a revolutionary blind alley.

We also feel that Trotskyist engagements, as well as those that uncritically accept the Trotskyist narrative of Maoism (i.e. Goldner, who is a "left communist" and not a Trotskyist, is a good example of this problem) have never succeeded in making sense of this theoretical trajectory. When we encounter articles about Maoism by so-called "critical Trotskyists" that see nothing valid in the Chinese Revolution and that ignore all of the great revolutionary movements at the global peripheries that were inspired by this revolution—when we read theoretical engagements that treat Maoism as a phenomenon that happened only in the 1960s and 1970s and that ignore the fact that Maoism-qua-Maoism did not crystallize until the end of the 1980s—we tend to assume that this bad faith on the part of our Trotskyist counterparts tells us more about their lack of theoretical understanding than any mistakes on our part. Moreover, when we see the great people's wars that have erupted since the emergence of Marxism-Leninism-Maoism treated by other communists as insignificant, or as "fake communism" despite the fact that they are successfully mobilizing the masses, and the failures of these revolutions promoted over their successes, we wonder whether these communists care about even trying to make revolution. As one Maoist comrade once put it, "these people don't even think we should dare to struggle!"

But we *should* dare to struggle and we should develop our theory from both the successes and failures of our struggles, just as we have done with the successes and failures of Russia and

China. If we fail again this does not mean we were wrong for even trying but that we have failed to overcome the problems aptly described by Marxism-Leninism-Maoism or that we have encountered new problems that themselves will need to be systematically theorized. For we are taught by failures and setbacks just as much as we are taught by successes. We can learn nothing when it comes to revolutionary theory unless we actually attempt, through a thorough historical-materialist systematization of past revolutionary movements (especially the world-historical socialist revolutions of Russia and China), to make revolution. Lenin once famously argued that without a revolutionary theory there can be no revolutionary movement, and this is correct. At the same time, however, without revolutionary movements and what we can learn through the experience of revolution there can be no revolutionary theory.

So we ask the question "Maoism or Trotskyism?" to clarify the grounds in which an ideological choice can and should be made. If the reader prefers a communism that has succeeded in keeping itself "pure" because it has remained, out of concern for this theoretical purity and because of its belief that a revolution must only happen if it is global, then Trotskyism is clearly the only viable option: after all, Trotskyism can boast a lack of revolutionary failure, and point out the failures of the so-called "Stalinisms", because it has never succeeded in approaching the point of revolutionary momentum where failure is even possible. But if the reader is willing to accept that making revolution is a difficult business that is prone to failures more often than it is prone to successes, desiring to understand how these failures and successes can be systematized, and willing to accept that the difficulty of making revolution will often produce more failures than successes as we stumble slowly but hopefully towards the next world-historical revolution, then Maoism, with all of its "impure" messiness, is the only relevant communist ideology. For the world is indeed messy, and we come to revolution drenched in the filth of capitalist ideology and all of the mistakes that "weigh upon us like a nightmare"; it may take decades of inspiring but ultimately failed successive people's wars to stretch beyond the next socialist horizon. But if we don't try, and instead attempt to preserve an ideal Marxism as we wait in permanence, we will be overtaken by the armageddon promised by capitalism.

Notes

1. Revolutionary Internationalist Movement, *Long Live Marxism-Leninism-Maoism!*.

2. Or if it *is* revisionism then it is *objectively* revisionist in the way that the aforementioned RIM document has proclaimed that any communism pre-Maoism is a form of revisionism-in-essence.

3. See here the response to Goldner's article and the assumptions it shares with Trotskyist critiques of Maoism (http://moufawad-paul.blogspot.ca/2012/10/message-to-insurgent-notes-please.html).

4. Trotsky, *The Three Conceptions of the Russian Revolution*.

5. Trotsky, *The Permanent Revolution* (third chapter).

6. Trotsky, *Results and Prospects* (eighth chapter).

7. Ibid.

8. Ibid.

9. Although Trotsky doesn't specifically argue that the capitalist mode of production is global, his theory of "combined and uneven development" implies this understanding due to its inability to make a distinction between capitalism as a mode of production and capitalism as a world system. Instead, for Trotsky, there is only one capitalism that is global, combined and uneven, and the unevenness is only due to the "anarchism" inherent to capitalism rather than a necessary fact of global imperialism imposed by capitalist modes of production that can only exist as modes of production at the centers of world imperialism. His most

succinct definition of "combined and uneven development", which can be found in the *The Third International After Lenin*, demonstrates this theoretical confusion.

10. *Theses, Resolutions and Manifestos of the First Four Congresses of the Third International*, 32.

11. Ibid., 31.

12. And sometimes, even with a single country, different regions have different class compositions—albeit united under a single state.

13. Mao's *On New Democracy* can be found at the Marxists Internet Archive (http://www.marxists.org/reference/archive/mao/selected-works/volume-2/mswv2_26.htm).

14. As an aside, as a friend and comrade who helped edit this polemic pointed out, it is "important to stress that Trotskyists confuse the theory of New Democracy or People's Democratic Revolution with the Stalinist and post-Stalinist theory of National Democratic Revolution. The latter practically instructs communist parties in the third world to subordinate themselves to the 'national bourgeoisie' [as with Li's line in the CPC pre-Mao noted above] and hence the debacles of Indian mainstream communism, which has morphed into just contesting elections repeatedly, and the far more tragic disaster of the PKI and Tudeh. New Democracy is very clear about the independent power of the party, of the working-class and peasantry, entering into alliances with the bourgeois forces of the Kuomintang only tactically, and subordinating the national bourgeoisie to the peasantry and working class—not subordinating the working-class and peasantry to the national bourgeoisie" (Noaman G. Ali).

15. Mao, *On New Democracy*, 14, emphasis added.

16. Ibid., 14–15.

17. Samir Amin once referred to this process as "delinking",

arguing that the emergence of socialisms at the peripheries, by opting out of the global capitalist market, would negatively affect the capitalist economies at centers of imperialism since it would deprive them of global surplus.

18. Although it is quite possible to twist around this distinction and argue, by cherry-picking quotes, that Lenin thought that socialism was something separate from the dictatorship of the proletariat, this is correct and incorrect. Socialism is indeed that part of the dictatorship of the proletariat where forces of production are socialized and centralized, whereas earlier parts of the dictatorship of the proletariat in semi-feudal/semi-colonized contexts may have a process of the dictatorship of the proletariat where, as the theory of New Democracy teaches us, these forces of production must be built. But this is a particularity of the global peripheries since a dictatorship of the proletariat emerging at the centers of capitalism would not have to develop the necessary forces of production. Hence, Balibar's argument in *On the Dictatorship of the Proletariat* that Lenin's conception of socialist is the dictatorship of the proletariat.

19. Enver Hoxha was the leader of the Albanian Revolution whose fidelity to Stalin as the pre-eminent Marxist-Leninist was quite dogmatic.

20. See Spartacist League, *Trotskyism, What it Isn't and What it Is!*, where these ortho-Trotskyists argue this precise point. And this is a rather ludicrous point considering that Gorbachev has openly stated that he wanted to end the Soviet Union, that he was an anti-communist and despised Stalin, and has now been quite open about his love of capitalist "democracy" (he even appears in Pizza Hut commercials!)... So how does this make him a "Stalinist"?

21. Here it is important to note the CPC's polemical exchange with the CPSU, *The Great Debate*, specifically "On the Question of Stalin" (which can be found online at

http://www.marxists.org/subject/china/documents/polemic/
qstalin.htm) where they uphold the Stalin period of the
Soviet Union against Khruschev's revisionism but, at the
same time, point out that Stalin was indeed guilty of
committing "errors of principle and... errors made in the
course of practical work". Here they accused Stalin of
metaphysical and subjectivist thinking on important
questions, of being divorced from the reality of the masses,
of treating contradictions between people as contradictions
between communism and its enemy, of wrongly convicting
people as counter-revolutionaries, of wrongly exposing the
scope of suppression, and of demonstrating chauvinism
within the international communist movement. But apparently to uphold the Stalin period against the Khruschev
period is, for Trotskyists, tantamount to "Stalinism".

22. I'm speaking here of the failed Spartacist insurrection in
Germany and the fact that Rosa Luxemburg and Karl
Leibknicht had written some pretty condemnatory things
about Trotsky vis-a-vis the Russian Revolution. And yet still,
despite the fact that the KPD at that time had no love for
Trotsky or anything that would be considered Trotskyist,
this has not stopped a notorious sectarian Trotskyist group
from appropriating the name of this insurrection for
themselves.

23. Some Trotskyist groups, such as the International Marxist
Tendency (IMT), have gone so far as to actually advocate
revisionism by claiming that revolutionaries at the centers of
capitalism can produce an insurrection by entering social-
democratic parliamentary parties and taking them over from
the inside. It should be noted, though, that other Trotskyist
and post-Trotskyist groups have critiqued the IMT for
practicing revisionism, just as it should be noted that other
Marxist traditions, including Maoism, have sometimes been
guilty, based on a dogmatic reading of Lenin's *Leftwing*

Communism an Infantile Disorder, of the same entryist revisionism.

24. Spartacist League *Trotskyism, What it Isn't and What it Is!*.

25. Canada's PCR-RCP, for example, have spent a lot of time trying to answer this question because they see it as essential to building a revolutionary movement in their social context. And the fact that this relatively new party is growing and demonstrating that it is a vital force is not only due to its militancy but to its creative and fresh application of Marxist theory to the context of Canada.

Bibliography

Ajith. *Against Avakianism*. Available at *The Naxalbari*. (http://thenaxalbari.blogspot.ca/2013/07/naxalbari-issue-no-4.html), 2013.

- - -. *The Maoist Party*. Available at *The Naxalbari*. (http://thenaxalbari.blogspot.com/2013/05/on-maoist-party.html), 2013.

Althusser, Louis. *Philosophy and the Spontaneous Philosophy of the Sciences*. New York: Verso, 2011.

Amin, Samir. *Class and Nation*. New York: Monthly Review, 1980.

Anderson, Kevin. *Marx at the Margins: On Nationalism, Ethnicity, and Non-Western Societies*. Chicago: University of Chicago Press, 2010.

Badiou, Alain. *Being and Event*. London: Continuum, 2005.

- - -. *Ethics: an essay on the understanding of evil*. London: Verso, 2012.

- - -. *Logics of Worlds*. London: Bloomsbury, 2013.

- - -. *Theory of the Subject*. London: Bloomsbury, 2012.

Balibar, Etienne. *On the Dictatorship of the Proletariat*. New York: Verso, 1977.

Biel, Robert. *Eurocentrism and the Communist Movement*. Montreal: Kersplebedeb, 2015.

- - -. *The Entropy of Capitalism*. Chicago: Haymarket Books, 2012.

Boer, Roland. *Sectarianism Versus Ecumenism: The Case of V.I. Lenin*. Available at *MRZine* (http://mrzine.monthlyreview.org/2012/boer140612.html), 2012.

Canadian Communist League (Marxist-Leninist). *Statement of Political Agreement for the Creation of the Canadian Communist League (Marxist-Leninist)*. Montreal: self-published, 1975.

Clark, Tom. *The State and Counter-Revolution: A Critical History of the Marxist Theory of the State*. Available at *The Encyclopedia of Anti-Revisionism Online* (https://www.marxists.org/history/erol/ncm-1a/tom-clark/), 1983.

Communist (Maoist) Party of Afghanistan, *A Response to the RCP-USA's May 1ˢᵗ 2012 Letter*. Available at *Shola Jawid* (http://www.sholajawid.org/english/main_english/A_respose _to_the_rcp_USA_sh28.html), 2012.

Communist Party of China. *A Basic Understanding of the Communist Party of China*. Montreal: Norman Bethune Institute, 1976.

Communist Party of Peru. *On Marxism-Leninism-Maoism*. Available at *Signal Fire* (http://www.signalfire.org/2011/12/23/ fundamental-documents-pcp/), 1988.

- - -. *The Mass Line*. Available at *Massline* (http://www.massline. info/Peru/ML_PCP.htm), 1988.

- - -. "To the Communists, To the International Proletariat and the Oppressed Masses of the World." In *Maoist Road* 1 (2011), 16–17.

Derbent, T. *Categories of Revolutionary Military Policy*. Montreal: Kersplebedeb, 2013.

Draper, Hal. *Marxism and the Trade Unions*. Available at *Marxists Internet Archive* (http://www.marxists.org/archive/draper/ 1970/tus/index.htm), 1970.

- - -. *Two Souls of Socialism*. Available at *Marxists Internet Archive* (http://www.marxists.org/archive/draper/1966/twosouls/9-6strains.htm), 1966.

Dunbar-Ortiz, Roxanne. *An Indigenous Peoples' History of the United States*. Boston: Beacon Press, 2014.

Elbaum, Max. *Revolution in the Air: Sixties Radicals Turn to Lenin, Mao and Che*. London: Verso, 2006.

Elements of a Sum Up of the WCP. Available at *The Encyclopedia of Anti-Revisionism Online* (https://www.marxists.org/history/ erol/ca.collapse/wcp-sumup.pdf), 1983.

Engels, Friedrich. *Ludwig Feuerbach and the End of Classical German Philosophy*. Peking: Foreign Language Press, 1976.

Ghandy, Anuradha. *Scripting the Change: Selected Writings of Anuradha Ghandy*. Delhi: Daanish Books, 2011.

Grant, Ted and Alan Woods. *Reason in Revolt: Marxist Philosophy and Modern Science*. Available at *In Defense of Marxism*. (http://www.marxist.com/rircontents.htm), 1995.

Horne, Gerald. *The Counter-Revolution of 1776*. New York: New York University Press, 2014.

James, C.L.R. *The Black Jacobins: Toussaint L'Ouverture and the San Domingo Revolution*. New York: Vintage Books, 1989.

Kasama Project, The. *Out of the Red Closet*. Available at the *Kasama* website (https://mikeely.files.wordpress.com/2012/01/out-of-the-red-closet-kasama-pamphlet.pdf), 2012.

Kuhn, Thomas. *The Structure of Scientific Revolutions*. Chicago: University of Chicago Press, 1996.

Laruelle, François. *Introduction to Non-Marxism*. Minneapolis: Univocal, 2015.

Leonard, Aaron J. and Conor A. Gallagher. *Heavy Radicals: the FBI's Secret War on America's Maoist*. Winchester: Zero Books, 2014.

Lewis, C.S. *A Preface to Paradise Lost*. Oxford: Oxford University Press, 1961.

Liebknecht, Karl. *Militarism*. Toronto: William Briggs, 1917.

Los Angeles Research Group. *Towards A Scientific Analysis of the Gay Question*. Available at *The Encyclopedia of Anti-Revisionism Online* (http://www.marxists.org/history/erol/ncm-3/gay-question/index.htm), 1975.

Losurdo, Dominic. *Liberalism: A Counter-history*. London: Verso, 2014.

Mao Zedong. *On New Democracy*. Peking: Foreign Languages Press, 1967.

Maoist Communist Party France. "The Communists' Unity on a World Wide Scale is Achieved Through Ideological Struggle." *Maoist Road* 1 (2011), 25–27.

Moufawad-Paul, J. *A Living Colonialism*. York University, 2010.

- - -. *The Communist Necessity*. Montreal: Kersplebedeb, 2014.

Popper, Karl. *The Logic of Scientific Discovery*. New York:

Routledge, 2002.

Post, Charles. *The American Road to Capitalism*. Chicago: Haymarket, 2012.

Rancière, Jacques. *Proletarian Nights*. London: Verso, 2012.

- - -. *Staging the People: the Proletarian and his Double*. London: Verso, 2011.

Revolutionary Communist Party of Canada. *It's Right To Rebel: Maoist Manual for Serving the Struggle of the Masses*. Available at the PCR-RCP website (http://www.pcr-rcp.ca/en/archives/1304), 2014.

- - -. *Programme*. Available at the PCR-RCP website (http://www.pcr-rcp.ca/en/archives/category/programme), 2007.

Revolutionary Communist Party of Canada (Organizing Committees). *Maoism Today*. Available at the PCR-RCP website (http://pcr-rcp.ca/en/en/pwd/2f.php), 2005.

Revolutionary Internationalist Movement. *Long Live Marxism-Leninism-Maoism!* Available at *Banned Thought* (http://www.bannedthought.net/International/RIM/AWTW/1995-20/ll_mlm_20_eng.htm), 1995.

Sapp, Jan. *Genesis: The Evolution of Biology*. Oxford: Oxford University Press, 2003.

Spartacist League, *Trotskyism, What it Isn't and What it Is!* Available at the Marxists Internet Archive (http://www.marxists.org/history/etol/document/icl-spartacists/1990/trotskyism.html), 1990.

Stalin, Joseph. *Foundations of Leninism*. New York: International Publishers, 1932.

Theses, Resolutions and Manifestos of the First Four Congresses of the Third International. London: Ink Links and Humanities Press, 1980.

Trotsky, Leon. *Results and Prospects*. Available at the Marxists Internet Archive (http://www.marxists.org/archive/trotsky/1931/tpr/rp08.htm), 1931.

- - -. *The Permanent Revolution*. Available at the Marxists Internet

Archive (http://www.marxists.org/archive/trotsky/1931/tpr/pr03.htm), 1931.

- - -. *The Three Conceptions of the Russian Revolution*. Available at Internationalist Group (http://www.internationalist.org/three.html), 1939.

Werner, J. *Beat Back the Dogmato-Revisionist Attack on Mao Zedong Thought*. Available at *The Encyclopedia of Anti-Revisionism Online* (http://www.marxists.org/history/erol/ncm-5/rcp-hoxha/index.htm), 1979.

Yami, Hisila. *People's War and Women's Liberation in Nepal*. Kathmandu: Janadhwani Publications, 2007.

Young, Robert M. *Darwin's Metaphor*. Cambridge: Cambridge University Press, 1985.

Žižek, Slavoj. *The Fragile Absolute*. London: Verso, 2000.

Acknowledgments

This book represents the culmination of three years of writing and six years of theoretical and practical experience. The idea of *Continuity and Rupture* began to percolate at the back of my mind during the days in which my blog started to gather an audience. I wrote a back-and-forth about the meaning of Maoism with my friend at *Worker's Dreadnought* (we called it "The Three-Headed Beast"), and was consistently asked to explain what I meant by Marxism-Leninism-Maoism. By the time I finally began to think through what Maoism meant as a theoretical terrain I was already engaged in supporting a Maoist project and had learned a lot from the comrades with whom I was working beside and those who had laid the groundwork for this project. When I wrote *The Communist Necessity* an early draft of *Continuity and Rupture* was already in existence; the former in fact came out of the latter, but was a much more complete polemic that, to my mind, would function as an introduction (or "prolegomena") for this book. Due to the context in which this book took shape and form I need to thank the influence and support of a lot of people.

First of all, and most importantly, I want to thank all of the comrades connected to the PCR-RCP and its mass organizations. The older comrades whose experience of struggle from the New Communist Movement to the present has provided us with a wealth of practical experience; the contemporary comrades who I have worked alongside (even those who have dropped out for a variety of reasons); and the younger comrades who have partici-pated in making the Revolutionary Student Movement the largest anti-capitalist student organization in Canada. Since any engagement with Marxist theory will be impoverished outside of practice, there is no way this book could or should exist without such influence.

Secondly, I need to thank all of my friends/comrades in the

CUPE 3903 circles whom I struggled with and against in those days where I was breaking from my union activism so I could find a project that transgressed economism. Despite the differences we might have, the experience and ongoing dialogue has always been precious to my development even in those times when it has functioned as a foil for critique.

Thirdly, I would like to express my gratitude to Gabriel Kuhn who, after reading and reviewing *The Communist Necessity*, initiated a thoughtful email exchange that indirectly contributed to early edits and additions to the draft of *Continuity and Rupture*. Although our anti-capitalist perspectives are somewhat different I've appreciated the creative ways in which they intersect, our ongoing discussion, and our shared love of *Moomin*.

Finally, as always, there is no way this book or any other similar project could exist without my partner, Vicky, who has been a constant source of joy and support for over a decade. Although she likes to deny it, the long road that led me to my current political commitments was initiated by her when, back during our undergraduate days and before we even started dating, she forced me to care about politics in a concrete manner, led me into the activist world, and initiated the process of arguing against some of my ideas regarding capitalism that we all begin by treating as common sense. There's nothing like being tear-gassed together in Quebec City in 2001 to create relationship solidarity! We've both come a long way since then.

Zero Books

CULTURE, SOCIETY & POLITICS

Contemporary culture has eliminated the concept and public figure of the intellectual. A cretinous anti-intellectualism presides, cheer-led by hacks in the pay of multinational corporations who reassure their bored readers that there is no need to rouse themselves from their stupor. Zer0 Books knows that another kind of discourse - intellectual without being academic, popular without being populist - is not only possible: it is already flourishing. Zer0 is convinced that in the unthinking, blandly consensual culture in which we live, critical and engaged theoretical reflection is more important than ever before.

If you have enjoyed this book, why not tell other readers by posting a review on your preferred book site. Recent bestsellers from Zero Books are:

In the Dust of This Planet
Horror of Philosophy vol. 1
Eugene Thacker
In the first of a series of three books on the Horror of Philosophy, *In the Dust of This Planet* offers the genre of horror as a way of thinking about the unthinkable.
Paperback: 978-1-84694-676-9 ebook: 978-1-78099-010-1

Capitalist Realism
Is there no alternative?
Mark Fisher
An analysis of the ways in which capitalism has presented itself
as the only realistic political-economic system.
Paperback: 978-1-84694-317-1 ebook: 978-1-78099-734-6

Rebel Rebel
Chris O'Leary
David Bowie: every single song. Everything you want to know,
everything you didn't know.
Paperback: 978-1-78099-244-0 ebook: 978-1-78099-713-1

Cartographies of the Absolute
Alberto Toscano, Jeff Kinkle
An aesthetics of the economy for the twenty-first century.
Paperback: 978-1-78099-275-4 ebook: 978-1-78279-973-3

Malign Velocities
Accelerationism and Capitalism
Benjamin Noys
Long listed for the Bread and Roses Prize 2015, *Malign Velocities*
argues against the need for speed, tracking acceleration as the
symptom of the on-going crises of capitalism.
Paperback: 978-1-78279-300-7 ebook: 978-1-78279-299-4

Meat Market
Female flesh under Capitalism
Laurie Penny
A feminist dissection of women's bodies as the fleshy fulcrum
of capitalist cannibalism, whereby women are both consumers
and consumed.
Paperback: 978-1-84694-521-2 ebook: 978-1-84694-782-7

Poor but Sexy
Culture Clashes in Europe East and West
Agata Pyzik
How the East stayed East and the West stayed West.
Paperback: 978-1-78099-394-2 ebook: 978-1-78099-395-9

Romeo and Juliet in Palestine
Teaching Under Occupation
Tom Sperlinger
Life in the West Bank, the nature of pedagogy and the role of a
university under occupation.
Paperback: 978-1-78279-637-4 ebook: 978-1-78279-636-7

Sweetening the Pill
or How we Got Hooked on Hormonal Birth Control
Holly Grigg-Spall
Has contraception liberated or oppressed women? *Sweetening
the Pill* breaks the silence on the dark side of hormonal contraception.
Paperback: 978-1-78099-607-3 ebook: 978-1-78099-608-0

Readers of ebooks can buy or view any of these
bestsellers by clicking on the live link in the title. Most
titles are published in paperback and as an ebook.
Paperbacks are available in traditional bookshops. Both
print and ebook formats are available online.

Find more titles and sign up to our readers' newsletter at
http://www.johnhuntpublishing.com/culture-and-politics
Follow us on Facebook at
https://www.facebook.com/ZeroBooks
and Twitter at https://twitter.com/Zer0Books